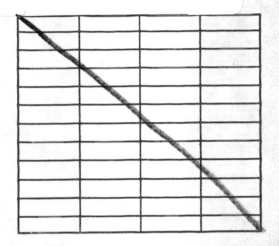

Rethinking School Choice

☆

Rethinking School Choice

LIMITS OF THE MARKET METAPHOR

☆

Jeffrey R. Henig

PRINCETON UNIVERSITY PRESS

PRINCETON, NEW JERSEY

Library of Congress Cataloging-in-Publication Data
Henig, Jeffrey R., 1951–
Rethinking school choice : limits of the market
metaphor / Jeffrey R. Henig.
p.   cm.
Includes index.
ISBN 0-691-03347-1
1. School, Choice of—United States.   2. Educational
planning—United States.   3. Educational change—
United States.   Education—United States—Marketing.
I. Title.
LB1027.9H46   1993
371′01—dc20   93-5411   CIP

This book has been composed in Bitstream Caledonia

Printed in the United States of America

1   3   5   7   9   10   8   6   4   2

TO MY FAMILY

☆

☆ *Contents* ☆

CONTENTS

ix

✩ Figures and Tables ✩

FIGURES

TABLES

☆ *Preface* ☆

I BEGAN THINKING about this book during the Reagan administration, wrote it during the Bush administration, and saw it published during the Clinton administration. Changes in national leadership *do* affect public dialogue about important issues. Under Presidents Reagan and Bush, school choice was raised higher on the policy agenda and its meaning came to be more deeply imbued with the premises of economic theories about how markets perform. The election of Bill Clinton introduced a new element, signaling a slight hitch in the broad privatization movement to shed governmental responsibilities in favor of market forces. Although he too is an advocate of school choice, Clinton's view of it differs from that of his immediate predecessors. He is more confident, generally, about the potential for government to do good. He is more wary, specifically, of the destabilizing potential of school-choice plans that extend to include private and parochial schools.

Bill Clinton's election, however, does not mark the end of the movement to restructure America's schools in the image of the marketplace. While the president can play a pivotal role in framing issues for public debate, other actors also are important. In the area of education policy more than most, the president shares the stage with public officials at the state and local levels. It is here—among the fifty states and more than fifteen thousand school districts—that most of the key decisions that affect public schools have been, and will continue to be, made.

Even those who favor restricting school choice to public schools fall victim to the seductive appeal of the market metaphor. In treating the distinction between public and private choice as if it relates simply to the question of whether privately operated schools ought to be included, they mistakenly accept the market advocates' terms of debate. Rather than simply focusing on the strengths and weaknesses of private versus public institutions and processes as *service-delivery mechanisms*, the message of this book is that we need to focus on the differences between private and public institutions and processes as *vehicles for deliberation, debate*, and *decision making*. As I conclude in chapter 9, the real danger in the market-based choice proposals is not that they might allow some students to attend privately run schools at public expense, but that they will erode the public forums in which decisions with societal consequences can democratically be resolved.

xiii

As with most books, this one has intellectual and motivational roots that spread too deep and too wide to be fully acknowledged. I owe a special debt to John Witte, of the University of Wisconsin, and Gary Orfield, of Harvard University, for the ideal combination of encouragement and perceptive criticism that they offered in their roles as outside reviewers for Princeton University Press. Norton Long, Ken Meier, Laura Salganik, and Clarence Stone provided helpful comments during the early stages of the project. Janice Kuhn was a cheerful and effective research assistant.

I also owe a debt of gratitude to my family. Other authors, in expressing such thanks, usually apologize for being inattentive and preoccupied during the writing stage, with the clear premise that things will be better now that the book is out of the way. My wife, Robin, and daughters, Jessica and Samantha, have a special cross to bear. They know that I am indiscriminately preoccupied; reversion to a prebook state does not offer them much promise of relief! That they suffer me in good humor is the gift for which I am most grateful.

PART ONE

DEFINING THE PROBLEM

☆

☆ CHAPTER ONE ☆

The Call for Choice and Radical Reform

To those who want to see real improvement in American education,
I say: There will be no renaissance without revolution.
(*President George Bush, April 18, 1991*)

MARK TWAIN observed that "the radical of one century is the conserva-tive of the next."[1] The topsy-turvy nature of education-reform politics re-affirms that principle with an added twist. In contemporary debates about education policy, normally conservative politicians and interest groups are calling for radical change.

"Blow up the current education system": the words come not from a nine-teen-year-old member of the Weather Underground, but from the chief executive of a major U.S. corporation. "No more tinkering at the margins," he declares.[2] "Band-Aids won't work anymore," announces another business leader; "we need a total restructuring."[3] "If we in business don't close ranks and insist on radical reform, and do this very soon, I say . . . forget it," reports still another.[4] "You can't tinker at the edges," comments a moderate Repub-lican and former governor. "You have to go to the center."[5]

The notion that education reform requires nothing less than the wholesale revamping of America's education system was a central theme of the Bush administration's approach to education policy. *America 2000: An Education Strategy* was the broad plan announced by the White House in April 1991. "Sweeping, fundamental changes in our education system must be made," it asserts. "Substantial, even radical changes will have to be made."[6] While Bill Clinton took issue with some of Bush's specific education proposals, he did not challenge the notion that dramatic changes were required. Indeed, as governor of Arkansas, he had been one of the first state officials to argue for nonincremental reform.

This call for radical reform is rooted in several strongly stated claims. The first is that the performance of American schools—especially American pub-lic schools—is so poor that we now face a crisis; unless strong and dramatic steps are taken, the nation risks a steep and irreversible slide into economic stagnation and mediocrity. The second claim is that conventional reme-dies—increasing spending, attracting better teachers, mandating tougher standards, redesigning curriculums—have been tried, and have failed. The final claim is that the fault for past failures lies in the very political processes and governing institutions to which we mistakenly turn in our search for a remedy. Simply coming up with better program ideas will not work, because the reigning decision-making processes systematically weed out or enervate good ideas. Simply implementing present programs more effectively will not succeed either, because existing institutions of school governance are neither willing nor able to make the sustained and serious efforts that are required.

To this dim diagnosis is added a prescription for a cure. The prescription is "restructuring," and the favored way of bringing this restructuring about is to introduce market pressures into the process by which educational decisions are made. The notion that market forces can solve domestic social problems more reliably than can government planning is not unique to the education-policy arena. It draws much of its intellectual legitimacy and political sustenance from a broader "privatization" movement that has been politically influential in both the United States and abroad.

In the education area, the impetus to privatize finds expression most directly in the call for increasing educational choice. Educational choice involves expanding the freedom of families to send their children to schools other than the public schools in their assigned attendance zones. Choice plans can be based on vouchers, tuition tax credits, or administrative procedures. They may allow parents virtually unconstrained freedom to select the school of their choice, or they may impose a complicated regulatory framework on both parents and schools. They may permit parents to select a school or they may force parents to select a school. Choice plans may be limited to public schools, may include nonparochial private schools, or may include all schools. They may be districtwide or cross district boundaries. They may be locally initiated, encouraged by state incentives, mandated by state law, or stimulated by federal grants. Most of these options may be mixed and matched with others to create distinct combinations, and all may be further distinguished by their relative emphasis on other objectives, such as achieving racial balance, empowering principals, empowering teachers, empowering parents, or empowering neighborhoods.

Educational choice, it has been argued, will force schools to compete among themselves for students, and the resulting market pressures will stimulate innovation, responsiveness, and improvements in school performance. Although framed in the language of microeconomics, the call for educational choice rests just as heavily on political ideas. Advocates of choice envision changing schools by shifting the distribution of authority among existing interests. School-choice proposals would shift the focus of educational decision making from the government arena—in which elected officials, public bureaucracies, and organized interest groups are central players—to a market-based arena, in which the personal preferences of children and their families presumably will have a more prominent place. To the familiar claim that market forces are *more efficient* modes for allocating scarce resources is added the claim that they are *more responsive* to the felt needs and desires of the average citizen. In a strange twist, the shift away from democratic processes and institutions is defended by reference to values we associate with democracy. Markets, it has been argued, can be more democratic than democracy itself.

This book challenges both the diagnosis and the proposed remedy. While there is much that is wrong with American education today, claims of broad-gauge failures have been overstated, and the link between school performance and the array of economic and social problems that are the real source of citizen distress is more tenuous than education reformers proclaim. More importantly, the market-oriented proposals favored by the "restructurers" are unlikely to work as projected and are more likely than not to make things considerably worse.

EDUCATION REFORM IN AN ERA OF PRIVATIZATION

The Impetus to Shrink Government

Americans feel toward their government the way many adolescents feel toward their parents: deep-seated feelings of love, respect, and dependence compete with—and often are overwhelmed by—immediate resentments over chafing restrictions and nettling intrusions. Not only in the United States, but in much of the world, dissatisfaction with the growing apparatus of government has sparked a privatization movement. Its goals are to shrink the public sector by selling government-owned assets and contracting with private firms to provide public services, and to replace large social-welfare "helping" agencies with simpler voucher-type programs that encourage recipients to help themselves.[7]

Interest in educational choice and attention to the line of demarcation between public and private education both predate this privatization movement, which did not begin to flower until the late 1970s. But this earlier attention was episodic. Discussion, for the most part, was contained within the educational community. In that setting, the focus was on practical applications, and it lacked theoretical coherence and breadth. Occasionally the issue of educational choice was put on the broader political agenda. Such breakthroughs were associated, for example, with southern resistance to racial integration, with conservative economist Milton Friedman's call for school vouchers in his 1962 book *Capitalism and Freedom*, with the federal government's attempt to stimulate local experimentation with vouchers in the early 1970s, and with various Supreme Court cases establishing the conditions under which government may or may not become entangled with parochial and nonparochial private schools. Much can be learned from these earlier experiences, and each will receive attention later in this book. Until educational choice was intellectually and politically grafted onto the broader privatization movement, however, its influence on public policy was marginal. Into the 1980s at least, the dominant trend in the United States, as in much of the world, was in the opposite direction, toward growth in government in general and toward a greater public-sector role in education as well.

At first glance, the juxtaposition of privatization with education reform may seem peculiar. Privatization calls for a more modest and restrained government, a preference for individual over collective solutions, and a particular wariness of central authorities' tendency to preempt or control decentralized efforts by local authorities responding more directly to citizens' perceived needs. The education-reform movement, though, has expressed itself most sharply as a declaration of a collective public goal issued by representatives of government, with the national government taking a leadership role. A report by a national government commission is widely credited with sparking the education-reform movement,[8] and George Bush took great pains, as candidate and officeholder, to portray himself as "the Education President." And, while the national government has been important in framing the public debate about school reform, when it comes to moving from words to action, it has been the nation's governors (including the then-governor of Arkansas, Bill Clinton) who have taken the lead.

In fact, the privatization movement and the education-reform movement are closely related. Even though public officials have been among the leading spokespersons for education reform, the language, symbols, and specific policy proposals of the dominant strain in the contemporary education-reform movement have been imbued with the same suspicion of government and collective enterprises that the privatization movement manifests. Like proponents of privatization, education reformers look to economic theory and corporate practice for their models. Plans to reform schools by giving families greater choice in selecting the schools their children attend are defended because of the greater "market" pressures that competiton will induce. Plans to devolve decision making to the school level—another favorite of those seeking educational restructuring—are defended by reference to parallel initiatives in the corporate sector, where encouraging a team approach rather than a hierarchical chain of command is credited with introducing innovation, flexibility, and better employee morale.

John E. Chubb and Terry M. Moe, two of the most prominent advocates of educational choice, take pains to deny the link between school choice and the privatization movement; their proposals, they say, "have nothing to do with 'privatizing' the nation's schools."[9] Denying the link helps them portray their proposals as less radical and threatening than would be a frontal attack on public schools.[10] Others are much less shy about acknowledging the relationship. This includes those who are primarily associated with the broader privatization movement,[11] as well as those whose background is in education.[12]

This book takes the relation between privatization and education policy seriously. Participants in the privatization and education-reform movements see the link differently than I do. They see the turn toward market-based ideas and processes in both instances as stemming from a common cause: the failure of government institutions to meet individual needs. I, too, see common roots, but I stand their causal argument on its head. The problems we face in our schools today, like the problems we encounter with many of our public programs, can be traced in large measure to our failure to develop and sustain a vision of collective purpose. This failure—in part one of intellect, in part one of political capacity and societal will—is something for which the privatization movement itself deserves considerable blame.

Delegitimation of the "Public Interest"

The case for relying on market forces to initiate and direct educational reform draws intellectual coherence from social-science—and particularly economic—theories about the relationships among popular values, electoral institutions, public bureaucracies, and market forces. The theoretical case for school choice was fully and forcefully developed by Milton Friedman more than three decades ago. Friedman directly challenged two presumptions, widespread at the time, that linked the growth of government to the pursuit of a common good. The first presumption held that there were important conditions under which market forces were inherently unable to perform efficiently and fairly; Friedman argued that such market failures were much less common than had been supposed, and disputed the claim that direct government provision of services was required even where such conditions existed. The second presumption held that public officials primarily acted to pursue the well-being of their constituents. Friedman suggested that the behavior of government could best be understood in terms analogous to those economists use to explain the behavior of businesses and consumers: as an outgrowth of profit seeking and personal self-interest.

These ideas drawn from economics gained added force from their integration into a political perspective based on the ideas of pluralism and public choice. In place of a vision of governance as the pursuit of a collective public interest, pluralism and public-choice theory emphasize the ways in which government is enmeshed in a political battle among individuals and groups with fundamentally conflicting interests.

Disillusionment with the Melting-Pot Ideal

Our schools are just one arena—more visible perhaps than most—in which ethnic, racial, and class-based loyalties and identities clash. The clatter they make is a loud one, and threatens at times to overwhelm efforts to define a common interest. Earlier waves of immigration posed similar difficulties, but the image of a social melting pot provided a sense of mission that helped compensate for them. As a broad social vision, this collective metaphor implied that a common culture could be forged from the separate elements of immigrant values and experiences. It also provided a special vision of the role of education. Public schools, open to and attended by children of disparate backgrounds, would emphasize the shared values that attracted all groups to the United States: religious freedom, individual rights, democracy.

The power of the melting-pot image has lessened over time. In small part, this probably is due to changes in the nature of the immigrants themselves. Then, more than now, immigrants brought with them elements of a common heritage. The Irish might hate the Italians, and Protestants might hate Catholics, but potent as these antagonisms were, they were balanced by shared presumptions associated with a Western, predominantly European background. Sharper differences separate the new American immigrants—Asian and Arabic, Buddhist and Islamic, Afghani and Ethiopian—from one another and from the dominant norms.

More significantly, though, the power of the melting-pot vision has lessened because the ideas behind it have lost legitimacy. In an earlier and perhaps more naive era, education reformers such as Horace Mann could base a call for common schooling on an unabashed confidence in the transcendent universality of American ideals. The ethnocentric imperialism with which such calls were imbued would not go unnoticed today. The growing use of what Mary Ann Glendon labels "rights talk"[13] further chips away at the melting-pot ideal by legitimating the claims of each subgroup—based on religion, race, nationality, gender, or place—to the non-negotiable right to an education tailored to their unique values and ideas. So powerful is this particularism that some parents in one of the wealthiest and best school systems in the country, in the suburbs of Washington D.C., argued that their children should be reassigned to a different high school solely because their neighborhood had a rural flavor while their children's current school had become "too urban."[14]

Faced with disparate groups—each with its own notions of which ideas and values are important to preserve and which to discard, and all protected from direct challenge by the widely accepted philosophy of "to each its own"—it is tempting to beat a retreat from the idea of collective purpose, and to settle more comfortably into bite-size communities of like-minded folks or to draw the wagons around the even smaller circle of the family or individual. It is this urge to retreat that ultimately accounts for much of the popular appeal of both the broad privatization movement and the specific segment of the education-reform movement that draws on market models for inspiration. Although the market metaphor reinforces the impression that privatization is directly deduced from economic theory, interwoven with this cognitive element is a more visceral, cultural impulse for privatization as a retreat from responsibility to a broader collectivity.

Democracy as the Problem

Chubb and Moe turned to markets and choice to save education after reaching the bleak conclusion that efforts to reform schools through normal political channels were destined to fail. Theirs is something more than mere frustration with the slow pace, uneven responsiveness, and bureaucratic inefficiency of government. They charge that the most fundamental causes of the problem "are, in fact, the very institutions that are supposed to be solving the problem: the institutions of direct democratic control."[15] In a heterogeneous and pluralistic society like ours, they argue, the will of the majority necessarily becomes expressed through hierarchical regimes and bureaucratic modes of implementation. These, in turn, create a stifling environment in which principals and teachers are discouraged from developing the teamwork, innovative spirit, and professionalism that effective education requires.

Drawing on a market analogy, Chubb and Moe portray an inherent tension between majoritarian principles and the privately held interests of families as education consumers. Unfortunately, in their eyes, democratic insti-

9

tutions and ideals give parents no favored status. "The schools are agencies of society as a whole, and everyone has a right to participate in their governance," they write. "Parents and students have a right to participate too. But they have no right to win. In the end, they have to take what society gives them."[16] If the interests of parents and students are to be accorded greater weight—and Chubb and Moe think they should be—key decisions about education will have to be removed from the traditional democratic arena. The sovereignty of the family can be won only by trimming the sovereignty of the majority.

But responding to the failures of our schools by turning away from government, politics, and public deliberation is like telling a patient with a broken leg to avoid doctors and "walk off" the pain; it will not make things better, and almost certainly will make things worse. For all its exasperatingly slow pace, democratic government plays an absolutely critical role in airing alternative visions, encouraging compromise, and enticing disparate groups to redefine their interests and find common ground. And for all its frustrating clunkiness, when democratic government manages to act decisively and authoritatively it can bring about broad social transformations in a remarkably short time.

Moreover, public schools represent something more than one in a laundry list of services that government can provide well, or poorly, or not at all. Because education is a process through which individuals come to richer and broader understandings of their interests and how they relate to those of others, and because public schools are the vehicle for education most feasibly and appropriately subject to democratic control, government policy toward public schools is the major opportunity that democratic societies have for upgrading the quality of insight and sensitivity on which future majority decisions will rely.

DRAWING LESSONS

Where did we get off track? My argument is that advocates of market-based approaches to educational "restructuring," as it is called, have misdefined the nature of the problem, misread the history of past reform efforts, and misinterpreted the empirical evidence based on studies of more recent experiments at the state and local level. By defining poor school performance as a "crisis" they have helped propel it higher on the nation's agenda and justified their claim that only radical change will suffice. By selectively retelling the history of education policy, they have reinforced prejudices about governmental ineptitude, benign markets, and intimate communities. By portraying empirical analyses as if they decisively establish the workability and effectiveness of experiments in choice, they have created the mistaken impression that fundamentally restructuring education is a low-risk enterprise with predictable results. And by suggesting that schools' performance should be judged exclusively by their ability to satisfy the express demands of today's education "consumer," they neglect the needs of the undermobilized, they discount future generations, and they fail to come to grips with the responsibility of schools to shape interests as well as respond to them.

Defining the Problem: Crisis as Symbol

Just how poorly are American public schools performing? And how many of the broader problems we face—declining economic competitiveness, a semipermanent underclass, social disorder and crime—are attributable in any substantial way to what does or does not go on in schools?

Part of the power of the call for restructuring education comes from a sense that an educational crisis exists. Such a crisis has been declared by a series of prestigious panels, and is backed up by quantitative presentations that show declining test scores and establish embarrassing comparisons to other nations to which we have always presumed ourselves superior. The label "crisis" carries connotations—that conditions may deteriorate rapidly and irreversibly, that conventional treatments have failed, that dramatic interventions are required and justified—that are laden with politically relevant symbolism.

The case that a crisis exists is not straightforward. While some measures of educational attainment show decline, others have held stable in spite of social and fiscal pressures that might have been expected to exact a toll. And some indicators show signs of improvement, particularly in those areas that public officials aggressively targeted and authoritatively set out to address two and three decades ago. By wrongly placing schools at the center of the matrix of social and economic problems, moreover, the focus on an education crisis may misdirect our attention from other problems, some more readily solved, or having broader consequences if solved.

Evidence and Interpretation

While economic and political theories helped nudge choice to the forefront as an alternative vehicle for dealing with an array of social problems, theories alone could not generate enough momentum to push choice over the transom that separates policy ideas from politically viable policies. The intellectual legitimacy provided by abstract and formal logic is valued more among academics and policy elites than by the broad public, which pragmatically looks for more concrete and immediate indications about what does and does not work.

The abstract appeal of these theories subsequently was supplemented by historical analysis and empirical evidence. The historical narrative developed by proponents of choice offers an explanation of how the current system evolved, and accounts for the public-school monopoly and centralization of decision making as cases of good intentions gone wrong. In addition to this historical narrative, proponents of choice argue that systematic policy evaluations of proposals for choice at all levels of government provide valid and reliable empirical support for their contention that market-based initiatives are both viable and effective. One advocate claims that the number of studies documenting the successes of school choice at the local level "undoubtedly . . . is now above one-hundred."[17]

The historical narrative and policy evaluations play an important role in alleviating the public's fear that radical change means venturing into the unknown. The claim for school choice is presented as something much less tentative than theory or hypothesis. What is offered, instead, is presented as "lessons learned." Later, I will reconsider the historical record and the empirical studies used by advocates to bolster their case. This review will challenge the empirical case for market-based restructuring on two grounds. First, it will reveal that the historical record is far more complex, and the empirical record much more mixed and problematic, than proponents of radical reform ask us to believe. Neither the failure of governmental intervention nor the success of market-based initiatives can confidently be deduced from the available evidence. Second, it will suggest that an almost directly contrary interpretation can be drawn: that choice can have predictably undesirable consequences *unless* undertaken in institutional and social settings that only authoritative government can sustain.

The manner in which evidentiary claims have been used in the school-reform debate highlights the informal and often ad hoc manner in which we arrive at collective judgments about what works and what does not, even now, several decades after the birth of the so-called policy sciences. My position is that it *is* possible for leaders and the public to learn from careful consideration of past experiences with policies, but that the lessons of history are never clear-cut and decisive (even to those working hard to adopt a neutral and objective evaluative stance). Because facts are elusive, relevant variables usually unaccounted for, and generalization problematic, the enterprise of drawing lessons necessarily depends on interpretation and judgment, both of which are usually flawed and certainly variable.

Functions of the Market Metaphor

A truly market-based school-choice initiative would include controversial elements that Americans thus far have been reluctant to endorse. It would include offering publicly funded vouchers that could be used to attend private and parochial schools. It would include minimizing regulations governing public education, in order to lower the obstacles to those who would like to form new schools that would qualify for governmental support. And it would include making the barriers between school districts much more permeable, so that inner-city students, for example, would be free to shop around within the metropolitan area and transfer to suburban schools without having to change residence.

The market metaphor functions in at least two ways to make these radical changes seem less intimidating. The first is simply to bridge the gap between this very different way of structuring education and other experiences with market arrangements that are familiar and comforting. "If you think shopping for sneakers is a kick, try shopping for a high school," a publication for one urban school system proclaims. "And if you're in the eighth grade, you can do just that: shop around and 'buy' the best high school for you."[18] Shopping, after all, may be *the* unifying experience in American culture. All people do it. They know how it works.

The second function of the market metaphor is to bridge the gap between evidence and prescription. Lacking any working examples of a truly market-based system of school choice, proponents have based their claim to empirical support on the implied analogy between certain existing practices and free-market models. They assert that existing practices that incorporate elements of choice—such as magnet schools, districtwide arrangements for public-school choice, and state-initiated open-enrollment options—are like free markets, only a little less so. It is this analogy that sustains the interpretive leap: if it can be demonstrated that these practices succeed in promoting educational achievement without undermining equality, then stronger steps to displace governmental with market forces are surely worth trying.

The use of metaphor in policy analysis is common, and perhaps unavoidable. "Metaphoric reasoning—seeing a likeness between two things—is essential to classification and counting," Deborah A. Stone points out.[19] While such metaphors are necessary to guide rational thinking, they carry a political content that is often unacknowledged. "Buried in every policy metaphor is an assumption that 'if a is like b, then the way to solve a is to do what you would do with b.' Because policy metaphors imply prescription, they are a form of advocacy."[20] In drawing out and making more explicit the influence of the market metaphor in structuring public debate about educational reform, this book is intended to open that hidden component to more careful scrutiny and reconsideration.

NONMARKET RATIONALES FOR EDUCATIONAL CHOICE

Market theory is not the only route to educational choice. Those favoring greater choice in education, as Paul Peterson has observed, "are a motley collection of diverse interests whose views of the appropriate alternative to the existing system are hardly congruent."[21] They are linked not by a common vision, but by a shared dissatisfaction with the current system and a pessimism about the prospects for incremental reform.

While the concepts and models associated with microeconomics have been particularly prominent in public debates, there are at least four other intellectual routes to choice that do not depend on the market metaphor. Each is marked by distinct intellectual traditions and value commitments, though currently followers of all five traditions are marching together under the banner of choice.

Individuality and Personal Growth

A rationale for educational choice that draws more on psychology than economics for its intellectual underpinnings starts with a commitment to the individual as a primary source of diversity, creativity, and social progress. According to this perspective, the evolution of the mature personality requires room for expression and experimentation. People learn by doing, not simply by being exposed to knowledge. While there may be broad patterns of development that are common to all children, individuals respond differently to each specific opportunity for learning because of the personal collection of prior experiences and preconceptions they bring to bear. By the same token, the individual is the source of the creativity that spurs social evolution; by combining and recombining concepts and experiences, the individual acts as a tiny factory producing a synthesis and mutation of ideas.

An emphasis on psychological individualism has its own tradition within the education community, unlike market perspectives, which for the most part have been promoted from outside the profession. One major strain in American pedagogical theory blends elements of Froebel, Pestalozzi, Piaget, and Dewey into an argument for a child-centered approach to education. Early in this century, this approach led to the establishment of a wave of alternative schools, including the University of Missouri Lab School, Baltimore's Park School, the Walden School, and Dewey's own Laboratory School at the University of Chicago. While many of these were privately offered, child-centered approaches also were incorporated into public school systems; the New York City Board of Education operated the Little Red Schoolhouse in Greenwich Village, for example, for over ten years before discontinuing support in 1931.[22] Another wave of alternative schools broke during the late 1960s; examples include the Parkway School in Philadelphia; the Murray Road School in Newton, Massachusetts; Rochester, New York's School without Walls; and the Wilson Open Campus School in Mankato, Minnesota.[23]

John E. Coons and Stephen D. Sugarman's emphasis on choice as a tool for maximizing chidren's capacity for intellectual and moral autonomy places them among those who come to choice through a focus on individual growth rather than market theory.[24] They criticize economists for elevating the household into the primary unit for economic decision making, arguing that this takes too much for granted the premise that the family is a "competent agent for the child."[25]

The child-centered orientation associated with the individual and personal-growth approach itself has little appeal among neoconservative proponents of educational choice. The do-your-own-thing extremes to which child-centered and open-school approaches occasionally have been taken strike many as emblematic of a dangerously undisciplined and misdirected liberalism. Chester Finn, a former assistant secretary of education in the Reagan administration and a general advocate of educational choice, warns that "to refrain from pressing children to learn, in the hope that more of them will come to love their studies and reap the innate benefits of intellectual effort, is quite consistent with a long tradition of progressive education doctrine and practice, but also seems to me to fly in the face of much other wisdom and experience in the United States and abroad."[26] To Finn, Diane Ravitch,[27] Allan Bloom,[28] and others, a focus on individual differences and self-development runs headlong into the greater need to build a common culture and shared base of knowledge.

Communal Values and Cultural Diversity

A second nonmarket rationale for educational choice is rooted in sociological theories and concepts. It begins with an attachment to a particular vision of the role and place of communities as integrating elements in social life. Communities—linked by religion and ethnicity, but not necessarily spatially defined—represent repositories of distinct values and worldviews. While these communities frequently strive to impose their values on others, social vitality and progress ultimately require pluralism and diversity.

One major function of schools, according to this perspective, is to transmit these community-based values and views across generations. Contemporary advocates of multiculturalism and Afrocentrism argue, for example, that young children from ethnic and racial minorities should be exposed to a curriculum that speaks to, and reinforces, the historical contribution and worldview that characterizes their particular cultural heritage. A project in California, for example, seeks to develop an "African Mind Model Technique" as a way to teach young black males "to think like Africans."[29] Another proposes to teach young Hispanics the system of mathematics developed by the Mayans.

While the call for cultural diversity tends to be associated with the political left, there is a strong and somewhat complementary component rooted in the desire of many conservative analysts to reintroduce values and religion into the school curriculum. Faced with what they perceive to be a majoritarian culture that is relentlessly secular, those who value communities based on religion, faith, and spiritual ties sometimes turn to cultural pluralism as an ideal that will provide them with a safe harbor.[30]

Because the power to inculcate norms potentially represents the power to impose norms, those who support communal values and cultural diversity feel they must be wary of the dangers that arise when the apparatus of schooling comes under the control of any faction, even one representing a democratic majority. Those holding this view, therefore, look critically at the "common school" movement that, beginning in the 1820s, shaped so many aspects of public education in the United States. The heart of the common-school agenda, Charles Leslie Glenn, Jr., has argued, is "the deliberate effort to create in the entire youth of a nation common attitudes, loyalties, and values, and to do so under central direction by the state."[31]

Educational choice is attractive to some proponents of communal values, accordingly, because it would allow parents to select among schools that emphasize distinct cultural and intellectual traditions. Society has a legitimate stake in proscribing indoctrination into bigotry, and in requiring transmission of some broadly integrating values and a common intellectual core. But this should not be taken as a mandate for state-imposed education. The fact that state-imposed education may be cleansed of any overt sectarian bias is beside the point, since diversity in sectarian beliefs is integral to the pluralistic vision the holders of this view seek to realize.[32]

For those committed to using schools to transmit communal values, however, alliance with market-based models of educational choice is often a matter of convenience, not principle. The logic of market theory holds that one set of consumer preferences is as good as any other. By this way of thinking, a good school might be judged to be one that offers students an array of diverse values from which they might select, just as a good super-market offers a variety of cheeses or breakfast cereals. Such value "relativ-ism" is precisely what some proponents of communal values see as eroding the foundations of faith and religious belief. That those motivated by a vision of communal values can ally with market models is a mark of their sense of political vulnerability. They consider value relativism less threatening in a market environment—where they at least can find safe harbor for their own views—than in an environment in which a majority can use the power of public authority to impose its views on them. Ultimately, however, many of them cling to the hope of converting others to their view. And, when local circumstance gives them access to political power, their bond with market proponents can fall apart.

The Community-Power Rationale

The community-power rationale for expanding educational choice sees schools as rooted in interest-group theories of politics. Communities—linked by race and class, and forced into spatial patterns by discrimination and economic inequities—represent legitimate units of political mobiliza-tion. Schools are an important prize in the battle among communities striv-ing to maximize their resources and status. But schools are more than a trophy; they are an important resource in the ongoing battle. Reliable and sustainable mobilization demands a shared identity, a sense of political effi-cacy, and experience in exercising power. Schools can augment a commu-nity's stock in these valuable commodities by reinforcing and transmitting local values, by providing skills along with opportunities to exercise them in ways that build self-confidence, and by giving students and parents a local arena in which they can be drawn into the collective experience of demo-cratic control.

The penetration of schools by higher levels of authority potentially under-mines these conditions, however, by imposing the norms of the dominant groups, by deemphasizing or belittling racial and class-specific heroes and history, by maintaining an atmosphere of reduced expectations, and by preempting positions of authority. During the late 1960s, the community-control movement confronted this threat by seeking direct delegation of for-mal governmental authority to community-based school boards. The highly visible controversy and the dissolution of New York City's experiment with community control discredited this approach in many people's eyes, but

17

whether the problem was the basic concept or its implementation remains unsettled.[33]

The foremost example today of the community-empowerment approach is the Chicago School Reform Act of 1988, which seeks to shift significant responsibilities from a hierarchical and hidebound central bureaucracy to 540 elected local school councils comprising parents, teachers, and community representatives. Each local council has been given such tasks as evaluating the principal's performance, selecting a new principal to fill a vacancy, modifying the principal's performance contracts, approving the principal's expenditure plans, and making recommendations about textbook selection and teacher hiring.[34] The early response to the Chicago experiment was dramatic. Over seventeen thousand candidates entered the first election, which the *Chicago Tribune* labeled "wildly successful."[35] Observers on both the political right and the political left have cited it as a model worthy of emulation. Democratic senator Robert Kerrey, for example, characterized the Chicago reform as "a triumph of grassroots democratic action."[36]

But not all supporters of community empowerment believe the marriage between decentralization and market theory is made in heaven. In Chicago, business interests supporting the school-reform plan wanted to couple it with provisions more explicitly rooted in the market metaphor, including open enrollment and vouchers that could be used for private schools.[37] These provisions were resisted by other components of the reform coalition, including Designs for Change, a research and advocacy group recognized as one of the key organizations responsible for the reform legislation.[38] The Chicago Urban League rejected choice provisions based on the "absence of a bona fide market." Its assessment of the availability and distribution of vacant seats throughout the Chicago system concluded that only 5,228 empty seats were in schools where quality was high enough that "student 'consumers' might improve by 'purchasing' them—i.e., changing enrollment. . . . Even if we regard educational freedom-of-choice as a theoretically well-grounded experiment in social engineering, it will still inspire legal and moral scrutiny if the Board of Education spends substantial public dollars on a program that is available to less than 2 percent of its public."[39]

Contingent Allegiance

The differing perspectives discussed above share a commitment to choice either as a primary value in its own right or as a critical prerequisite to the pursuit of other values to which choice is intimately tied. For some education reformers, however, the commitment to choice seems purely tactical.

This contingent allegiance is rooted in a pragmatic assessment of perceived organizational obstacles to change, and the calculation that—in the current political and social environment—choice proposals represent a strategically appropriate vehicle for advancing a particular reform agenda.

Organizations like the National Governors' Association, the Committee for Economic Development, and the Education Commission of the States moved to their positions in favor of choice in a roundabout way. These organizations are part of a mainstream tradition of public reform, one that looks to address social problems through more effective government involvement, not through bypassing government itself.

Those with a contingent allegiance to choice orient their agenda for education toward desired outcomes—higher achievement scores, lower dropout rates, basic literacy, technical and scientific skills. Their readiness to embrace a potentially radical solution such as choice is born in part of a frustration with the apparent failure of more conventional means. Added to this, however, is a rudimentary causal theory that links these desired outcomes to a growing body of research findings concerning the characteristics of successful schools and, in turn, to a political strategy in which choice plays a facilitating role.

Research on effective schools identifies with surprising consistency a series of preconditions to improved student performance.[40] These preconditions include high expectations, order, a strong principal, motivated teachers, and an academic, college-oriented curriculum. Since these are "apple pie" goals that occasion little public challenge, the question emerges why these preconditions are not more easily and widely met.

It is here that education theory gives way to political theory. The primary obstacles to bringing about these preconditions are seen to be entrenched bureaucrats and teachers' unions, which successfully blunt or co-opt reforms periodically launched in response to public concern. The primary appeal of choice, in this view, is not its inherent value or its presumed relationship to individual freedom, personal development, community solidarity, or community power. The appeal of choice lies, instead, in its potential for outflanking interests resistant to institutional change. This potential rests in part on the newly demonstrated political viability of choice, which until recently was considered to be too closely linked with the political albatross of voucher proposals involving private schools. Plans for public-school choice as instituted in Cambridge, Minnesota, and Seattle—and as favored by the Clinton administration—are capable of generating enthusiasm and support among diverse constituencies, forging a coalition broad enough to stand up to tightly organized resistance from within the education community. Once put in place, choice plans further weaken the antichange forces by replacing familiar rules and traditions of decision making with new rules that allow previously marginal interests to assert themselves on an ongoing basis.

Strange Bedfellows Make Risky Partners

Differences in the underlying rationales for educational choice are submerged in the contemporary debate. This should not be surprising. Predictable political dynamics encourage proponents of choice to deemphasize the differences among them, in order to forge the broad coalition needed to carry their proposals onto the public agenda. Moreover, while economic underpinnings have provided much of the intellectual coherence and legitimacy that mark the choice movement, these alternative visions provide much of the spirit and spark.

Market-based rationales, however, ultimately point to different types of policies than do other rationales for educational choice. And these differences have meaningful consequences in the long run. Those inclined to favor choice because of its potential role in facilitating the pursuit of values such as individual development, cultural diversity, community empowerment, and effective schools should be wary of accepting a ride on the back of the market paradigm.

The risk is partly that pursuit of the values associated with freely operating markets will obscure the required trade-off between choice and other values, such as stability, equity, and community. Maximizing individual choice, while desirable on its own terms, must be limited by our need to consider other consequences. But there is a further and even less acknowledged risk as well. Focusing on the trade-off between choice and other social values concedes that pursuing the reforms outlined by advocates of choice will indeed increase choice. This book raises challenges even to this claim. Ironically, pursuit of the particular, individualistic vision of choice may actually reduce the aggregate range of choice that our society currently enjoys.

EDUCATION BY AND FOR DEMOCRACY

A Political Perspective

The argument for turning to market forces to stimulate and guide radical education reform has at its core a tangle of assumptions relating to governance, power, democracy, and control. In this sense, it can fairly be said that this is a movement driven by political theory, not by educational theory or research on childhood development. But the political ideas have not always been fully articulated, and they certainly have not undergone the kind of sustained scrutiny that usually is accorded intellectual challenges to conventional political beliefs.

The language of economics and the language of policy evaluation have displaced the language of political theory in contemporary debate. Economics provides a coherent, though somewhat abstract, rationale for relying on nongovernmental forces to pursue collective goals. Policy evaluation employing social-science techniques brings those abstractions down to earth with seemingly "hard" evidence that choice initiatives work.

This has helped maintain an air of nonpartisan pragmatism by disengaging debate from more contentious issues, but it has done so at a cost. As a political movement animated by political ideas, the contemporary call for educational restructuring ought to be analyzed in explicitly political terms. So understood, the limitations of this reform movement come into clearer focus.

Whose Choice?

The word "choice" is a potent political symbol. Its connotations of personal freedom and abundance of opportunities make it a slogan that is easy to rally around. It is no coincidence that choice is a central issue outside the education arena as well, most notably in the abortion debate. And, given the combination of potent appeal and fundamental ambiguity, it is not surprising that choice is a label simultaneously pursued by the political right and left alike. Overhearing one woman say to another "I'm pro-choice" tells you little about her political agenda without further clues. She may be a liberal feminist thinking about a woman's right to choose whether or not to carry an unwanted pregnancy to term, or a conservative mother hoping for legislation that would make it easier for her to transfer her children to parochial school.

In the thin, pure air of abstraction, educational choice can be presented as a universal goal, opposed only by those so mean-spirited and daring as to claim allegiance to repression, suppression, and force. This illusion fades when theory is translated into specific programmatic forms. There are many visions of what school-choice programs should comprise, and the distinctions among them are far more significant than acknowledged in the pro-versus-con format of the current debate. They are linked, however, in this regard: each and every proposal to expand school choice has the potential to impinge on the free exercise of choice by some groups as the price exacted for increasing the options for others.

Embracing educational choice, then, does not lift us out of the messy political world in which interest is pitted against interest, and within which one group's victory usually rests on another's defeat. This highlights the importance of making certain that public debate about education reform consider not only the likely consequences of policies *if implemented as envisioned*, but also the possible consequences of policies *as they are likely to evolve*.

The Implementation Hurdle

Proponents of choice sometimes acknowledge that variations in school-choice programs can lead to highly variable results, and that—done incorrectly—options might actually make things worse. But they do not take this issue of variable implementation seriously. Their response is simply to affirm their insistence that school-choice plans be put in place according to the particular blueprint they offer.

While advocates of choice insist that the debate over their proposals focus on the merits of the ideal model they construct, there are good reasons to expect this model to change in the transition from idea to functioning program, and to change in ways that are not at all peripheral. Indeed, I will argue that there is either a basic naïveté or a fundamental inconsistency in the way some advocates of choice take into account the problematic nature of the transition from idea to practice. In order to make their vision more palatable to those wary of unregulated market forces, they ask us to imagine choice operating within a framework guaranteeing the protection of minorities, the poor, the uninformed. But the actualization of such a framework, I will argue, would require a government that is well informed, authoritative, sensitive, and willing to stand up to powerful interests. The market theory animating the radical choice proposals not only questions that government has these attributes, but, by aggressively challenging the notion that government ever can have these attributes, it reinforces those who deliberately would reduce the capacity of and authority for government to act.

Choice within Limits

There is no need to throw out the baby with the bathwater; choice, in its place, has much to offer. Rather than seeing choice as a single solution to all the educational problems that face us, we should look at it as one in a series of tools to be selectively employed as conditions warrant. Educational choice can help improve our schools by providing a safety valve for the discontented, a source of information to policymakers about shifting preferences and school performance, a way to reduce pressures on school administrators to micromanage the classroom, and a way to limit the need to resort to coercion in order to enforce the law and promote social goals.

This is a much more modest vision of choice and what it can accomplish. And it is a vision that relies on public officials and collective institutions for its realization. Whether choice as a tool will be used wisely or not depends in large measure on the ability of public officials and the capacity of the citizens to hold them to account. While this leaves just as much uncertainty in outcome, perhaps, as the grander views held by advocates of choice, it places the responsibility for making it work just where it should be: in the public eye and subject to public control.

Education for Democracy

Making government work is difficult. It especially is difficult to work through democratic procedures that invite and accept as legitimate views from disparate actors with conflicting agendas and incompatible styles. Calls for radically restructuring education through market processes appeal in part because they promise to sidestep this process. In the grand bazaar of education, families would be free to negotiate their own bargains on their own terms, paying only as much attention as they wish to the hubbub around them.

It is seductive, but misleading, to look for miracle cures that propose painlessly and speedily to solve problems that are rooted in fundamental political tensions. Rather than looking around for the idea or the technique that will do the trick, it is necessary for us to hunker down for a long-term commitment to ongoing deliberation, unending adjustment and reconceptualization, and contingent—but nonetheless authoritative—collective action.

This may sound a bit intimidating in prospect. We all want to put problems behind us; that is how we are used to measuring progress, and we are accustomed to thinking in such terms. First get the schools straightened out, we reason; then we can tackle ozone depletion, the cost of health care, or whatever the next challenge in sequence may be.

Ultimately, however, the argument sketched out in this book is somewhat more optimistic than the reigning view. The reigning view is that government has failed and is doomed to fail whenever it attempts to fashion collective solutions to social problems. My view is that government has succeeded many times, and it has done so most often when it has enunciated clear goals and mobilized public support based on appeals to concepts of what is right and just and in the broader interest. Individual choice is a value worth protecting; it can also be a useful tool in the collective arsenal. But its effectiveness in addressing social problems depends on its being used in the context of confident and legitimate government authority, not as an alternative to such authority.

Democratic procedures and institutions have a central role to play in building the deeper and broader-based coalition that is needed if attention to education is to be serious and sustained. Rather than substituting one proposed panacea—choice—with another, this book will conclude by considering what is needed to mobilize such a receptive coalition. Part of the answer, happily, leads us to a richer concept of education: education not just as one among many services that governments may provide, but as one of the most important ways in which democracies can create the conditions for their own vitality and growth.

Chapter 2 discusses the power of the "crisis" label as a political symbol, and reconsiders the evidence used to buttress the claim that existing institutions of educational governance are fundamentally incapable of mounting a proportionate response. Chapters 3 and 4 trace the intellectual underpinnings and evolution of the market metaphor and its application to education and politics; overextension of the analogy has led to a thinner conception of democracy and government that makes it easier to underestimate how much can be lost by jettisoning the conventional institutions for democratically defining collective interests and authoritatively pursuing them through government.

The focus in chapters 5 through 7 turns from the world of ideas to the world of practice. Proponents of market-based choice understate the relevance of the nation's earlier experience with freedom of choice in education—an experience that demonstrated the corrosive and divisive consequences that choice can have under some circumstances. And they misinterpret the lessons appropriately drawn from more recent experiments with school choice by failing to understand how much those efforts depended on strong political leadership, authoritative government, and the will to insist that parochial interests sometimes be challenged in the name of broader societal goals.

The final chapters look to the future. There are many ways that elements of choice might be introduced into our educational system. Most call for an ongoing and substantial role for government rather than a one-shot conversion to a market arrangement. Chapter 8 looks at the literature on public-policy implementation to see what can be learned about the role of public institutions of governance and open processes of democratic deliberation in making it more likely that the policies we want are the policies we will get.

Chapter 9 concludes the book by offering a positive agenda for education reform. School choice plays a role in this agenda, but it is a role properly limited by an understanding of the institutional, cultural, and political milieus in which individuals' values are shaped and their interests pursued. Rather than specific pedagogical innovations or new organizational techniques, this agenda focuses on what is necessary to build the civic capacity to undertake and sustain schooling fit for a democracy.

The Political Meaning of "Crisis"

THE CALL for a radical restructuring of America's schools has gone hand in hand with the declaration that a crisis exists. *A Nation at Risk*, the 1983 report prepared by the National Commission on Excellence in Education, almost certainly played the largest role in promoting the crisis label.[1] Its striking charge that "the educational foundations of our society are presently being eroded by a rising tide of mediocrity that threatens our very survival as a Nation and a people" sensitized the media and the alert public to the issue, and ensured that subsequent studies would garner attention they might not otherwise have received.

Other education reports issued over the past decade have adopted less dramatic metaphors than *A Nation at Risk*, but they also promote the notion that the problems are severe, that they are not localized, and that left unaddressed they will sharply worsen. "The nation's public schools are in trouble," we are warned.[2] Public education today faces "a crisis in confidence . . . a crisis in performance . . . and a crisis in the concept of democracy."[3] Another report declares that "it is possible that our entire public education system is nearing attack."[4] "A real emergency is upon us," writes yet another expert panel, noting "a conviction that we must act now, individually and together."[5]

But is there really an education crisis, and, if so, what precisely does that mean? Paul Peterson notes that almost every decade has witnessed intense bursts of concern about schools in the United States. The focus of concern differed from one decade to the next. In the 1920s it was inefficiency, in the 1930s fiscal problems, in the 1950s Russia's scientific challenge, in the 1960s racial segregation and excessive bureaucratization. "The frequency with which crises have been identified in American education," he argues, "suggests that caution be exercised in characterizing educational difficulties, so that the rhetoric used does not automatically escalate problems into something more."[6] Critics of the educational system point to declining test scores, the poor performance of American students in international competitions, and growing public dissatisfaction as compelling proof of crisis, but others—reviewing the same evidence—say the case is not so clear. Indeed, according to Gerald W. Bracey, the "evidence overwhelmingly shows that *American schools have never achieved more than they currently achieve*."[7]

In this chapter I review the evidence on both sides of the issue. While it is clear that substantial problems exist, I suggest that the crisis label is both misleading and potentially dangerous. In spite of plenty of statistics of various kinds, we do not really have a clear picture of what our schools are accomplishing. The technical disputes about measurement obscure one straightforward conclusion: the available data do not speak for themselves. Both historical and cross-national comparisons present a mixed picture. In some areas, American educational achievement appears to be poor or declining; in others it is stable or on the upswing.

In the context of ambiguous and incomplete information, drawing the right lessons for public policy requires interpretation and judgment. And in this context, arguments about the appropriateness of the crisis label are not simply word games. In addition to reviewing the available evidence, I examine why so much energy is invested in this terminological skirmish. Behind the verbal thrust and parry are important issues about social priorities and the capacity of existing political institutions and processes to meet pressing needs. Proponents of radical school-choice plans use the crisis label to bolster their claim that existing public institutions for setting and implementing educational policy have been completely discredited. In so doing, they risk eroding the very institutions on which our capacity for collective and democratic responses depends in the long run.

EVIDENCE OF CRISIS

How does a social problem get labeled a "crisis"? One way to answer this question is to look closely at how various reform-oriented reports have characterized the problem, how they have attempted to measure school performance, and the standards they explicitly or implicitly have applied. Proponents of radical reform point to four types of evidence to buttress their claim that a crisis exists: standardized test scores, international comparisons, evidence of popular dissatisfaction, and anecdotal reports from businesses about the difficulty of finding well-prepared employees.

Standardized Test Scores

The decline in average scores on the math and verbal Scholastic Aptitude Tests (SATs) is perhaps the most widely cited proof that a serious problem exists. A Nation at Risk reported "a virtually unbroken decline from 1963 to 1980." Average verbal scores during that period fell by more than fifty points, and average mathematics scores by nearly forty points.[8]

27

SATs are taken primarily by students intending to go on to college; this makes interpretation of the decline extremely tricky. At least some of the decline is attributable to the greater number of students taking the test. The proportion of minorities taking the SAT has risen from 13 percent in 1972 to 28 percent in 1991.[9] The growing pool of test-takers includes higher numbers of students who would be expected to do worse—because they come from lower-income backgrounds, because they are members of ethnic or linguistic minority groups that historically do not perform so well on standardized exams, or because they have had poorer records in high school.

But advocates of restructuring argue that this "composition effect" does not account for all of the decline. Diane Ravitch, then the assistant secretary of education, reported that, while it is true that minorities tend to score lower on the SAT, "it is not true that this demographic change alone has dragged down the scores, because the white average fell by 10 points since 1976, the first year scores were available by ethnic group."[10] The expansion of the pool of test-takers could not account for the decline in scores of the top students, yet *A Nation at Risk* noted that "both the number and proportion of students demonstrating superior achievement on the SATs (i.e., those with scores of 650 or higher) have also declined."[11]

Other standardized exams, because they are taken by all students at specific grade levels, do not present the same ambiguities. But overall scores on most of them also tell some sad stories. After reviewing the evidence, the National Commission on Excellence in Education reported that high school student achievement scores on most standardized tests are "now lower than 26 years ago when Sputnik was launched."[12] One of the best sources of data is the National Assessment of Educational Progress (NAEP), a congressionally mandated series of tests designed periodically to monitor U.S. students' achievement in such areas as reading, mathematics, science, and writing. Based on the NAEP results, the commission concluded that "about 13 percent of all 17-year-olds in the United States can be considered functionally illiterate," with failure rates for minorities over three times the average. Science achievement as measured by the NAEP, the report further noted, declined steadily from 1969 to 1973 to 1977.[13]

Unfavorable International Comparisons

Some of the most graphic and most distressing reports focus on the comparison between American students and those in other countries. A 1987 analysis of the Second International Mathematics Study, which compared American eighth and twelfth graders with students in twenty other countries, concluded that Americans were competitive in computation and other basic math skills, average in algebra achievement, but "among the bottom 25 percent of all countries" in geometry. In advanced mathematics, the best American students performed only "at or near the average" of all students in the other countries.[14]

Finn indicates that, in an even more recent comparison of thirteen-year-olds from five countries and four Canadian provinces, the U.S. students came in "dead last" in math and tied for last place in science.[15] American adults, in another example, came in "well behind" Sweden, West Germany, Japan, France, and Canada in a 1988 test that called for them to locate on a map fourteen countries and two bodies of water.[16]

American Dissatisfaction with Public Schools

What gives political life to the notion of an education crisis is the sense that broad segments of the American public are disenchanted with public education and ready to sign on for radical change. That many Americans are angry about schools is evident in several ways. Letters to newspaper editors, for example, show that some citizens are intensely upset with what they see to be school officials' unreasonable requests for greater funding, especially when those requests are explicitly linked to the possibility of increased taxes.

In extreme cases, voters have simply refused to provide the funds necessary to keep the public schools operating. The small town of Wales, Massachusetts, for example, was forced to lay off five of its seven elementary school teachers because of budget problems. This left only two teachers and a principal to teach 199 children. Early in 1992, residents were given the chance to vote on a measure that would have allowed Wales to rehire the five teachers immediately. The measure, which would have raised yearly property taxes by about two hundred dollars for each household, was defeated by a vote of 407 to 249. This was not simply a knee-jerk resistance to taxes; on the same day, and by a similar margin, they approved a tax increase to fund garbage collection.[17]

Citizens also show their dissatisfaction with the schools by voting with their feet. Advocates of radical reform argue that the willingness of parents to incur the costs of residential relocation or transfer to private schools is an additional indicator that a crisis exists. The sixty largest public-school systems in the nation lost almost 1.2 million students (15 percent) between 1967 and 1986.[18] Nearly five and a half million children attend private elementary and secondary schools in the United States, and the number of private schools seems to have increased. While the proportion of children attending private schools has been stable over the past ten years,[19] some reform advocates insist that only the tuition burden prevents a more substantial exodus from the public system.[20]

Perhaps the most direct way to find out how the public feels about schools is to ask. While acknowledging that Americans sometimes seem complacent about their own children's educational progress, Finn asserts that "whenever they are asked on surveys, most people place the decrepitude of the nation's education system near the top of their lists of societal problems."[21] "Dissatisfaction with the performance of United States educational systems has regularly been registered in public opinion polls," the President's Commission on Privatization declared in building its case for structural reform. "When people were asked to rate their *local* community schools on the four-point scale commonly used for academic purposes, their schools' grades declined from 2.63 (B-) in 1974 to 2.12 (C) in 1983."[22]

Business Hiring Complaints

Corporate leaders' expressions of dissatisfaction with the capabilities of new high school graduates is the fourth category of evidence offered to justify the crisis label. *A Nation at Risk* indicated that "business and military leaders complain that they are required to spend millions of dollars on costly remedial education and training programs in such basic skills as reading, writing, spelling, and computation."[23] There are plenty of specifics to back up this broad claim:

- According to Motorola, 80 percent of its job applicants fail an entry-level test at the levels of seventh-grade English and fifth-grade math.
- New York Telephone received 117,000 applications for jobs in 1988, but only 2,100 of the applicants passed the company's employment exam.[24]
- One Florida manufacturing company estimated it could save $1.2 million a year if its workers had stronger math and reading skills.[25]
- Pacific Telesis Group has entrance tests requiring the equivalent of a seventh-grade education, but six of ten job applicants still fail. According to a corporate vice president, "American companies are being forced to adapt to these low skills by organizing their businesses around people with 7th grade skills and a day and a half of training. Then, to remain competitive, they must lower wages and increase hours."[26]

A poll of more than 301 private business employers, conducted during September 1991, found that 59 percent rated recent high school graduates as more poorly prepared than graduates of ten years before. More than 70 percent indicated that they had to screen more graduates in order to find those who could meet their employment standards, and just about half felt that their ability to retain new employees had declined as a result of graduates' lack of proper preparation.[27]

EMPIRICAL CHALLENGES TO THE CRISIS CLAIM

When applied to a newly discovered problem—such as the depletion of the ozone layer, or the failing financial health of the savings and loan industry—a declaration of crisis is little more than a societal wake-up call. It is an assertion of a new claim on collective attention and a plea to realign priorities. When applied to a problem like education, which has long been subject to public attention and governmental action, the crisis label carries an additional politically potent message: that traditional institutions and processes have failed, and that incremental change will not suffice.

This is the position staked out so strongly by Chubb and Moe, for example. They take pains to emphasize the wide range of governmental initiatives that followed the *Nation at Risk* report. State governments toughened graduation requirements, increased testing of students and teachers, raised teacher salaries, and experimented with innovative reforms such as career ladders, merit pay, school-based management, and magnet schools. To all appearances, they write, the "problem of declining academic performance had been met head-on with a revolutionary program of reforms that promised a brighter future for the nation's schools."[28] That a crisis persists in spite of this head-on effort, they reason, proves that the problems are more fundamental than we have been willing to realize. In our search for solutions, we should not look to the institutions that caused the problems in the first place—the public bureaucracies that run the schools and the democratic mechanisms that direct them—any more than we should expect a car that stalls at every stoplight to give its own engine the requisite tune-up. In the context of the contemporary debate about education reform, therefore, the claim that a crisis continues to exist in spite of volumes of research, rising expenditures, and aggressive governmental reform initiatives represents more than an assertion of priorities; it is the groundwork for the subsequent assertion that anything short of a radical overhaul of the educational system is destined to fail.

The declaration of an education crisis, however, rests on a partial and one-sided reading of the available data. Just as powerful are figures that tell a somewhat different story: one of progress in expanding educational achievement, lowering dropout rates, improving performance as measured by some tests of reasoning and substantive knowledge, narrowing educational differences between whites and racial minorities, and maintaining a stable base of public support and appreciation. These victories are not complete; most fall short of what we might hope for. But several demonstrate steady progress, and a few are dramatic. Moreover, some of the clearest gains are in precisely those areas that had been collectively identified as high priorities warranting authoritative governmental action.

Staying in School

Sometimes it is necessary self-consciously to step outside our time, our country, and our expectations to gain perspective on social change and accomplishments. We take it for granted in the United States today that young people should stay in school, that personal success will require at least a high school education, and that postsecondary education should be an opportunity available to all and availed of by most. We are shocked by reports that nearly one million American young people drop out of school each year, because we know that, for many of them, "prospects will be grim. Often moving in a shadowy world of drugs or crime, they suffer chronic unemployment, and end up on welfare, supplemented by part-time jobs or even petty theft."[29]

That our standards are so high, however, should not blind us to the substantial progress that we have made in expanding educational attainment. Just half a century ago the picture looked quite different. As Lawrence A. Cremin notes, "Throughout most of the history of popular education in the United States, people assumed that children would obtain as much schooling as they and their parents deemed appropriate or financially feasible, and they would go off to work, or, in the case of young women, begin the business of homemaking or childrearing."[30]

Americans only gradually developed a collective commitment to the goal of universal education. Government simultaneously led and responded to this shift in collective expectations; state governments, during the second two decades of this century, passed legislation requiring older children to stay in school, and state and local governments provided the financial backing to make this feasible. That government was not simply reflecting a popular consensus becomes apparent when one reviews the record of controversy and resistance that met these measures in many instances.[31]

While attitudes were shifting, it was still the case in 1940 that the average American adult had finished only 8.6 years of schooling, and even the new generation—those between twenty-five and twenty-nine years of age—had completed only 10.3 years. "Clearly, the normal expectation for the average American child on the eve of World War II was the completion of elementary schooling and the continuation on to some secondary schooling," with only about half graduating from high school.[32] In the wake of the war, the commitment to expand educational attainment was taken further in two ways. First, it was more explictly made a responsibility of the national government. Second, it was stretched to cover higher education as well as high school.

The articulation of this social goal, and its codification in government policy, was followed by dramatic and continuing progress. With a few dips (accounted for by wars), the percentage of young adults in school has risen dramatically, and continues to rise (see fig. 2.1). So has the percentage completing high school and four-year colleges. While it may be true that any dropout equals one too many—and while it certainly is true that the economic consequences of dropping out today are greater than they were fifty years ago—the data indicate that dropout rates, too, are in decline. In 1967, 17 percent of sixteen- to twenty-four-year-olds had dropped out; by 1989, the figure had declined to 12.6 percent.[33] The lesson may be that we have not done enough, or that we need to do more. But in this instance at least, it cannot fairly be concluded that working through conventional democratic institutions and administrative structures has not worked at all.

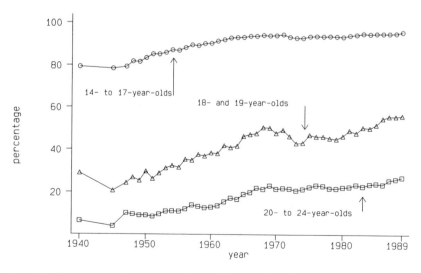

FIG. 2.1 Percentage of young people enrolled in school. *Source*: Compiled from National Center for Education Statistics, *Digest of Education Statistics, 1990* (Washington, D.C.: U.S. Department of Education, 1991), table 6.

Recent Trends in Test Scores

Staying in school is one thing; learning something while there may be quite another. Data to assess long-term trends in educational achievement are much more limited than those on years of school completed.[34] But within the time frame that we can measure, the same trend that showed steady deterioration of test scores in the early 1980s showed signs ten years later of leveling off and reversing. Moreover, the clearest evidence of improvement is in the two subject areas—math and science—that received the most emphasis in the major reform reports, and that have been most explicitly addressed by state and local governments through curricular change, teacher recruitment, and specialty schools.

Figure 2.2 presents mean SAT scores from 1966 to 1990. The steady drop from the mid 1960s through the late 1970s makes it clear why alarm bells began to sound. Since then, however, verbal scores have stabilized and math scores have begun to improve.

The rebound may even be stronger for the average student than it is for the highly self-selected pool of students who choose to take the SAT. To get a better sense of the performance of the average high school student—who

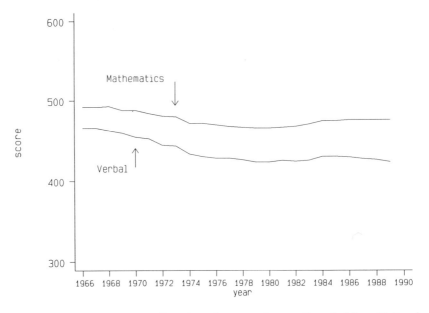

FIG. 2.2 Mean SAT scores, college-bound seniors. *Source*: Compiled from National Center for Education Statistics, *Digest of Education Statistics, 1990* (Washington, D.C.: U.S. Department of Education, 1991), table 119; updated with information from the *New York Times*, August 28, 1990.

may have no intention of going to college or who may apply to the generally less prestigious institutions that do not require the SAT for admission— Charles Murray and R. J. Herrnstein investigated trends in two other standardized tests: (1) a series of five Preliminary Scholastic Aptitude Tests (PSATs) administered to a nationally representative sample of high school students in 1955, 1960, 1966, 1974, and 1983, and (2) the Iowa Test of Educational Development, which has been given to all Iowa high school students for fifty years. "Conservatively, high school students *as a whole* seem to be as well prepared in math and verbal skills as they were at the beginning of the 1960s," they conclude. "They may be better prepared than they have ever been."[35]

The National Assessment of Educational Progress, as discussed earlier, also is a more dependable measure than is the SAT of educational achievement trends among average students.[36] While not providing as long a time-series as the PSAT and Iowa tests employed by Murray and Herrnstein, the NAEP tests have the advantages of being more substantively focused and of including elementary-level students. Figures 2.3 through 2.6, which present

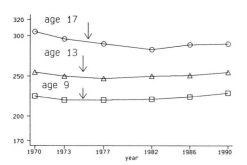

FIG. 2.3 NAEP science achievement.

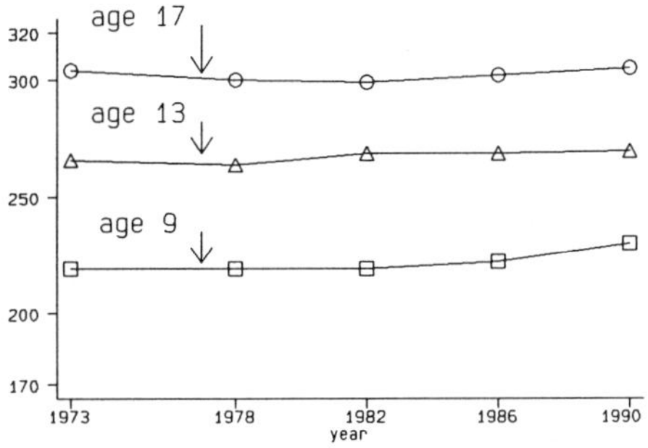

FIG. 2.4 NAEP math achievement.

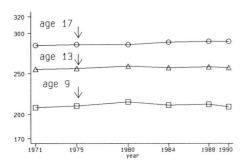

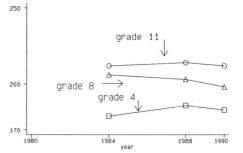

FIG. 2.5 NAEP reading achievement.

FIG. 2.6 NAEP writing achievement.

FIGS. 2.3–2.6 *Source*: National Center for Education Statistics, *Trends in Academic Progress* (Washington, D.C.: U.S. Department of Education, 1991), 19.

NAEP trends for science, math, reading, and writing, also seriously challenge the crisis label. Patterns are not consistent across subject areas or age groups. To the extent we can unravel things, however, it appears that modest declines during the 1970s or early 1980s have been followed by modest improvements in recent years. After declining during the 1970s, for example, science achievement has increased for all age groups tested over the last decade.[37] Mathematics scores declined or were level through the 1970s, and have subsequently increased for all age groups.[38] The only exceptions to this pattern are in reading scores for the youngest students and writing scores for eighth-grade students.[39]

Minority Gains in Access and Test Scores

Progress and failure are most informative when judged against explicitly held goals. You may never have hit a home run, or read a novel by a South American writer, or learned to distinguish a symphony by Mozart from one by Beethoven; this reveals a little about your accomplishments, but unless you have tried to do these things, it tells almost nothing about your capabilities. Similarly, it makes sense to judge the capacity of schools to effect desired change by considering their performance in high-priority areas. From the mid-1950s into the 1970s, it seems fair to say that improving racial equality was the dominate item on the nation's public-education agenda. While the experience was wrenching, and while the results rarely matched the hopes of those who spearheaded the effort, America's public schools accomplished much in this area.

Figure 2.7 sets forth the percentage of twenty-five- to twenty-nine-year-olds, white and nonwhite, who have completed high school and who have completed four years of college. The racial gap has narrowed dramatically. In 1940, only 1.6 percent of minorities in that age range had completed four years of high school or more; by 1988, 18.1 percent had done so. This amounts to an increase of over 1,000 percent; for whites, during the same period, the increase was 267 percent. At least through 1980, moreover, the narrowing of the gap is attributable entirely to improvements among minorities; since 1980, continued improvements for minorities are coupled with a leveling off among whites.[40]

Differences in achievement, as measured by standardized tests, have substantially narrowed as well. Between the 1975–76 and 1988–89 school years, as illustrated in figure 2.8, the gap in combined math and verbal SAT scores between whites and blacks declined by over 22 percent (from 258 to 200).[41] The NAEP tests of reading, mathematics, and science proficiency show a

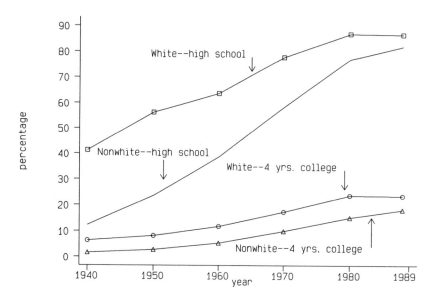

FIG. 2.7 Schooling completed by 25- to 29-year-olds, by race. *Source*: National Center for Education Statistics, *Digest of Education Statistics, 1990* (Washington, D.C.: U.S. Department of Education, 1991), table 8.

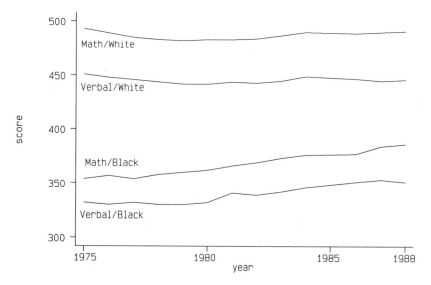

FIG. 2.8 SAT scores, black and white college-bound seniors. *Source*: National Center for Education Statistics, *Digest of Education Statistics, 1990* (Washington, D.C.: U.S. Department of Education, 1991), table 120.

similar pattern. For thirteen-year-olds, for example, the reading gap from 1971 to 1990 dropped 48.7 percent; the science gap declined 20.8 percent between 1977 and 1990, and the math gap declined 35.7 percent between 1978 and 1990.[42]

Exaggerating the International Education Gap

"Ever since international comparisons of science and mathematics test scores began in the 1960s, Americans have believed the myth that U.S. students are outclassed by those in other nations," writes education researcher Iris C. Rotberg.[43] Yet the rankings on which such comparisons are based "are meaningless," she argues, due to the difficulty of comparing test scores from nations with fundamentally different school systems, curriculums, and educational goals.

The most serious problem with many of the international comparisons has to do with the way national samples of test-takers are derived. Some nations have much more selective educational systems than does the United States. They begin weeding out, or channeling into vocational tracks, many of their poorer performers at a younger age than does the United States. As a result, their test-takers—while perhaps representative of those still in school—are an elite group of proven performers carefully culled from the population at large.

This problem was especially severe when international comparisons were first conducted. During the 1960s, for example, a Netherlands-based organization—the International Association for the Evaluation of Educational Achievement—released results that showed U.S. students doing poorly compared to high school students in several European countries. Over 75 percent of U.S. students in that age group were still in school. But their scores were compared, without adjustment, to the average scores for West German students, who comprised the top 9 percent of their age group, Netherlands students (13 percent of their age group), and Swedish students (45 percent). Much more recently, a 1987 mathematics comparison showed Hong Kong twelfth graders ranked first among fifteen nations, with Hungarians ranked near the bottom. But rather than reflecting how well the schools in those countries are doing, the relative rankings largely reflect the Hong Kong educational system's policy of screening all but the top 3 percent of students from taking mathematics, while Hungary provides advanced mathematics to about half of its twelfth graders.

This type of selection bias does not fully explain away American students' poor performance. This becomes apparent when we look at comparisons for younger children, since the major industrialized nations do not differ so widely in the selectivity of their educational systems prior to the high school years. For example, the 1988 mathematics assessment in the United States, Ireland, Korea, the United Kingdom, Spain, and Canada (in which the U.S. students came in "dead last," in Finn's words) compared thirteen-year-olds, an age group for which enrollment is nearly universal in those countries. A similar study released in 1992 showed U.S. thirteen-year-olds again doing poorly, although U.S. nine-year-olds performed very well on the science exam (coming in behind only Korea and Taiwan, but ahead of Canada, Hungary, Spain, the Soviet Union, Israel, Slovenia, and Ireland).

But even in the comparisons among younger children in nations with fairly similar educational systems a selection bias may be exaggerating the U.S. performance gap. As Rotberg points out, "what isn't stated is that the samples of children actually tested were not representative of the entire country." While the entire United States was included in the 1988 assessment, it was compared with only selected Canadian provinces, only the largest of several language groups in Spain, and a sample from the United Kingdom that excluded students from London, the largest inner-city district.[44] The 1991 data for the Soviet Union included only Russian-speaking students in fourteen republics, and that for Israel included only Hebrew-speaking schools. Figures for thirteen-year-olds in Brazil were based on students in just two cities, and the Italian tests were administered in only one province. While the extent of the bias introduced this way cannot be precisely determined, we can be certain that the U.S. scores would have been higher if, for example, New York City students or those from districts with high percentages of Spanish-speaking immigrants had been excluded.[45]

The international education gap, so measured, is a useful social indicator that may help us realign priorities and policies. That American students seem to do poorly relative to other nations is an appropriate reason for concern, especially as the quality of these international comparisons increases. But whether this indicates a genuine "crisis" is another matter. To some extent, it may simply reflect different priorities in the United States. Compared to other nations, we devote a considerably greater portion of our educational expenditures to postsecondary education, for example.[46] Part of what we have "purchased" with this expenditure is a more forgiving system, which allows those who drop out in their teens a variety of options for resuming their education later, as adults. As Michael Kirst points out, "the General Education Development (GED) examination that adults study for in a variety of settings, including community colleges and the military, helps bring our graduation rate up to 87 percent by age 29."[47] In addition, our universities are recognized generally as much more demanding than those in Japan, for example, leading Kirst to suggest that many American students may make up lost ground quickly, once they have managed the difficult transition from high school. Reflecting the high quality of the U.S. higher-education system, the number of students from South Asia and Southeast Asia enrolling in U.S. institutions for their higher education increased by 102 percent between 1981 and 1989; the number coming from Europe increased by 68.9 percent.[48]

In applying the crisis label, reformers suggest that the gap is large and growing, and that responses through conventional channels simply will not suffice. Yet the evidence of a *growing* gap simply does not exist. The premise that our economic successes in earlier decades were based on the kinds of skills tested is questionable. There are no comparable assessments for the 1960s and 1970s, and even the evidence from international assessments over the past ten years is too uncertain and erratic to establish a clear trend.

More Demanding High School Programs

One apparent reason why American students perform poorly on standardized math and science tests is that many simply stop taking coursework in those subjects as soon as they are allowed. Particularly unsettling have been reports that American students have been taking coursework that is less and less demanding even as the level of knowledge needed to be considered literate in today's world has been increasing. The proportion of public high school students enrolled in math and science courses dropped from 1960 to 1977, for example; in science the drop was precipitous, from 60 percent to 48 percent.[49]

What recent calls for reform do not often acknowledge, however, is the speedy and convincing fashion in which the supposedly recalcitrant education-policy community responded to reports such as these. The National Commission on Excellence in Education recommended that all college-bound high school students take at least four years of high school English, three years of social sciences, three years of science, one semester of computer science, and two years of a foreign language. In 1982, the year before its report was issued, only 1.9 percent of high school graduates followed that program; by 1987 this had increased to 12 percent. In 1982, only 29.2 percent had taken a 4–3–2–2 load in English, social studies, science, and math; by 1987 this had increased to 54.6 percent.[50] The proportional increases in demanding courses were especially sharp among minority students. Between 1982 and 1987, the proportion of black high school graduates who had

TABLE 2.1
Average Number of Carnegie Units[a] Earned by
High School Graduates

Subject Area	1982 graduates	1987 graduates	Percent increase
English	3.80	4.03	6.1
History/Social Science	3.10	3.33	7.4
Math	2.54	2.97	16.9
Computer Science	0.11	0.43	290.1
Science	2.19	2.59	18.3
Foreign Language	1.05	1.46	39.0
Vocational ed.[b]	3.98	3.65	−8.3
Arts	1.39	1.43	2.9
Physical ed.	1.93	1.97	2.1
Other[c]	1.14	1.14	0.0
Total	21.2	23.0	8.5

Source: National Center for Education Statistics, Digest of Education Statistics, 1990 (Washington, D.C.: U.S. Department of Education, 1991), table 126.

[a] Each Carnegie Unit represents one credit for the completion of a one-year course.

[b] Includes nonoccupational vocational education, vocational general introduction, agriculture, business, marketing, health, occupational home economics, trade and industry, and technical courses.

[c] Includes personal and social courses, religion and theology, and all other courses not included in the other subject fields.

met the standard for college-bound students rose from .07 to 8.3; for Hispanics the increase was from .05 to 5.5.

There was also a growing emphasis on academic coursework (see table 2.1). High school graduates in 1987 took substantially more courses in computer sciences, foreign languages, math, and science than did their counterparts in 1982. These increases occurred both in public and private schools, but for the most part were greater, both proportionally and in absolute terms, within the public schools.[51]

Public Dissatisfaction with Schools Exaggerated

By claiming that there is a crisis in the public's confidence in its schools, proponents of radical education reform endow their crusade with a populist sheen. Public-opinion polls, movement to suburban and private schools, and resistance to greater expenditures for education suggest that there is a nagging dissatisfaction with schools in the population at large. But this is not at all the same thing as claiming that the public is experiencing deep, broad, and rapidly increasing alarm. To the contrary.

Most Americans do not pay much attention to schools or to education policies generally. Only 22 percent of Americans indicate they know "quite a lot" about local public schools in their communities, for example, while about 30 percent admit they know "very little" at all. The *Times Mirror News Interest Index* found that during the week of May 23, 1991, when President Bush announced his education-reform plan, only 14 percent of Americans followed the story "very closely." Comparable figures for other stories in the news that week were: Bush's heart fibrillations (38 percent followed very closely), the situation of Kurds in Northern Iraq (36 percent), reports on the national economy (33 percent), concerns about Vice President Quayle's ability (26 percent), Chief of Staff Sununu's use of military airplanes for personal trips (24 percent), and rape allegations against Senator Kennedy's nephew (21 percent).

This is important since, generally speaking, the more Americans know about schools, the more they seem to like them. For example, when asked to grade public schools *in the nation*, only 21 percent assigned a grade of A or B in 1991, but 42 percent gave As or Bs when asked specifically about schools *in their own community*. And when parents who actually have children in the public schools are asked to assign a grade to the school their oldest child attends, they are even more satisfied: fully 73 percent assign an A or a B.[52] Moreover, public dissatisfaction with community schools peaked in 1983, the year *A Nation at Risk* made its media splash (see fig. 2.9). But after that, dissatisfaction dropped and has remained relatively stable since. Many more citizens believe that their community schools are good or excellent than believe they are poor or failing.

Part of the public's responsiveness to appeals for educational restructuring may be accounted for by population and other broad changes that are shrinking the relative size of the public schools' natural constituency. A declining proportion of the voting public has a direct stake in the issue. The combination of the aging of America's population and the growing readiness of Americans to defer marriage and childbearing has reduced the proportion of families with school-age children. In 1970, 44.2 percent of American families had no children under eighteen; by 1988 this figure had increased to 51 percent. What is more, those families that do have children are increasingly likely to be poor and headed by females—the segments of the population least likely to vote.[53]

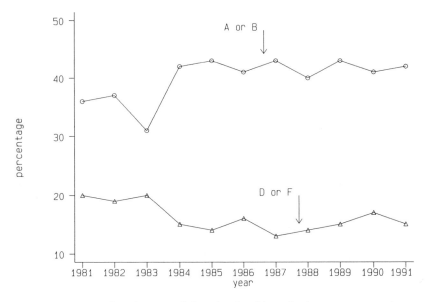

F<small>IG</small>. 2.9 Americans' evaluation of their local public schools. *Source*: Stanely M. Elam, Lowell C. Rose, and Alec M. Gallup, "The Twenty-third Annual Gallup Poll of the Public's Attitudes toward the Public Schools," *Phi Delta Kappan* (September 1991).

C<small>RISIS BY</small> A<small>SSOCIATION</small>: L<small>INKING</small> P<small>ROBLEMS TO</small> S<small>CHOOLS</small>

The picture that is emerging differs from the crisis scenario favored by proponents of radical education reform in several respects. Rather than an across-the-board decline in educational performance, one can see a mixed pattern in which declines in some areas are coupled with improvements in others. Where declines are apparent—as in performance on many standardized tests—the rate of decline has decelerated and in many instances has been substantially reversed. In addition, improvements have been most apparent in the very areas that have been collectively defined as high priorities for governmental remediation, such as expanding educational attainment, narrowing the racial gap, extending to "average" students the opportunities previously reserved for an academic elite, and, most recently, toughening curricular standards. This is a direct challenge to the premise that existing institutions have proved themselves unable or unwilling to respond. Possibly reflecting this pattern, there is almost no evidence that Americans are building toward a fever pitch of dissatisfaction with schools—especially not those Americans who actually have some direct experience with them.

What, then, accounts for the apparent credibility of the crisis claim? Part of the answer is the ability of education reformers to build an association in the public's mind between public schools and other social problems that more tangibly and immediately impinge on Americans' sense of well-being. Through this association, reformers are seeking to boost school reform higher on the public agenda by means of a kind of "coattail effect."

The phenomenon of the coattail effect is familiar in national elections. A popular candidate at the top of a party ticket can help sweep into public office lesser-known candidates who benefit from the association in the voters' minds. A similar coattail effect seems to operate in the realm of agenda-setting. An issue or policy that attracts narrow or shallow attention on its own may be propelled into greater prominence by its association with other issues that are in the front of the public's mind. John N. Kingdon refers to this process as "coupling," and suggests that a major role played by political entrepreneurs is the strategic effort to hook favored solutions to problems that already have political momentum.[54]

Historically, in the United States, the issue with the longest and strongest coattails has been national security. During the period of the cold war, for example, the surest way for politicians to garner support for new governmental initiatives was to make a convincing case that the expenditure was necessary to combat the Soviet threat. Today, we tend to think of highway expenditures as quintessentially domestic in impact and developmental in purpose, but, as Robert B. Reich notes, the federal government's initial legislation launching the national highway system "was called the National Defense Highway Act, and justified in the halls of Congress as a means of speeding munitions across the nation in the event of war."[55]

It was on the coattails of national-security concerns that education was propelled onto the national government's agenda in the fall of 1957. On October 4 of that year, the Soviets launched *Sputnik I*, the world's first satellite. President Eisenhower responded quickly. He interpreted the Soviets' proven technological expertise as signaling an increased security threat, and he identified education policy as a major avenue of response. The result, in 1958, was the National Defense Education Act, which set the course for expanded federal government involvement in education through categorical grants provided to local districts and the states.[56]

In the post–cold war era, national-security concerns have lost much of their impetus, at least for the time being. In the case of the contemporary education-reform movement, the coattails belong to two broad issues of genuine and appropriately held public concern: (1) increases in violent crime and drug use, particularly among young Americans, and (2) the economic stagnation associated with the growing strength of our competitors in international markets.

Schools and Social Disorder

Even when social problems are immediately and directly felt, our ability to grasp them intellectually, to capture them with appropriate words and analogies, can be fumbling and imprecise. In this, we are like the young child who can tell the doctor only that "it hurts," and unleash a wail to prove we mean it. If the pain is sharp enough, lasts long enough, and provokes a sufficiently loud scream, we become confident that something needs to be done. But cataloguing the problem and linking it to the right remedies are far from straightforward.

There seems little question that many Americans today suffer a general sense of uneasiness, an undifferentiated feeling that things are going wrong. This sense is not really new. President Jimmy Carter, in 1979, referred to it using the term "malaise." Political scientist James Q. Wilson wrote, in 1968, about "urban unease."[57]

Although people might express their uneasiness initially by referring to recognized and major social problems like violent crime, deteriorating neighborhoods, and racial conflict, Wilson argued that an underlying factor was a concern about the unraveling of traditional norms and values, particularly the open flouting of "standards of right and seemly conduct." In this context, behavior that was not necessarily criminal—teen rowdiness, lewd language, littering, and the like—stirred deeper apprehensions about social disorder. During the late 1960s and early 1970s, this apprehension provided fertile ground for political entrepreneurs, who, calling for more police, tougher judges, and more prisons, rode a "law and order" wave to victory.

Some of the public's receptivity to the claim that there is an education crisis similarly reflects undifferentiated concerns about unraveling social values rather than issues that are more directly under the schools' control. When the people give the nation's schools poor or failing grades, they are apparently registering their unhappiness with things like teenage drug use and rowdy behavior, not curriculum, teacher quality, or inadequate academic standards.

Asked in a 1991 Gallup poll to name "the biggest problems with which the public schools in this community must deal," 22 percent said "drugs," and 20 percent said "lack of discipline." By way of contrast, only 10 percent pointed to "poor curriculum/poor standards," 2 percent to "teachers' lack of interest," 2 percent to "lack of attention to/understanding of students," and 2 percent to "school not interesting." Dissatisfaction with discipline, moreover, is aimed more at other parents than at teachers; in the national sample, more than three times as many respondents identified parents' lack of interest as a major problem than identified teachers' lack of interest. Twenty-three percent assigned a grade of D or F to parents of students in the local schools for "bringing up their children," while only 9 percent gave Ds or Fs to local teachers.[58]

Similarly, employers' unhappiness with today's high school graduates reflects concerns about behavior, values, and appearance as much as it does dissatisfaction with academic skills. Asked to evaluate the preparation of recent high school graduates, in a 1991 Harris poll, 60 percent of private business employers expressed dissatisfaction with students "learning how to dress and behave well," 62 percent were dissatisfied with graduates' "attitude toward supervisors," 72 percent were dissatisfied with students' "motivation to give all they have on the job," 77 percent were dissatisfied with the "sense of dedication to work," and 81 percent were dissatisfied with graduates' preparation for "having real discipline in their work habits."[59]

Results like these highlight the intricate way that perceptions about schools can be interwoven with perceptions about other problems we face. Schools are like a social magnifying glass. Because attendance is mandatory, schools are perhaps the public institution that reaches most deeply into our private lives.[60] Because they focus on children, they provide a glimpse into social problems—poverty, dependency, violence, alienation, crime—at an early, developmental stage. But even though certain serious problems first show up in the school environment, that should not be taken to mean that the schools can be held responsible.

Schools and the World Economy

The United States' flagging ability to compete in the world market—like concern about drugs, crime, and disorder—is another issue with momentum. Because it seems so directly tied to jobs and economic growth, it is a classic "pocketbook" issue that citizens are unlikely to ignore. And because it pits the country against others, it infuses this decidedly material issue with the emotionalism of old-fashioned nationalism and a dash of the excitement of a spectator sport. By linking it to economic performance, proponents of educational restructuring give their agenda a sense of tangible urgency that an objective review of the empirical record of school performance might not otherwise sustain. According to Thomas Toch, this link is "the principal reason that the nation supported the push for excellence in education so strongly; more than anything else, it was the competitiveness theme that defined the education crisis in the nation's eyes."[61]

The argument is based on a simple causal chain: poor education leads to less knowledge and innovation, less knowledge and innovation lead to faltering economic productivity, and faltering economic productivity leads directly to a decline in the quality of life. And this message is sharpened with direct references to the current and growing economic threat posed by Germany, Korea, and Japan.

The Task Force on Education for Economic Growth of the Education Commission of the States, for example, warns that "Japan, West Germany, and other relatively new industrial powers have challenged America's position on the leading edge of technological invention."[62] The commission, which included the top corporate officers from companies like IBM, RCA, Texas Instruments, Xerox, Dow Chemical, and Control Data, goes on to note that "Japan's improvements in education, of course, correspond in time to Japan's postwar economic miracle—a correspondence which suggests a direct link between education and productivity."[63] A National Science Foundation report, *Educating Americans for the Twenty-first Century*, similarly observes that "in terms of class hours, a typical Japanese secondary school graduate will spend three times the number of hours in science than even those U.S. students who elect four years of science in high school."[64] "Our children could be stragglers in a world of technology," it warns. "We must not let this happen; America must not become an industrial dinosaur."[65]

Finn goes further than many others by venturing to place a dollar figure on the potential economic losses that can be ascribed to poor education. "There is good evidence," he suggests, "that faltering academic achievement between 1967 and 1980 sliced billions of dollars from the U.S. gross national product."[66]

But the explanation for the United States' failure to maintain its post–World War II position of unchallenged economic dominance is more complex than is allowed by this simple equation of national educational performance with national economic performance. Bracey argues that some of the handwringing of business leaders about the poor skills of their workers is a disingenuous effort to distract attention from their own failures. "Are the schools responsible for the management decisions that kept Detroit turning out self-destructing, two-ton gas guzzlers until it lost its dominance of the market?" he asks. "Did the lack of emphasis on 'basic skills' produce the savings and loan debacle?" Or "decree that Korean workers would toil for low wages?"[67]

Some of the most important factors accounting for the growing intensity of international economic competition have to do with broad social changes unrelated to what goes on inside the classroom. One simple factor is the absence, in this half of the century, of brutal and debilitating clashes of the scope of the two world wars; although nominally worldwide, the destruction wreaked by those conflagrations fell almost exclusively on Europe and Asia. Changes in communications and transportation technologies, in addition, have radically altered the rules under which global markets operate. One result is that some of the factors that previously provided the United States with a competitive edge are becoming less relevant. Among these are natural resources, capital endowments, and the concentration of intellectual brainpower in what Robert Reich refers to in *The Work of Nations* as "symbol-analytic zones."

"If you read a 19th century history book about why we became rich, the answer is that America had more resources than anybody else," Lester Thurow has observed. "We didn't work harder than the rest of the world; we didn't save more money than the rest of the world; we were resources abundant."[68] Similarly, Japan's relative lack of natural resources was pointed to as a major economic restraint (and as an incentive to engage in militaristic expansion). But technological changes not only make it possible to produce more efficiently, thereby decreasing the relative importance of production,[69] but they compensate for shortages of national resources in other ways as well. Thurow argues that technological change is primarily responsible, for example, for the agricultural turnaround in Europe, which went from importing 20 million tons of grain in 1975 to exporting the same amount fifteen years later. A similar case can be made regarding the relative advantage in capital equipment that once gave the United States a substantial head start. Capital-rich countries like the United States could count on higher levels of productivity from their workers, and as a result could afford to pay higher wages. But with today's technology, we have developed a worldwide capital market that erases that initial advantage. "Capital," Thurow insists, "has dropped out of the equation."[70] Reich makes the case that the United States' concentration of creative problem-identifiers, problem-solvers, and intellectual brokers in distinct geographic clusters is one of its continuing competitive advantages.[71] The face-to-face interaction and experiential reinforcement that goes on in such concentrated areas as Los Angeles (music and film), New York (global finance and advertising), or Boston (computer software and engineering) cannot be readily matched in other countries. But

changes in communications technology that make possible the instantane-
ous global transmission of ideas and images clearly attenuate the advantages
that spatial concentration once provided.

Even if the United States had maintained an educational edge over other
nations, in other words, it is likely that its economic competitive advantage
would have narrowed due to other forces.[72] To acknowledge this is not to say
that education is unimportant; to the contrary, a strong case can be made
that changing world conditions make national differences in education *more*
important.[73] But suggesting that changing conditions impose new educational demands has quite different implications from suggesting that deteriorating education accounts for our current woes. The former implies that we
may need to reorder national priorities, that education may demand more of
our national attention and resources, that we may benefit from public debate
about the content of education and the way it is allocated among different
social groups. The latter serves primarily to underscore the fundamental
inadequacy of the institutions that have led us to the brink of ruin. Accordingly, it invites indiscriminate condemnation of those bodies; not only the
schools themselves, but the democratic institutions that failed to correct
them.

THE RISKS OF CRYING WOLF

Twenty-five years ago the "urban crisis" dominated public debate. President
Nixon spoke to Congress about the "crisis in the cities." The League of
Women Voters released a report called "Crisis: The Condition of American
Cities." The president of a major university wrote "What We Must Do: Uni-
versities and the Urban Crisis." The U.S. Catholic Conference of Bishops
released a statement called "The Church's Response to the Urban Crisis."
Even *Glamour* magazine got into the act, with a cover story entitled "The
Urban Crisis: What Can One Girl Do?"[74]

Political scientist Edward Banfield was one of the few who recognized,
even then, the potency of the crisis label. He noted that the application of
the label represented a claim on public resources and attention. It would be
interpreted as a demand to "do something . . . now." To Banfield, who believed that conditions in America's cities were in fact getting better, this
seemed dangerous. Applying the crisis label where no crisis really exists, he
warned, "may cause us to adopt measures that are wasteful and injurious
and, in the long run, to conclude from the inevitable failure of these measures that there is something fundamentally wrong with our society."[75]

Regardless of the extent to which the actual severity and scope of a problem can be established, to claim that it represents a crisis can be an important political strategy for those who are seeking nonincremental change. The term *crisis* connotes both extreme severity and the need for immediate intervention. Advocates of radical reform may need to convince others that a crisis exists in order to justify the greater disruption and greater reallocation of resources that their recommendations would entail.

Proponents of radical market-based choice solutions to America's education problems have additional reasons to wave the crisis banner. Besides legitimizing their claim that existing public institutions of deliberation and control cannot be counted on, promoting an atmosphere of crisis also may help motivate and hold together a fragile reform coalition. The obstacles to mobilizing and sustaining a collective movement of any kind are daunting.[76] Leaders have various tools with which they can attempt to surmount these obstacles: providing selective incentives to participants, encouraging the belief that success is likely, or appealing to emotions and higher values that transcend the narrower attraction of being a "free-rider" who lets others do the work. Another may be to create a sense that the problems are so pressing, and the costs of inaction so dear, that intragroup differences should be put aside, at least for the short term.

Although it presents itself as a unified and single-minded movement, the education-reform coalition is loosely stitched, comprising groups whose values, interpretations, and interests are quite different and inconsistent with each other. Libertarians, laissez-faire economists, social conservatives, pragmatic administrators, political entrepreneurs, and disgruntled parents are drawn to the call for educational choice for different reasons and with differing visions. Affixing the crisis label is one means of combating the centrifugal pressure that otherwise would cause the coalition to fly apart.

A broad and evenhanded review of the relevant evidence suggests that the crisis label is problematic. The data are too mixed and too uncertain to sustain such a strong characterization. One reason for this is that the research designs of the various studies leave something to be desired; we are overly dependent on standardized examinations as a measure of performance; the quality of historical data is suspect, especially where international comparisons are involved; there has been little effort to make certain that the performance indicators chosen reflect what schools actually are trying to do. Making the picture much cloudier is the fact that public elementary and secondary education in the United States is carried out in over eighty-three thousand schools in approximately fifteen thousand districts.

We know that some of these schools are doing much better than others, but looking at national trends necessarily obscures this.

To the extent that we are able to speak meaningfully about the performance of American schools, the available evidence calls for a more moderate and balanced assessment. This need not and should not translate into complacency. Our schools can and should do a better job; in the final chapter of this book I will outline in broad strokes what I think needs to be done.

Unyoking the education-policy debate from the notion of crisis can free us to better assess the options available to us. First, it should help disabuse us of the misperception that the current enthusiasm for radically restructuring the education system reflects a broad and unified popular movement. The perception of crisis helps submerge political differences. But as the focus shifts from broad abstractions to practical implementation issues, latent cleavages in the coalition are likely to emerge more visibly.

Second, it alerts us to several risks. One is the risk of looking for one-shot cures. It may be reasonable in true life-or-death crisis situations to try miracle cures; the press of time and the gravity of the situation may rule out more conventional treatments. But when the patient is ill but not gravely so, the preferred alternative combines proven techniques, calculated experimentation, monitoring of response, and readjustment based on feedback.

Another is the risk of reinforcing public cynicism. Banfield worried that a false sense of crisis would provoke unchecked government intervention. Where he saw a tendency to set collective aspirations too high, however, today we see a tendency to set them too low. Americans have had their confidence shaken in the capacity of government to meet social needs. A declared crisis, followed by a frenzied, short-term, and ultimately ineffectual response, is likely to erode our sense of efficacy further still.

Finally, a falsely declared crisis runs the risk of short-circuiting public deliberation and setting the stage for structural changes that may not be readily reversible. The market-based reform plans that are my primary focus can be antidemocratic in substance, a fact that the current momentum of the "do something now" movement temporarily obscures. Market-based choice reforms are intended to change the process by which school-related decisions are made. Advocates presume that such changes in process will translate into changes in what actually goes on inside the classroom—the substance of education—but the link between process and substance is at best indirect. Part of the popularity of the choice proposals depends on different groups projecting their own vision of what the substantive consequences will be. More of them than not are destined to be disappointed. If we are not careful a critical area of collective interest will be drawn at least partially into a more private decision-making arena, an arena in which fragmentation increases and inequality is reinforced, and in which subsequent opportunities for public deliberation will be substantially impaired.

An atmosphere of crisis tends to promote an orientation to action, but—other than implying that past responses have been inadequate—it provides no clear signal about the content of what should be done. Logic does not require that a finding of critically poor performance by today's schools must point us in the direction of privatization and market-based choice. Reformers might just as logically call for a radical expansion of governmental authority—an assertion of a stronger claim to tax revenues for funding new initiatives, for example, or a willingness by higher levels of government to challenge local funding and zoning provisions that have the effect of buffering well-to-do citizens from the responsibility to confront the needs of those trapped in deteriorating school systems.[77]

A quarter of a century ago, the natural response to social crises was more likely to involve an expansion than a contraction of the mechanisms of the welfare state. Faith in governmental institutions as the appropriate vehicle for social reform was strong, with the general public and among the policy elites. In the next chapter, I turn to a consideration of the intellectual evolution that has helped create a broader receptivity to market-based appeals.

PART TWO

EVOLUTION OF AN IDEA

☆

Any new formula which suddenly emerges in our consciousness
has its roots in long trains of thought; it is virtually old
when it makes its first appearance among the
recognized growths of our intellect.
(*Oliver Wendell Holmes, Sr.*, The Autocrat of the Breakfast Table)

WE ARE ACCUSTOMED, in the United States, to seeing innovative proposals met by an array of veto groups predictably arranged according to the interests they represent. Given that background, the breadth of support behind choice as a tool for educational reform is, at first blush, almost mind-boggling. Advocates of choice include presidents,[1] governors,[2] Republicans,[3] Democrats,[4] scholars,[5] citizens,[6] professional educators,[7] corporate executives,[8] blacks, and whites.[9] Educational choice, it has been said, "is gushing with the same kind of force as Old Faithful."[10] One observer likened the movement for public-school choice to "an onrushing train."[11]

The appeal of choice seems evident. It is a term with unmistakable and unfailingly positive connotations. It is defined in part by its opposites: coercion, submission, monotony. And it is defined in part by its associations: freedom, abundance, self-expression, personal fulfillment. As one supporter puts it, "The principle of consumer choice has a revered position in democratic societies."[12] It is not surprising that proposals to expand choice in education are politically popular; the warm glow of the word promises even the most timid of public officials that this is an issue with a ready-made constituency.

Yet, in spite of this surface appeal, U.S. citizens and policymakers historically have reacted warily to proposals that would inject market forces (via expanded parental choice) into the education arena. They have approached it gingerly, much like a young child might approach a dog for the first time—edging forward, fascinated and strongly drawn, then suddenly pulling back. Milton Friedman placed the issue of school choice on the nation's intellectual agenda over thirty years ago. His proposal for school vouchers attracted favor and attention in the academic world and among some policymakers, but ultimately fell on barren political ground. Why did the economic arguments for choice fizzle then, and why do they sizzle now? Does the explanation lie in refinements of the initial ideas that have made the basic theory more consistent, more sophisticated, more accessible, or more empirically well grounded? Or is this a story of gradual public enlightenment? Have changing conditions made feasible and attractive an idea that was once judged speculative and extreme? Or will the contemporary choice movement prove as evanescent as the enthusiasm that once greeted Friedman's plan?

There are two distinct threads to the history of educational choice. One is a thread of ideas and theories; the other is a thread of practice and adjustment. The two chapters in part 2 focus on the former. They outline the market metaphor as applied to education by Friedman, and trace its evolution into the theoretical argument most commonly associated with the choice movement in its current guise, that offered by John E. Chubb and Terry M. Moe in their *Politics, Markets, and America's Schools*. As is typical of many policy ideas, the theories behind school choice germinated and grew within a fairly narrow community comprising academics, political staffers, civil servants, interest groups, and other experts.[13] Within this community, ideas were debated openly and sometimes vehemently, with an emphasis on logical consistency, constitutional legitimacy, political and administrative feasibility, and compatibility with broader theories about the nature of governments, markets, and people. The particulars of these interchanges, though, did not penetrate far into the consciousness of most Americans.

The particular formulation of the school-choice issue that characterizes the contemporary debate, I shall argue, is attributable in no small degree to the push and pull among competing ideas. Friedman's arguments themselves represented an attempt to elaborate and reinterpret traditional economic ideas so as to counter intellectual challenges that arose in the context of the New Deal and the growing welfare state. His formulation subsequently was the focus of new intellectual challenges framed in terms of political feasibility, judicial theory, administrative practicality, and democratic ideals. Arguments for market-based school choice in the 1990s evolved from this intellectual give-and-take. Although the reemergence of a strong choice movement in some respects represents a cyclical trend, the issue returns in a somewhat different guise, reflecting its exposure to counterarguments and the attempt by its proponents to rebut, co-opt, preempt, or otherwise disallow these challenges.

Ideas, of course, do not evolve in an abstract realm according to an internal logic of their own. Subsequent chapters will carry us forward to consider the interaction between ideas and practice, between theory and experience.

Application of the Market Model

As I pass through my incarnations in every age and race,
I make my proper prostrations to the gods of the Market Place
(*Rudyard Kipling*, The Gods of the Copybook Maxims)

THE MARKET METAPHOR

Proposals to increase the freedom of parents to choose their children's schools typically are associated with economic theories of market behavior.[1] The central premise of these theories is that the provision of schooling can be understood in much the same way that economists understand the provision of other goods and services—like used cars or a good haircut. According to economic theory, goods and services are provided most efficiently and at the highest quality in a market setting, where consumers can compare prices and quality and make informed decisions about how best to allocate the money they have available to spend. If Carl's Cars charges too much for five-year-old Chevys, or if Harry's Hair Salon overcharges for a shave and a trim, customers will look elsewhere; if no alternatives are readily available, some sharp-eyed entrepreneur soon enough will seize the opportunity to open shop and capture Carl's or Harry's disaffected patrons. Shady car dealers, who turn back odometers, and shaky barbers, with a tendency to nip the earlobes, also will not last long in such a competitive environment, because consumers will abandon them for firms providing a better and more reliable product.

Similarly, it is reasoned, if parents are freed to act as rational education consumers—able to take their business elsewhere if unsatisfied with the product that their local school provides—schools will be forced to increase the quality of education and the efficiency with which they deliver it, or else risk going out of business. The problem with schools, from this perspective, is traceable to government's intrusion: confusing, through its school funding arrangement, the relationship between price paid and service received, constraining free choice by its mandatory assignment procedures and its effective monopoly, and limiting competition by imposing regulatory hurdles that make it difficult for new schools to be formed.

This simple analogy has a lot to do with the popular appeal of market-oriented educational-choice plans. Particularly in the United States—but in many other industrialized nations as well—average citizens are quite familiar with the rudiments of economic theory. By this, I do not mean that they know or understand the fully elaborated, highly formal models, mathematical proofs, and graphs of demand curves that leave many undergraduates gasping through their first serious class in microeconomics. But they are familiar and comfortable with the more concrete and accessible lessons of supply and demand as expressed in simple stories about how a Florida freeze drives up the price of oranges in Brooklyn, or how a shrewd entrepreneur, with an aggressive marketing strategy or a more efficient production technique, can underprice competitors and grab a bigger market share.

There are at least two important sticking points, however, that keep translation of the market metaphor to the case of schooling from being straightforward and wholeheartedly accepted. The first obstacle has little to do with economic theory as understood by scholars and much to do with many people being left distinctly uncomfortable by experiences with market forces in their everyday lives. Economic models and comforting allusions to the Invisible Hand notwithstanding, a trip to a shopping center for most of us is as likely to confirm apprehensions about shoddy merchandise and inflated prices as it is to demonstrate the self-regulation of market forces. Where market forces and consumer choice have been introduced in education, moreover, they frequently have been associated in Americans' experience with inequalities rooted in economic advantage and racial discrimination.

The second sticking point is a bit more abstract, and has proved more troubling to those who grapple with economic theory on its own terms. For there are important ways in which education is not like haircuts, or cars, or other material goods that are privately purchased and consumed. Conventional economic theory allows for the existence of some goods and some conditions to which market forces do not readily apply, and the emergence of a vast public-school network in the United States is presumed by many to mean that schooling is a "public good" that requires a direct governmental role. The evolution of the market metaphor that begins with Milton Friedman is the story of how a school of economists elaborated and redefined basic concepts in order to rebut the charge that schooling is a public good that must be provided by government, just as government is necessary to provide for the national defense.

Schools as Public Monopolies

More than thirty years ago, Friedman used schools to illustrate his general belief that unregulated market forces of supply and demand can do a better job than government programs in helping meet society's needs.[2] His reasoning—which still lies at the foundation of much of the education-reform movement today—took the debate beyond a simple celebration of the wonders of the marketplace. The core of Friedman's contribution was his detailed and vivid description of the generally harmful consequences of permitting public schools to operate as monopolistic providers.

Friedman, and others who apply a competitive-market model to education, argued that public schools have become lazy public monopolies. Public schools are monopolies because most parents are impeded from exercising their option to switch to alternative, private providers by the hefty price tag that tuition represents when added to a continued legal obligation to support public education through their taxes. Most are unable to switch to alternative public providers, because mandatory assignment policies make it necessary to move to another neighborhood or jurisdiction to accomplish this, and this route is also too expensive for most households to consider. Like private monopolies, they argue, public monopolies have little incentive to keep costs low or keep quality high, since the absence of competition allows them to translate high prices and low quality into higher salaries and less-demanding work conditions, without fear that their patrons will be lured away.

Public monopolies, moreover, can be even more insidious than private monopolies. There are at least three reasons why this may be so. First, public monopolies greatly limit the potential for citizens to exert influence through the exit option. Faced with a private monopoly, consumers have the option of withdrawing patronage (unless, of course, the product is an absolute necessity). Because public monopolies are supported by tax revenues, they suffer no financial loss if consumers opt out.[3] Second, public monopolies obscure the relationship between price paid and service received. Although patrons of private monopolies may not like the high prices they encounter, they at least are in position to compare price to value and make an informed judgment about whether they are being taken advantage of. When services are funded through general tax revenues, citizen-consumers are in no position to disentangle the budgetary twists and turns in order to assess just how much they are paying for each pothole filled, each crime successfully solved.[4] Finally—and here the argument slides from economic theory to political hypothesis—public monopolies may be further shielded from criticism and control by the aura of legitimacy and authority that they gain by their association with democratic processes and their presumed allegiance to the common good.

The result is that public schools are free to do a poor job without fear of consequences. Even more disturbing, it would be economically *irrational* for them to expend the energy and resources that would be required to improve the education they provide. They have no incentive to pursue innovations or reevaluate standard procedures, since doing a better job may not generate greater revenues or higher salaries, and it might even lead to more overcrowding and more difficult working conditions if aggressive parents respond by moving into their attendance zone.

Education as a "Public Good"

This elaboration of public schools as monopolies is the most familiar element of Friedman's argument, and the aspect most frequently echoed in the contemporary school-choice debate. But it is also the least original in some respects. Such laissez-faire notions had been around for quite some time, but their audience had been shrinking while Keynesian economic ideas captured the foreground.[5]

What made Friedman's argument so potent was his further elaboration of the market analogy so as to rebut directly the intellectual and political challenges that seemingly knocked the wind out of laissez-faire economics. Rather than insisting that education was directly analogous to the goods and services that markets were well equipped to handle, Friedman acknowledged that education could not be effectively provided by a purely market-driven process. But he directly challenged the reigning presumption that this both accounted for and justified the nation's heavy reliance on public schools. Government could assume some responsibility for ensuring that education is provided without necessarily taking on the task of providing education itself.

That a competitive market offers advantages over a public monopoly is an article of faith among most economists. In spite of this, at the midpoint of this century, mainstream economics generally had accepted the principle that schools have characteristics making market arrangements infeasible. Most economists considered education to be a "public good"—like national defense—that naturally required a strong government role.

When parents make certain that their children are educated, for example, the benefits of their efforts are shared by the broader community (in the form of a better-trained work force, a source of civic leadership and entrepreneurial innovation, reduced demand for social welfare, lower crime, and so forth). These positive "spillovers" (or "externalities," or "neighborhood effects") presumably do not play a role in a family's calculation of how much of an investment to make in its children's education.[6] This suggests that, left to their own devices, some families acting rationally will tend to underinvest in education, relative to what is good for the society as a whole. Purely market processes, in such cases, will produce a suboptimal level of support for schools.

Even when they recognize the collective social benefit that comes from a well-educated population, moreover, all citizens have a self-interest in reducing their own contribution to the funding of schools, while shifting the burden to others. This is what economists label the "free-riders" problem.[7] Citizens who act like rational, self-interested consumers will figure that they can enjoy the benefits of living in a highly educated society even if they do not pay their own fair share. In cases like this, economists generally agree that government must become involved. Through its taxing authority, government can demand contributions from citizens, essentially forcing them to do what is in their collective best interest.

Government Funding versus Government Provision

In an important elaboration of the economic ideas about government and markets, Milton Friedman drew a distinction between government funding and government provision. He acknowledged that there might be a legitimate role for government in taxing citizens to ensure sufficient educational funding, but he challenged the conventional wisdom that the "public good" aspects of education necessitated that governments get directly involved in operating, or even regulating, schools.

Starting from the premise that competitive markets generally are preferable to government as a mechanism for allocating social resources, Friedman sought to determine deductively the minimal governmental role required to deal with the special complications that education presented. The danger that a totally free-market approach would lead to an aggregate underinvestment in education could be eliminated most simply, Friedman argued, by a legal requirement that all children attain some minimal specified level of education. "Such a requirement could be imposed upon the parents without further government action, just as the owners of buildings, and frequently of automobiles, are required to adhere to specified standards to protect the safety of others."[8]

61

The minimal step of simply requiring parents to educate their children to a certain level—and then leaving the rest to market forces—might suffice for building construction and auto safety, but perhaps not, Friedman acknowledged, for education. Some families would simply be too poor to pay the required tuition. Americans accept the consequence that a low-income car owner might be forced to sell a car if unable to keep it repaired to minimal standards, but "the separation of a child from a parent who cannot pay for the minimum required schooling is clearly inconsistent with our reliance on the family as the basic social unit and our belief in the freedom of the individual."[9]

Government subsidy of the costs of education is justifiable, therefore, in order to make it possible for low-income families to obtain the basic level of education for their children that is required for the society as a whole to thrive. Whether government should subsidize education beyond that basic level is open to question. If there are positive spillovers from such additional education—for example, if funding the higher education of middle- and low-income families expands the pool of individuals able to serve in social and political leadership roles—citizens might decide through democratic processes to undertake that responsibility. Vocational training that primarily increases the students' ability to obtain higher wages is a different story. It would not be justifiable, in economic terms, publicly to fund such education, since its benefits are appropriated fully by the individual student and no externalities are involved.

Most relevant to contemporary education policy debates, Friedman argued that there was no justifiable reason to leap from governmental subsidy to governmental provision. Government could meet its obligations to ensure an adequate level of education without instituting a public school system at all. The secret to doing so—and the policy mechanism for smoothly moving toward such a "denationalized" alternative—is the education voucher.

EDUCATION VOUCHERS: HOT IDEA, COOL RESPONSE

Public schools in the early 1960s were firmly entrenched as valued community institutions, symbols of democratic ideals, and presumed channels for upward mobility. Even individuals attracted by the logic of market theory might hesitate to risk the disruption that a sharp shift to markets would entail. Friedman offered a new policy model—education vouchers plus deregulation—that he argued could facilitate a smooth and somewhat gradual transition from a governmentally managed to a market-responsive system.

The Voucher Concept

Economic theories suggested that a voluntary market exchange would do a better job of matching the needs of citizens to educational products. Subsidizing parents directly, to ensure that they could afford to provide their children with a legally specified minimum level of education, would suffice to meet the complications arising from the positive spillover effects of education.

As a policy direction this suggested two things. On the demand side, it meant that parent-consumers should be free to select the school of their choice, and to carry with them to that school a government allotment—in the form of an education "voucher"—that could be cashed in by the receiving school. Friedman assumed that the receiving schools could be either public or private, and that the size of the voucher would cover the estimated cost of a child's education.

On the supply side, the voucher concept implied to Friedman the need to ensure that governmental requirements and regulations do not stifle the emergence of small, innovative, and possibly transitory schools that might emerge to fill underserved market niches. Friedman suggested that the regulatory role of government could "be limited to insuring that the schools met certain minimum standards, such as the inclusion of a minimum common content in their programs, much as it now inspects restaurants to insure that they maintain minimum sanitary standards."[10]

Today, the concept of providing an in-kind government subsidy in a voucherlike form is a familiar one. The best-known example is the federal food stamp program. Begun in the early 1960s, the program quickly grew; each month it now provides over twenty million lower-income Americans with coupons that can be used to purchase groceries. Section 8, a housing program, represents another important voucher program. Initiated in 1974, Section 8 provides certificates to some lower-income families to supplement their ability to afford to rent in the private housing market. Programs like Medicaid and Medicare, which provide government reimbursement to medical providers who treat, respectively, the eligible poor and the elderly, are not literally voucher programs, in that they do not provide a redeemable chit to the beneficiary. But they are philosophical kin in most important respects. Like vouchers, they provide in-kind benefits rather than cash, and like vouchers they are intended to enable beneficiaries to meet their needs in the private sector.

Vouchers expanded as a proportion of the nation's social-welfare expenditures between the mid-1960s and the mid-1970s. At least three factors contributed to their appeal to lawmakers. First, because their use is restricted to designated purchases, they appeal to those who believe that some recipients will waste or misuse more fungible benefits, such as direct cash payments or tax credits. Second—also because they can be used only for designated purchases—they attract important political support from provider groups that benefit indirectly from increased demand for their products.[11] Third, voucher plans have ideological appeal to market-oriented conservatives, who see them as a vehicle for shifting responsibilities out of the hands of government bureaucracies.

The precedents were less apparent when Friedman first floated the education-voucher idea, however. The GI Bill, which Congress adopted in 1944,[12] authorized federal payments to veterans to subsidize their tuition costs at accredited institutions of higher education or vocational schools. School-voucher mechanisms quite similar to what Friedman was proposing also had been stumbled upon by some Southern districts seeking to evade integration, a fact of which he was aware.[13]

The Initial Response

Discussions of education vouchers often trace the idea back to the publication of Friedman's *Capitalism and Freedom* in 1962, although he had laid out the basic proposal seven years prior to that. His 1955 article seems not to have stirred much broad interest.[14] *Capitalism and Freedom* set the discussion of schools in the context of a much broader and more fully articulated thesis about the nature of government and markets. While this broader argument eventually gave the school-voucher proposal greater authority, initially it seems to have overwhelmed the idea. Early reviews of *Capitalism and Freedom* paid little attention to the education discussion, to which Friedman devoted one of his twelve chapters.[15]

The voucher idea eventually found a receptive audience, however, primarily among academics attracted by its intellectual power,[16] among some spokespersons for parochial schools attracted by its potential to provide additional resources and students,[17] and among a few conservative think tanks and foundations attracted by the laissez-faire message of Friedman's broader arguments.[18] By 1971, one observer concluded that "on the intellectual circuit . . . vouchers are the hottest thing going."[19]

In the United States, somewhat surprisingly, the school-voucher idea reached the national government agenda because its appeal extended to elements on the ideological left. Christopher Jencks, at one time education editor for the liberal *New Republic*, began questioning the viability of American public schools as early as 1966.[20] In the late 1960s and early 1970s, he worked with others, under contract to the U.S. Office of Economic Opportunity (OEO), to flesh out a voucher proposal and to design a policy experiment to test it in selected school districts. The OEO had been the governmental home of some of the most ardent proponents of community action and Lyndon Johnson's War on Poverty, and although President Nixon took steps to reassert his own control over the agency, the OEO's interest in the voucher model rested more on its potential to redistribute opportunity to the benefit of minorities and the poor than on its market rationale.[21]

Accounting for Strange Bedfellows

That liberals like Jencks and conservatives like Friedman could jointly support the call for educational choice is partly explained by their shared aversion to heavy-handed and unresponsive bureaucracies. But they also agreed because, in principle, vouchers may be either regulated or unregulated, redistributive or nonredistributive.

Market principles, at least as he interpreted them, pointed Friedman in the direction of unregulated vouchers, and made him resistant to using vouchers to offset existing inequalities in income and wealth. As already noted, he favored an unregulated voucher in order to ensure easy entry into the market by alternative suppliers. He envisioned a voucher of the same amount for all district residents, but took two things for granted: that wealthier individuals should be free to supplement the voucher if they wished to provide their child with entry to a more costly school; and that wealthier districts would be free to award their residents vouchers with a higher face value than districts with weaker property bases might be able to afford.[22]

Liberals envisioned a much more regulated and redistributory voucher system. Under Jencks's proposal, for example, participating schools would be required to fill at least half their openings randomly and to accept each voucher as full payment, in order to minimize discrimination based on race, ethnicity, or ability to pay. Extra payments would be offered to schools that accepted lower-income students: "These 'compensatory payments' might, for example, make the maximum payment for the poorest child worth double the basic voucher."[23] A voucher system that did not include and enforce such safeguards for the interests of disadvantaged children "would be worse than no voucher system at all."[24] Theodore Sizer, then dean of the Harvard Graduate School of Education, similarly supported vouchers only on the condition that the government's role in regulation and redistribution simultaneously be strengthened. He favored vouchers only if they were structured to "discriminate in favor of poor children," and warned that "a voucher plan for all children (not just poor children) that replaced some existing sources of public aid would cripple the public schools and would give excessive power to middle-class parents."[25]

The Cooling of the Response

But vouchers—at least as linked to the market ideas that hatched them—failed throughout the 1960s, 1970s, and 1980s to make the transition from attractive notion to actual policy. Full-scale voucher proposals faltered in the face of intense opposition within the educational community combined with the wary skepticism or relative indifference of broad segments of the American public.

The first indication that vouchers faced severe political obstacles came in reponse to the OEO effort to carry out a voucher experiment. National interest groups representing teachers and school administrators aggressively challenged the voucher model. A spokesperson for a coalition that included the American Federation of Teachers, the National Education Association, the National Association of Elementary School Principals, and the American Association of School Administrators told a congressional committee that pursuit of the voucher experiment meant that the "original purpose of OEO—assistance to the poor—has been redirected into an ill-conceived attempt to reprivatize our social services."[26]

This mistrust of vouchers was not restricted to the national leaders of the education profession. *Nation's Schools* surveyed a sample of local school administrators in January 1970; fully 82 percent indicated they were unwilling to see some kind of experimental voucher plan tried out in their district.[27] Another survey found that only 8 percent of school superintendents liked voucher plans. To put that in perspective, 80 percent said they liked Sesame Street, 58 percent liked sex education, 56 percent liked Spiro Agnew, and 2 percent liked long-haired men and boys.[28]

The OEO "failed to generate a local constituency for vouchers," despite its efforts to build grass-roots support among community organizations, teachers, and parents' groups in Minneapolis, Rochester, Kansas City, Milwaukee, Gary, and Seattle.[29] The sense that vouchers represented a political potato too hot to handle was so widespread that local school officials almost uniformly resisted the OEO's advances, even though the project would presumably have provided both additional federal resources and a reputation for innovation.[30]

Six school districts accepted OEO funding to study the feasiblity of operating a voucher project, but only one—Alum Rock, California—ultimately agreed to participate in the experiment. Even there, state and local officials made participation contingent on a series of conditions being met that markedly "tamed" the degree of reliance on market forces that Friedman had in mind.[31] Even before federal support ended after five years, key elements had been further eviscerated; once the federal aid ended, the local district could not or would not absorb the costs of maintaining the core of what remained of the voucher plan.

In spite of public-opinion polls showing growing support for the broad concept of education vouchers, both elected officials and voters continued, into the 1980s, to shy away from embracing specific plans. Working along with federal officials, New Hampshire and East Hartford, Connecticut, conducted voucher-feasibility studies, but both dropped the plans in 1976. In New Hampshire local residents eventually turned down the proposal in a "resoundingly negative" vote;[32] in East Hartford the stumbling block was opposition from school principals.[33] In 1978, the U.S. Congress defeated a proposal that would have allowed parents to claim a tax credit equal to half the tuition they paid to send their children to private school. In 1980, and again in 1982, efforts failed to get a regulated voucher system put in place through California's initiative process.[34]

THE REACTION AGAINST VOUCHERS

The notion of expanding individual choice is a potent one, which resonates particularly well in the echo chamber of American political culture. The United States was born in a revolution that pitted free individuals against the claims of the state; some even trace the seeds of the voucher idea to Thomas Paine's thoughts about funding for education in *The Rights of Man*.[35] The archetypal American hero in history and fiction is the lone pioneer who scoffs at the pretensions of formal authority—Daniel Boone, Henry Ford, Paul Newman's character in *Cool Hand Luke*, Jack Nicholson's character in *One Flew Over the Cuckoo's Nest*, *Catch 22*'s Yossarian.

The failure of the voucher idea to take hold initially is all the more intriguing when considered in this light. This section describes some of the intellectual challenges that were mounted against the voucher concept in response to these early efforts to place it on the policy agenda. These challenges—not simple lethargy or bureaucratic intransigence—explain why the initial spark of enthusiasm for vouchers so quickly was dampened. And the particular form and phrasing of the school-choice proposals that have reemerged in the debate over education reform are attributable, in large part, to deliberate attempts to sidestep these challenges.

Although numerous objections to vouchers were raised,[36] for the most part they fell into four types. These involved concerns about separation of church and state, inequality, administrative feasibility, and impact on the public schools.

Church and State

Of the twenty-five thousand to thirty thousand private schools in the United States, approximately eight out of ten have a religious orientation. Of these, the most prominent are Catholic schools, which enroll about 60 percent of all private-school students.[37] This association between private schools and parochial education accounted for many of the philosophical and legal objections to early voucher proposals, like Friedman's, that would involve the government in subsidizing the costs of private-school tuition.[38]

Philosophically, the association raised questions regarding both the substance of education and the threat of hyperpluralism. Religious beliefs and principles may clash with the beliefs and principles that most Americans expect to be introduced as part of a solid education. Religion is anchored in faith and tradition; science is based on skepticism and experiment. Could religious institutions be expected to instill in young Americans the modes of rigorous and critical thought on which scientific and economic progress are believed to rest? Could they be counted on to teach scientific theories, such as Darwin's theory of evolution, that may challenge their accepted interpretations of their holy scriptures? In the face of racial and ethnic tensions already apparent in the nation's large cities, might it not be injudicious for central governments to underwrite the cost of educating students in institutions that may more deeply indoctrinate them in separatist views and ideals?

The concern that voucher proposals would excerbate conflict among religious groups was emphasized by the president of the American Federation of Teachers in 1971. At several meetings he attended, he said, "the line-up of religious teams was as apparent as if they had worn colored jerseys"; he warned that proposals for vouchers that would include parochial schools were "dynamite which lies ready for detonation."[39]

Such popular concerns might not have slowed vouchers' momentum alone without the added influence of the Supreme Court. Legally, the overlap between private education and parochial education raised specific challenges centering on the stipulation, in the First Amendment to the Constitution, that "Congress shall make no law respecting an establishment of religion, or prohibiting the free exercise thereof." Precisely what the Founding Fathers meant to accomplish with this prohibition is not easily determined. At the time, six states had laws on their books that clearly favored certain religious orientations. Maryland required Christianity; Pennsylvania and South Carolina supported belief in one eternal God; Delaware required acceptance of the doctrine of the Holy Trinity.[40] The Court, however, determined that the amendment means more than that the federal and state governments are not to set up official religions or punish individuals for their personal religious beliefs. Any "excessive entanglements" between the government and religions must be avoided. Any public policy with "the purpose or primary effect of aiding or inhibiting religious education" is considered to be unconstitutional.[41]

As it has turned out, this standard may not rule out all conceivable forms of vouchers. The Court generally has taken the position that laws that have the direct effect of establishing religion are unconstitutional, even though they may benefit all religions alike and not aid one religion over others. But it also has held that laws that have an indirect, remote, or incidental effect of aiding religion may be constitutionally valid. Thus the Court recognizes a distinction between direct government aid to parochial schools (unconstitutional), and aid to families to reimburse certain costs associated with attending parochial schools (may be constitutional). It also sees a distinction between laws that are specifically targeted to families with children attending parochial schools (unconstitutional) and those offering benefits to all families with children, even if some of the latter may use those benefits to defray the costs of parochial school (may be constitutional). And it sees a distinction between support for instruction with religious themes (unconstitutional) and support for certain secular activities that may take place in, or in association with, parochial schools (may be constitutional).

There is no clear trend to the Court's thinking on these issues. As one review of the decisions made between 1969 and 1986 concludes, the pattern has been "often change, reversal, confusion, and at times some justices were unpredictable."[42] The Supreme Court of the 1990s, however, is more likely to be receptive to some sort of voucher arrangements than the Court that was sitting when these proposals first arose. At that time, the legal obstacles loomed large. Proponents of vouchers knew that any plan would face long and costly legal challenges. Referring to constitutional reservations helped opponents avoid the charge that their position rested on hostility to Catholicism or to religion in general.

Inequality

Concerns about inequality related both to socioeconomic class and to race. Critics charged that voucher schemes almost certainly would work to the detriment of the poor. Unless vouchers were steeply progressive, unless they included free transporation, and unless schools were prohibited from charging tuitions higher than the voucher amount, the effect of vouchers might be primarily to subsidize the private education of middle- and upper-class children.

Although proposals like those of Jencks included such redistributory elements, some critics argued that the poor were too weak politically to ensure that such provisions would be approved, implemented, and sustained over time. Concerns about the impact of vouchers on racial equality centered on the risk that vouchers would underwrite the cost of white flight from integrating public schools. This was a concern built on historical experience, not simply on intellectual speculation.

Administrative Feasibility

A third category of challenges involved the translation of the voucher idea into an adminstratively feasible plan. Critics argued that voucher plans would impose tremendous organizational burdens on local schools, which would find it impossible to predict with any precision the number of students to expect or the particular mix of educational skills and deficiencies they might bring with them.

Most voucher plans, in addition, envisioned public officials taking on some new roles, such as collecting and disseminating information to help parents make informed decisions and making sure recipient schools met basic health, safety, and curricular standards. According to Cohen and Farrar, some of the reticence about vouchers arose from uncertainty about how theoretical models of economic behavior really related to the concrete problems schools administrators faced: "Insiders and intellectuals saw vouchers as a solution to vague and abstract problems, such as monopoly power in education—not as the solution to the day-to-day problems of running a school system."[43]

Undermining Public Schools

Voucher plans "would certainly cut the throat of our public schools," a school-board member of a moderate-sized Oklahoma district complained during the fall of 1971.[44] Critics feared that vouchers would immediately drain the best and brightest students from the public schools. Over the longer term, they worried that vouchers would erode the political constituency that historically had sustained the public system.

These concerns were probably felt most sharply by those—such as teachers and administrators—whose livelihoods were directly connected to the public system. Because teachers and administrators were politically mobilized and aggressive in conveying their concerns, elected officials at the state and local level also were wary. It was this kind of transmission of concern that helped account for the taming of the Alum Rock experiment. Partly in order to assuage fears within the education community, provisions in the voucher experiment prohibited the inclusion of private schools, guaranteed that no public school would be closed due to lack of "business," and protected teachers from the threat that their jobs might be lost.

It seems likely, however, that reticence to put the public schools at risk was felt by a rather broad segment of the American public. General support for the public schools could be evident even at the height of concern about the so-called education crisis. In spite of its readiness to express support for the concept of educational choice when queried generally and in the abstract, the public showed little inclination forcefully to demand such change.

Concerns about the impact of vouchers on public schools led some proponents of choice to suggest that some of its presumed benefits could be obtained in a system restricted to public schools. Mario D. Fantini, in 1973, argued that "using education vouchers to make options outside the public school system—the external voucher plan—is far less important, far less desirable, than creating options within the system."[45] By then, the impetus behind vouchers already was waning. His recommendation for what he called "public schools of choice" did not attract much attention at the time, but his argument would be resuscitated more than ten years later as part of market-oriented conservatives' efforts to wrap choice schemes in a more politically acceptable package.

THE REEMERGENCE OF SCHOOL CHOICE

Ronald Reagan took office in 1981 with a simple education-policy agenda. In line with his antibureaucracy stance and his commitment to states' rights, he proposed to abolish the U.S. Department of Education. Reflecting his belief in the importance of religion and values, he proposed to seek a constitutional amendment allowing organized prayer in public schools. And reflecting both his emphasis on values and his faith in private market forces, he proposed to seek legislation that would provide financial support to parents with children in private and parochial schools—either through tuition tax credits or through public vouchers. According to one account, "So strongly did [the Reagan administration] hold to these objectives that in April 1983, when the National Commission on Excellence in education came up with a report that ignored them, the White House came close to canceling President Reagan's picture-taking ceremony with the commission in the Rose Garden."[46]

During his first two years in office, Reagan was remarkably successful in bringing about legislative and regulatory changes in line with his domestic policy goals. He presided over increases in military spending, cuts in non-defense discretionary programs, and the largest tax cut in the nation's history.[47]

Such success did not carry over into the realm of education, however. The White House tried unsuccessfully—in 1983, 1985, and 1986—to get Congress to approve an education-voucher plan. None of the voucher proposals was as extreme as the model originally envisaged by Milton Friedman, and the 1986 version was especially modest. It would have given local districts the option to use vouchers, not required that they do so. It also would have left to the local districts the decision whether to allow such vouchers to be used for private schools. And it would have limited the use of vouchers to remedial education for children not able to get adequate help within their own public schools; the vouchers could not be used to pay general tuition for children without such special needs.

The administration's willingness to settle for a scaled-down school-choice package in 1986 reflected its reading of the limits set by political realities. Opposition to a broader conversion to market-oriented educational choice was too deeply embedded. Rather than "send up another voucher bill that wouldn't go anywhere," a top Education Department official indicated that the administration was willing to narrow its objectives so that it could "become a player in the game."[48]

But even this milder proposal could not overcome broad resistance from groups concerned about its impact on public schools and its potential to expand into a larger program involving public support for parochial schools. The chairman of a powerful House committee stated flatly, "I'm not in favor of vouchers, period." A key Republican Senate staff member, while supportive of small-scale, voluntary voucher experiments, indicated that the White House could not even count on strong support from its own party: "Anything that would mandate a voucher plan would not be supported by a majority of Republican members."[49]

Within a few years, however, the political landscape had shifted dramatically. "Efforts to Allow Choice of Schools Stir Debate," a January 1989 article in the *New York Times* announced. Showing the bipartisan nature of the developing support, the article quoted Rudy Perpich, the Democratic governor of Minnesota, as saying that "without choice, school districts have little incentive to change and to provide alternatives for those whose families want them."[50] By 1990, the chairman of the board of a major U.S. corporation was claiming that the "most promising approaches to school reform are those that promote competition between schools and that come from providing parents a choice among schools."[51] And a member of the Congress declared educational choice the "most potent education restructuring reform being discussed today. . . . Choice changes how education is controlled and managed. The idea works."[52]

It is little wonder that President Reagan's secretary of education expressed some bewilderment. "When I started talking about choice a couple of years ago it was still regarded as somewhat heretical," William J. Bennett noted in 1987. "Now it seems to be the conventional wisdom."[53]

Figure 3.1 illustrates the cycles in attention given to the issues of vouchers and educational choice; it graphs the number of articles dealing with those subjects that were listed in the *Readers' Guide to Periodical Literature*, which indexes most popular magazines and journals.[54] There were few articles directly focusing on vouchers and school choice until the federal

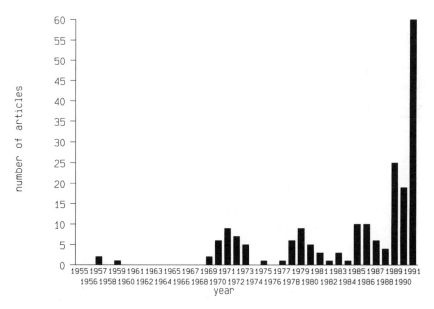

FIG. 3.1 Articles on vouchers or school choice, 1955–1991. *Source: Readers' Guide to Periodical Literature*, various years.

73

government's interest in a voucher experiment began to attract attention around 1970. Attention fell off within three years, then picked up again during the late 1970s, primarily in relation to the efforts to pass a school-choice initiative in California. Interest rose in 1985 and shot up dramatically as the 1990s began.

What happened? Proponents of choice generally explain the turnaround in the latter half of the 1980s in one of two ways: as an example of collective enlightenment, or as the gradual assertion of the will of the majority. Both perspectives promote the notion that the current choice movement is inevitable, desirable, and a reflection of democratically expressed values. Yet both are misleading in key respects, and both underplay an important dynamic that helps account for the political rejuvenation of the school-choice movement. By reformulating choice proposals and the arguments offered in their behalf, advocates of choice were simultaneously able to neutralize some of the traditional opposition and to expand their coalition by attracting support with nonmarket appeals. The resurgence of choice, in other words, is not just a story of policies coming to reflect latent or newly developing interests; it is also a story of how actors can reshape the political landscape through the theories, ideas, and interpretations of evidence they present.

Collective Enlightenment?

The enlightenment explanation presumes that confusion and lack of information account for the resistance to educational choice. Not until recently, it is argued, have Americans shed the myths that mistakenly led them to believe that choice was dangerous and that good education depended on a dominant role for the government.

According to the enlightenment perspective, the vast expansion of governmental responsibilities during this century rested on myths about the risks of irresponsibly exercised choice, the limitations of markets, and the benevolence of government. But the failure of the expanded governmental apparatus to eliminate social problems, it is suggested, finally is setting the stage for reconsideration. Average citizens are learning through experience that public schools provide neither the skills nor the moral environment they desire for their children. This grass-roots experience is reinforced by social science policy research, which authoritatively demonstrates that choice can simultaneously promote excellence and foster desegregation, and that private schools subject to market pressures outperform public schools beholden to hierarchical bureaucracies.

When Milton Friedman first introduced the notion of vouchers, Americans' confidence in the beneficence and capability of government was high. Aggressive governance, in the form of Franklin Roosevelt's New Deal, had convinced many that federal policy could wrestle to the ground the wild tiger of economic cycles. In 1960, Americans elected a charismatic president who stimulated broad enthusiasm for the notion that the national government could apply goodwill and technical know-how to tackle social problems related to poverty and race.

By 1980, advocates of choice argue, Americans' confidence in government—particularly the federal government—had been shaken. Trust in government dropped sharply. Dissatisfaction with high taxes and high inflation, governmental scandals such as Watergate and Abscam, the apparent inability of government successfully to address domestic problems (for example, poverty) and international problems (for example, the hostages in Iran) helped set the stage for the broad privatization movement and the antigovernment, antibureaucracy message that was the unifying dimension of Ronald Reagan's campaign. Studies comparing public versus private forms for delivering services traditionally provided by the government, such as sanitation and fire protection, built a case that contracting out to private firms could save money without reducing the quantity or quality of services.[55]

Education policy had its own story of gradual disillusionment with government. Part of that, as discussed in chapter 2, is the story of declining indicators of educational attainment. More potent in shaping the public's attitude toward government and the schools, however, was the nation's collective experience with efforts to bring about racial desegregation. As federal courts shifted their attention from blatant segregation in the South to the more subtle situation in the North, and as government involvement came to be associated most visibily and immediately with its imposition of mandatory busing, the public sector's role in education was transformed, in the eyes of many Americans, from crusader for a moral cause to misguided and heavy-handed oppressor.

Popular Victory?

Rather than gradually becoming enlightened about the limitations of government, this second perspective adhered to by some proponents of choice presumes that the majority of Americans always have favored market approaches and the principle of unfettered individual choice. Until recently, this majority sentiment was submerged, effectively intimidated and suppressed by the better-organized educational professionals, who had a direct stake in expanding public-sector involvement in the schools.

From this perspective, a shift in political forces—the erosion of the power of unions, growing divisions within the minority community, the growth of an educated middle class with the confidence to challenge the experts—accounts for the reemergence of choice. The centrality of freedom to the American psyche and the deep preference for private over public mechanisms explains why choice is "The Idea that Will Not Die."[56]

An Uncertain Public

Both the enlightenment and popular-will explanations overstate the public's aversion to government, in general and in the specific case of the schools. To the extent that it is meaningful at all to talk about a national psyche, it is more accurate to speak of an uncertain public. This is a public distressed about the course of national affairs yet far from ready to embrace radical change. It is a public in which mistrust of government coexists with a ready impulse to ask government to take on greater responsibility. Instead of a fixed and confident national will, there is a fluid situation in which concerned citizens are open to new answers and looking for leadership, guidance, and illuminating discussion about where the boundaries of public and personal responsibility should lie.

Claims that an enlightened public has suddenly recognized the limits of government usually are based on sudden declines in public confidence as measured by one or two questions in opinion polls. But consideration of a fuller range of relevant questions, and review of the complete historical record, reveal these drops to be selective, cyclical, and short-term.

Linda Bennett and Stephen Bennett analyzed surveys about trust in government and concerns about government power from 1935 to 1988. They found that the public's aversion to government is neither unambiguous nor fixed. "There continues to be some ambivalence in Americans' opinions about big government. Many Americans will offer that the national government is involved in too many issues and yet expect it to do more. . . . Americans still express belief in 'individualism,' and many hold to their personal responsibility to surmount the obstacles they confront in life. But belief in individualism does not preclude the possibility of a helping hand from government."[57] Belief that the federal government has too much power peaked in the period between 1978 and 1982, but then it started to decline. Experiencing the government-shrinking policies of the Reagan administration led some Americans to have second thoughts about government's place in society. By 1988, "the percentage of the public predisposed to agree with President Reagan's call for more cuts in Washington was no larger than in 1964, at the height of LBJ's popularity."[58]

This same kind of uncertainty and fluidity is evident in Americans' views about the proper role of government in education. The same polls that show strong public support for vouchers and other pro-choice reforms also show support for policies that presumably would centralize and increase government involvement. In 1991, for example, Americans favored by a margin of five to four the adoption of a voucher system including parochial schools—seemingly indicating a preference for market-based solutions over government management and control. Yet those same respondents, by even wider margins, favored government action to equalize school expenditures across districts, initiation of tax-supported public preschool programs for three- and four-year-olds, and requirements that local schools use a standardized national curriculum.[59]

Because neither firm evidence nor united will dictates the superiority of market forces over governmental authority, the process through which educational reforms are adopted is sure to be conflict-ridden and open-ended. In this environment, political leaders and organizations with a stake in the structure of education have an opportunity to shape the terms of debate by offering an interpretive framework that most people find more compelling, convincing, and comfortable than that offered by their opponents. Ideas are a potent weapon in this battle to set the definitions and reinterpret history.

Repackaging Choice

It's time parents were free to choose the schools that their
children attend. This approach will create the competitive
climate that stimulates excellence in our private and
parochial schools as well.
(*President George Bush, April 18, 1991*)

E ARLY IN 1988, President Ronald Reagan went to Suitland High School,
a public school in Prince George's County, Maryland, and announced to
twenty-two hundred students and guests that its magnet program was "one
of the great successes of the education-reform movement." In doing so, he
was using his considerable powers of rhetoric and symbolism to initiate an
interpretive revision of history and a political reclamation of a foundering
idea. Previously, choice proposals had been associated with private schools
and market principles; previously, magnet schools had been associated with
authoritative government action to bring about racial integration rather than
educational quality. Linking the choice agenda to existing public magnet
schools helped the Reagan administration make the case that school choice
was feasible and demonstrably successful. Understanding how this was
accomplished can tell us quite a bit about the way we learn—and fail to
learn—from our collective experience.

Part of this process of social learning is rooted in the hard soil of personal
experience, practical application, and systematic analysis. In chapters 5 and
6, I will review the historic record of magnet schools and educational choice
to make clear why that record does not support the strong claims made by
advocates of school choice. But my focus for now is on the evolution of ideas.
This chapter highlights the repackaging of school choice begun during
Ronald Reagan's second administration. This repackaging made choice appear less threatening to some traditional opponents, and helped to launch it
back onto the national political agenda. Although this reformulation in some
respects reflected a continuation of the strategic retreat that proved unsuccessful in 1986, it set the stage for calls for a more radical and comprehensive
market-based voucher system to reemerge.

THE POLITICS OF CHOICE

Reagan's Turnaround or "Strategic Retreat"

By January 1988, a seemingly sharp transformation had taken place. Rather than seeking to abolish the Department of Education, Reagan was working with his energetic and highly visible secretary of education, William Bennett, to place the White House in the forefront of the education-reform movement. The President's rhetorical commitment to school prayer remained unchanged, but no substantial efforts to pursue a constitutional amendment were on the horizon. And, in place of an emphasis on tuition tax credits, vouchers, and private schools, Reagan was touting the notion that choice among public schools would suffice to stimulate educational reform.

The strategic retreat to a public-schools-only emphasis was a defensive maneuver. Proposals to expand parental choice among public schools were shielded from the strongest historical challenges to vouchers: the fears that the best and brightest students would be drained from the public schools, that popular support for public-school funding would be eroded, that government would become inextricably involved in the finance and regulation of religious schools, and that the threat of a growing private-school alternative would be used as a political tool to weaken the negotiating power of unions representing public-school teachers. The suddenness of the administration's change in approach is indicated by the surprise reported by Albert Shanker, president of the American Federation of Teachers, at a January 1989 White House Seminar on School Choice: "Many of us feared that the seminar would be a reiteration of Reagan's support for vouchers and tax credits to pay for students to switch from public to private schools and that Reagan would be passing that torch on to Bush. But . . . Reagan, Bush and [then Secretary of Education] Cavazos spoke *only* of public schools and pushed the idea that having a choice of which public schools you could attend would strengthen *public* education. Bush went so far as to say that if parents were not required to send their children to the one assigned public school, many who now patronize private schools would re-enter public schools of their choice."[1]

The kind of market-based voucher concepts that had never managed to make the transition from academic theory to viable policy option were still staggering in the political ring, bruised and battered—even with the considerable power of Ronald Reagan backing them up. The effect of the shift in tactics was dramatic. This was not just a case of throwing in the towel, to save a bleeding fighter so he might fight again another day. By associating the concept of choice with ongoing activities in the public sector, the Reagan administration launched a multidimensional counterattack. It preempted the kinds of legal and philosophical challenges that had stymied previous efforts to enact choice plans that included parochial schools. Simultaneously, it defused the potent racial issue, addressed concerns about administrative feasibility, furthered its effort to shift debate from issues of equity to issues of effectiveness, linked its educational-reform stance to its central ideological commitments to New Federalism and privatization, and—perhaps most important—set the stage for the claim that empirical evidence supported its proposals. This repackaged vision of educational choice had so immediate and broad an appeal that it became a central element in George Bush's presidential campaign and subsequent domestic program.

Defusing the Issue of Racial Inequality

Fears that school choice would exacerbate economic and racial inequality were strongest in the late 1960s and early 1970s when Friedman's voucher notions were first introduced. While partly based on theoretical grounds, such fears had been fed by the nation's shared experience with resistance to the Supreme Court's 1954 and 1955 mandates for school desegregation. Southern states and school districts had turned to freedom-of-choice and voucher plans as a way to avoid the implications of *Brown v. Board of Education*,[2] forging in many Americans' minds a permanent link between educational choice and racial bigotry. By the 1980s, the nation's memory of the experience was attenuated. The median age of the American public in 1980, when Ronald Reagan was first elected, was thirty; half of all Americans were younger than five years old when the *Brown* decision was declared. The expansion of a black middle class, the election of blacks to public office in many cities, the growing perception that affirmative action was effectively compensating (some would say overcompensating) for historical inequalities—all these factors fed a national mood that had grown somewhat weary of the racial issue.

This national mood about racial matters was complex. On the one hand, it meant that Americans tended not to respond with the same moral outrage to charges of racial discrimination as many did in the 1960s. On the other hand, they exhibited a wariness of actions or rhetoric that might pull the scab off old wounds. The Reagan administration had confronted and misjudged this complex mood when it attempted to ease regulations intended to prevent federal grants from going to private colleges or universities that practiced discrimination.[3]

The shift to a public-schools-only stance made credible the association between the administration's goals for choice and certain magnet schools, like those in Prince George's County, that had been operating for years throughout many American communities. Magnet schools were initiated with the specific intention of promoting racial integration. Associating their long-term choice agenda with magnets gave advocates of choice the opportunity to defuse the racial concerns that threatened to bedevil the administration's education policy. Using the magnet-school experience as his reference point, Assistant Secretary of Education Chester E. Finn, Jr., declared that "the research uniformly fails to support" the charge that choice would "torpedo desegregation goals."[4]

Administrative Feasibility

For similar reasons, the retreat to a public-schools-only stance assuaged many of the concerns raised about the administrative feasibility of educational choice. While public-school administrators might continue to fret about the difficulty of undertaking enrollment planning once deprived of the ability to assign children mandatorily to designated schools, many public-school systems already were allowing students and their parents more choice than conventional wisdom acknowledged. Some of this choice took place within the context of magnet initiatives tied to racial integration. Some was related to programs instituted to meet the needs of students with special needs. Some simply reflected a loose implementation of residential requirements, wherein parental requests for reassignments were usually granted with little attention or scrutiny. If so many school districts already were managing to handle public-school choice without undue administrative stress, it seemed reasonable to conclude that fears of mass confusion and misallocation of resources were overstated.

From Equity to Excellence

The Reagan administration, although relying on the magnet-school association to blunt charges that choice initiatives necessarily entailed backtracking on the goal of racial integration, nonetheless shared neoconservatives' concern that the unchecked pursuit of racial equality had distorted the federal domestic-policy agenda. Reports that magnet schools, in addition to aiding integration efforts, were delivering higher-quality education provided an opportunity to shift the focus of debate from racial equality to educational excellence. In this sense, the repackaging of school choice served more than the defensive function of neutralizing opponents' traditional concerns. By reaffirming the link between choice and excellence, proponents of choice sought to broaden their constituency to include groups concerned about the "mediocratization" of American life.

The neoconservative insight into domestic policy distinguishes between efforts to equalize opportunity (good) and efforts to equalize outcomes (bad). Charles Murray and others argue that the 1960s marked a sharp shift in the orientation of the national elites who shaped government policy.[5] From the founding of the republic, they suggest, America's stance on social welfare issues was dictated by a consensus that a civilized society "does not let its people starve in the streets."[6] By the beginning of the 1960s, this historic consensus had evolved to incorporate the somewhat more ambitious ideals of the New Deal. Beyond averting destitution, according to this more contemporary view, government could play the additional role of giving the disadvantaged timely aid to help them pull themselves out of poverty. The Kennedy administration carefully characterized this in the slogan "Give a hand, not a handout." The idea that government should provide the poor an opportunity to succeed—not be the guarantor of their eventual success—underlay the early War on Poverty programs and major civil-rights legislation.

Murray dates rather precisely the point at which things began to go wrong. The transformation started in 1964 and was substantially complete by 1967. Economic prosperity combined with expanded social-welfare programs failed to eliminate poverty. Supreme Court decisions combined with civil-rights legislation and a general public rejection of overt racism failed to bring about racial equality. The tenacity of the problems was dramatized by hundreds of violent riots in some 250 cities all across the United States.[7] The relatively small group of intellectuals who confer legitimacy on public ideas took these as evidence that society—specifically, its deep and institutionalized racism, and the inability of its economy to provide sufficient numbers of well-paying jobs—was to blame. In light of this, providing opportunity was not enough. "If society were to blame for the riots, if it were to blame for the economic and social discrepancies between whites and blacks, if indeed it were to blame for poverty itself among all races, and *if society's responsibility were not put right by enforcing a formalistic legal equality*, then a social program could hardly be constructed on grounds that simply guaranteed equality of opportunity. It must work toward equality of *outcome*."[8]

This notion that people had a *right* to a certain level of income, education, housing, and the like led, the argument continues, to new and reoriented programs that unintentionally enticed people into dependency.[9] Programs that effectively guarantee a minimum standard of living, that give criminals so much protection that they rarely are punished for their crimes, that permit the indifferent student to get Bs and the bad student to get promoted, lower and obscure the costs of irresponsible behavior. They provide "incentives to fail."

Emphasizing equality of outcomes, it was argued, perverted the education process—and undermined educational quality—in several ways. Advocates of equality promoted a pedagogical philosophy that deemphasized structure and discipline. Supreme Court decisions like *Gault v. Arizona* (1967) set boundaries on the authority of school officials to punish or expel students; fearing lawsuits, many schools "gave up the practice of making a student repeat a grade."[10] And, finally, the awkward fact of racial differences in academic performance led schools to deemphasize achievement altogether.[11] As theories of economic rationality would predict, schools, teachers, and students all took the easy way out. It was no coincidence, Murray argued, that the educational gains urban blacks had been making began to level off at this point.[12]

Carefully constructed arguments such as Murray's nicely complemented Ronald Reagan's less academic, more intuitive worldview. "We've created the greatest public school system the world has ever seen, and then have let it deteriorate," he said in the spring of 1983. "I think you can make a case that it began to deteriorate when the federal government started interfering in education."[13] Receiving an honorary degree from the University of South Carolina in the fall of 1983, he emphasized that the problem with education was not lack of money, but insufficient "homework, testing . . . and good old-fashioned discipline."[14]

Reagan's 1988 speech at Suitland High School linked excellence with school choice in a new way. Previously, choice and excellence were often presumed to be values in tension.[15] Magnet schools—one of the most visible options for exercising school choice—were so closely tied historically to desegregation goals that policymakers as well as the broader public associated them with the overemphasis on racial results that the neoconservatives decried. Many of the other "choice" schools within the public system had been started in the 1960s and 1970s as part of the "alternative" schools movement; the pedagogical bent of these schools was precisely the nontraditional emphasis on "open education" and "experiential learning" that neoconservatives believed had done so much damage. Many analysts, too, had a pessimistic view of the average American's commitment to excellence and capacity to pursue it; parochial values and lack of information might lead many families to choose schools that would provide a poor education.

The location of Reagan's speech—at a public magnet school—symbolized the expansion of the vision of choice to include an emphasis on quality.[16] Federal aid for magnet schools through the Emergency School Aid Act had been justified exclusively by the potential for magnets to bring about desegregation. The Carter administration took the position that there simply was no evidence supporting the view that magnets provided better education. Presidents Reagan and Bush insisted that excellence be given equal, if not higher, billing. "Right now, all of the Federal money is tied to desegregating magnets," a deputy assistant to President Bush indicated. Magnet schools could do more than just desegregate: they "increased competition and choice and improved the education of students." In its first year in office, the Bush administration proposed that eligibility for federal aid to magnet schools be expanded to include recipients that might be using magnets for purposes other than desegregation.[17]

Linking Education to Broader Themes: New Federalism and Privatization

By linking the rhetoric of market ideas to the practice of public-school choice, the Reagan administration accomplished something else as well. The two broadest unifying themes of the Reagan presidency involved New Federalism and privatization. The goal of New Federalism was to shift power from the national government to the state and local level. The goals of privatization were to shrink the size of government at all levels and to increase reliance on market forces and voluntarism to achieve social ends. Switching focus from an abstract, national voucher system to models of choice already in place at the state and local levels integrated the administration's education policy into this broader agenda.

In his inaugural address, Ronald Reagan declared, "It is my intention to curb the size and influence of the Federal establishment and to demand recognition of the distinction between the powers granted to the Federal Government and those reserved to the States or the people." His program for a New Federalism comprised several components: a reduction in the amount of grants to state and local governments, an easing of the regulations and requirements imposed on those governments as a condition of receiving federal grants, and a return to the states of responsibility for certain functions (such as providing cash assistance to poor families) that he believed had been inappropriately taken over by the national government.[18]

Central to the political viability of New Federalism was the claim that such a downward shift of responsibilities would lead to greater innovation, efficiency, and responsiveness to citizens' concerns. Focusing attention on magnet schools and emerging state-level programs for public-school choice testified to the claim that subnational governments were "laboratories of democracy," where new policy ideas were constantly being tried, tested, and fine-tuned to best fit local circumstance and local norms.[19]

The goal of privatization was more radical and potentially unsettling than New Federalism. Conflict over the particular allocation of responsibilities among the levels of government is a constant theme throughout American history, and, while the period from Franklin D. Roosevelt through Lyndon Johnson saw a general drift toward the national level, the claim that states should not be eclipsed had never been pushed to the margin. For at least a decade prior to Reagan's election, a backlash against centralization had been gathering steam. President Nixon had introduced the term New Federalism, and even Jimmy Carter, a Democrat, had picked up on the theme of an expanded state and local role in a "partnership" to address social needs.

Privatization challenged conventional wisdom more directly. Since the Progressive Era, the presumption that government was (or at least could be) the primary vehicle for social improvement had deepened its roots in the American psyche. The New Deal experience reinforced that idea, and produced a political coalition to give it muscle and staying power. Familiar and comfortable though they were, abstract arguments for market processes made little headway in this context.

Accordingly, conservative advocates of privatization were especially anxious to establish the credibility of their claim that less government need not mean fewer benefits. They found some of what they needed in studies indicating that contracting out for various urban services—garbage collection, fire protection, street repair, and the like—generated fiscal savings without necessarily reducing the quantity or quality of the service provided.[20] But these were not services that stirred great passion or enthusiasm among the people. Nor was it clear whether successes in relying on private contracting to deliver such straightforward, technical, and measurable services could be extrapolated to the "more complex, undefinable, long-range and 'subjective' services"—like education—that were involved in meeting the more troubling problems of social welfare.[21]

Referring to education vouchers as a model did not give advocates of privatization the credibility they needed; the historic resistance to vouchers only reinforced the impression that reliance on private markets would be disruptive, conflict-ridden, and ultimately infeasible. Redefining educational choice in terms of activities that were already underway and operating smoothly rendered such reservations moot.

Linking educational choice to New Federalism and privatization simultaneously accomplished two goals. First, it expanded the potential constituency for the administration's specific education proposals beyond dissatisfied parents. State and local officials, traditional advocates of states' rights, and other groups that might benefit from less aggressive national government were given an incentive to ally with the education-reform movement, even when they might not have any direct stake in the schools themselves. So were natural allies of the privatization movement, including conservative think tanks and philanthropists, antitax forces, and private firms specializing in the provision of contracted services.

Second, the linkage injected new political life into the broader movements, which had begun to flag. The Reagan administration implemented some of its New Federalism initiatives in the early years of its first term, when it generally enjoyed its greatest legislative success.[22] But state and local officials that had complained for years about federal mandates and constraints on the use of federal funds became increasingly wary of New Federalism, as they came to the conclusion that responsibilities were being shifted downward without the concomitant resources to meet those responsibilities—with the likely result that they would be left holding the bag.[23] The privatization movement managed to get onto the national government's agenda a series of proposals that would have been unthinkable several years before,[24] but moving those ideas from the talking stage to the action stage was proving more difficult.[25] In the aftermath of *A Nation At Risk*, both the decentralization and privatization movements had something to gain by being associated with education reform.

BACK TO THE MARKET

An old saying suggests that sometimes it is necessary to take one step backward in order to move two steps ahead. Retreating to a public-schools-only position was a step backward for the Reagan administration. Taking that step, however, succeeded in clearing the way for choice to rise high on the public agenda. Almost immediately upon gaining legitimacy and a broader audience, some proponents of choice began pushing hard, once again, for much more radical choice plans based on market theories.

John Chubb and Terry Moe, by virtue of the tremendous amount of attention sparked by their *Politics, Markets, and America's Schools*, have become the most recognized spokespeople for such radical market-based choice plans. Several factors probably help account for the impact of their book. Their professional credentials may have been a factor; both are well-regarded political scientists, who had published extensively on other topics. Institutional affiliation almost certainly played a role. The Brookings Institution, which published the book, is perhaps the nation's premier think tank; that it has had a moderately liberal reputation made its endorsement all the more potent.[26] Had the study been released by the Heritage Foundation, or some other organization publicly linked to the conservative cause, its reception undoubtedly would have been more wary and skeptical.

These perhaps superficial factors aside, there are at least three substantive reasons why the book won—and earned—more attention than most other calls for educational choice. First, rather than simply repeating familiar market-based arguments for competition and choice, Chubb and Moe link their proposal to a broad theory of politics and democracy. Second, rather than relying on abstract theoretical arguments—economic or political—they anchor their proposals in the existing empirical literature and in their own original research. Third, rather than proposing a broadly worded call for greater choice, they take pains to spell out a model in unusual detail. The basic elements of their theory of politics and democracy were outlined in chapter 1: they argue that democratic, majoritarian institutions are irretrievably linked to bureaucracy and hierarchy, at least in heterogeneous environments like those that typify our major urban centers. Their empirical analysis, which I review more closely in chapter 6, purports to prove that hierarchy and bureaucracy serve, in turn, to bind schools in ways that keep them from achieving educational quality. In the following section I review their specific proposals. Although framed somewhat differently and couched in a strategically refurbished terminology, the Chubb and Moe proposals reiterate in their essentials the market-based voucher proposals that have come and gone before.

Chubb and Moe's "Scholarship" Plan

Table 4.1 summarizes the basic components of the Chubb and Moe plan. Its most obvious difference from those that have preceded it is its substitution of "scholarships" for vouchers. Vouchers go from the government to parent

TABLE 4.1

The Chubb and Moe "Scholarship" Plan

A. Schools.

 1. Schools will be chartered under state law based on minimal criteria currently used to accredit private schools.
 2. Existing private schools can choose to participate.
 3. States decide whether religious schools are included.

B. Funding.

 1. The state establishes a Choice Office in each district. Schools are compensated through this office.
 2. "Scholarship" amounts would be allowed to vary among districts based on district choice; states may choose to undertake equalization policies to supplement revenues available to poorer districts.
 3. "Scholarships" could also vary within districts to compensate poorer families and students with special needs.

C. Student Choice among Schools.

 1. A student will be free to "attend"[a] any school in the state.
 2. Choices and applications will be handled by the district Choice Offices, within which there will be Parent Information Centers.
 3. Transportation will be provided "to the extent tax revenues allow."

D. School Choice among Students.

 1. "Schools will make thier own admission decisions, subject only to nondiscrimination requirements."
 2. "Schools will set their own tuition." They are free to accept students with different-sized scholarships and they can keep scholarship money above the tuition amount. It is "unwise" (but apparently not prohibited) to allow schools to accept supplementary out-of-pocket payments from families.
 3. Schools will be free to expel students or deny them readmission when they believe the situation warrants.
 4. Students not selected by any school after two application rounds will be assigned a school based on a "safety net" procedure that could include lottery assignment to neighborhood schools.

E. School Governance and Organization.

 1. "Each school must be granted sole authority to determine its own governing structure."
 2. This specifically includes all personnel policies, curriculum, textbook choices, preparation time, and homework standards.
 3. Teachers will have the right to belong to unions and bargain collectively, but the unit will be the school and teachers need not join the union or be bound by union bargains.
 4. "Statewide tenure laws will be eliminated."

TABLE 4.1 *(cont.)*

F. *The Role of the State.*

  1. "The state will continue to certify teachers, but requirements will be minimal—corresponding to those that, in many states, have historically been applied to private schools."

  2. The state will hold schools responsible for meeting procedural requirements of the choice process.

  3. The state *will not* have any say in school organization, in governance, or in assessing student or school achievement.

Source: This table is adopted, with minor modifications, from John F. Witte, "Market versus State-Centered Approaches to American Education: Does Either Make Much Sense?" Paper prepared for delivery at the 1991 Annual Meeting of the American Political Science Association, Washington, D.C., August 29–September 1, 1991. Witte's reconstruction is based on John E. Chubb and Terry M. Moe, *Politics, Markets, and America's Schools* (Washington, D.C.: Brookings Institution, 1990), 219–225.

[a] They use the word "attend." However, given the rest of their plan, especially on school selection, "apply to" is the correct term. Chubb and Moe, *Politics, Markets, and America's Schools*, 221.

to school; scholarships are funded by the government, assigned to students, but sent directly to the schools in which those students enroll. "At no point will it go to parents or students."[27]

This distinction is a fairly transparent attempt to avoid the negative associations that historically have accompanied voucher plans. Asserting that the educational community has "consistently and vehemently" opposed voucher proposals and portrayed them as "the embodiment of everything that is threatening to public education," Chubb and Moe seek to dissociate their proposal from "the unwarranted stigma that the establishment has succeeded in attaching to the very concept of vouchers."[28] But the distinction is formalistic and shallow; in all significant respects Chubb and Moe's scholarships are intended to serve exactly the same function as vouchers, and in all significant respects they do.

Apart from this substitution of mechanisms for reimbursing schools, the Chubb and Moe proposal, for the most part, represents an elaboration of the Friedman model. Like Friedman's, it emphasizes freedom of mobility on the demand side. Students and their families would be free to shop around for the school that best meets their interests without regard to whether the school is in their neighborhood or their city, public or private (A2; A3; C1). Chubb and Moe leave it to the individual states to decide whether parochial schools should be eligible, but indicate their "own preference would be to include religious schools as well."[29] Like Friedman's, too, their proposal emphasizes deregulation on the supply side (A1; D1; D3; E1; E2; F1; F3), in order to make it easy and attractive for new schools to form and to establish distinctive identities.

The Chubb and Moe proposal is designed to accommodate a few redistributory and regulatory provisions that Friedman did not mention, but that are not directly contrary to his basic design. Their emphasis on the establishment of information centers (C2), their indication that transportation costs should be provided to the extent possible (C3), and their introduction of "safety net" provisions for students otherwise unable to obtain admission (D4) are intended to alleviate concerns that lower-income families will be unable to take advantage of the choices available to those with more educational and financial resources.

Chubb and Moe do indicate that their "preference is for an equalization approach,"[30] and it is here that they cross swords, at least symbolically, with the purer market mechanism that Friedman prefers. They recommend three major redistributory elements. Significantly, however, in each of these cases they draw a distinction between what they personally prefer and what should be regarded as necessary components of their scholarship plan. They prefer (but would not require) states to provide supplemental funding to poorer districts (B2). They prefer (but would not require) districts to provide larger scholarships to students with educational disadvantages (B3). And they prefer (but would not require) that parents be prohibited from supplementing scholarship amounts with their own funds (D2).[31]

The Bush Administration Signs On

The Reagan administration's strategic retreat to a public-schools-only stance broadened the political viability of school-choice initiatives, and through the first half of his administration President George Bush's actions suggested that he had learned this lesson. Early in 1989, the secretary of education, Lauro F. Cavazos, was emphasizing the intent only to fine-tune the Reagan proposals, and the necessity for the federal government to limit its activities largely to finding and publicizing success stories at the state and local levels.[32] Although the relative lack of activism on the education-policy front generally disappointed those who had taken seriously Bush's stated intention to become the "Education President," the administration continued to offer pro-choice pronouncements. These heavily emphasized choice initiatives in the public sector, like those in Minnesota, East Harlem, and Cambridge, Massachusetts. Asked early in his presidency whether it was unfair that private-school parents have to pay tuition in addition to supporting the public system through their taxes, Bush indicated that it was "their right" to send their children to private schools, but "I don't think they should get a break for that."[33]

By the end of 1990, though, there were a few clues that the White House was becoming favorably inclined toward choice schemes that included private schools. Vice President Quayle was sent to Oregon to support a state initiative that would have given parents the right to have their children attend any school in the state and provided a tax credit of twenty-five hundred dollars to parents if their children attended either public or private schools.[34] In announcing the launching of the new federal Center for Choice in Education in December 1990, Cavazos indicated that the president supported the new Wisconsin program that provided some low-income Milwaukee families state support to pay tuition costs at private schools.[35]

The heavily publicized *America 2000* proposal, with which President Bush articulated the broad outlines of his education program in April 1991, gave little specific attention to choice; as Harold Howe II noted, "one 85 word paragraph is all there is on the subject."[36] Most commentary and public reaction focused instead on proposals for national testing and the establishment of model "break-the-mold" schools. But a question-and-answer section in the back of the booklet summarizing the plan makes it clear that the preference was to include parochial schools if legally possible: "It will apply to all schools except where the courts find a constitutional bar."[37]

Suddenly, early in 1992, the Bush administration began taking more visible and affirmative positions on market-oriented, private-school choice plans. With the Senate considering legislation that might have given poorer families the right to use federal aid to attend private schools, Bush drew an analogy between proposed programs to provide government support to families with children in private elementary and secondary schools and well-established programs supporting college students. "We don't exclude [college] students who choose private schools, including religious schools," he told a group in Columbus, Ohio, on January 26. The *Washington Post* article reporting the speech observed, "Education Secretary Lamar Alexander frequently has spoken of broadening the meaning of public education to include schools that are not directly controlled by local governments, but Bush has never been so direct."[38] On January 29, Bush and Alexander included a proposed "G.I. Bill for Children" as part of their budget plan for the following fiscal year.

Coming less than one month before the New Hampshire primary, the explicit inclusion of parochial schools in the Bush administration's school-choice proposals may have reflected the growing political pressure on the president to take strong stands on domestic issues, and to forestall the rising support for Patrick Buchanan among more conservative elements in the Republican party. Indicative of the latter was an address Bush made to a group of officials of Christian radio and television stations, just two days after the Columbus speech. Using religious themes and language "seldom heard in his oratory except in election years,"[39] Bush supported voluntary prayer in public schools. "In Sunday school, children learn that God is everywhere, but in public school, they find that He's absent from class," he told the group. "I want to thank you for helping America, as Christ ordained, to be a light unto the world."

In January 1992, popularity polls were still suggesting that Bush had little to fear from his potential Democratic challengers. But as the Buchanan challenge faded later in the spring, the threat from a surging Bill Clinton loomed in its place. Clinton was a proponent of school choice, but only of choice plans that were restricted to public schools. On June 25, the president transmitted his proposed GI Bill legislation to Congress. With the threat from the political right diminishing, emphasizing the religious aspects of school choice no longer served the tactical interests of those seeking the reelection of George Bush. Now the focus turned from religion and values back to the language of economic theory. By emphasizing the free-market aspects of school choice, Bush put himself in position to draw a stark distinction between his domestic agenda—rooted in markets and the entrepreneurial spirit—and that of the Democrats, which could be portrayed as being bogged down in bureaucracy and governmental solutions imposed from on high.

The GI Bill for Children

Bush's "Federal Grants for State and Local 'GI Bills' for Children" proposed allocating four-year grants to states and local school districts that provided thousand-dollar scholarships to children in low- and middle-income families. Families could use these scholarships to send their children to any lawfully operated school, whether public, private, or religious. Up to half of the scholarship amount could be used to pay for supplementary academic services (such as summer, weekend, or after-school programs); these, too, could be in a public or private setting. The state and local grantees could set their own income-eligibility levels, with the proviso that this not exceed the higher of the state or national median income adjusted for family size. Participating schools would be required to comply with federal antidiscrimination provisions relating to race, gender, and disability, but otherwise the proposed program would impose no regulations about admission, curriculum, testing, teacher qualifications, or the like.[40]

Officially known as the Servicemen's Readjustment Act (P.L. 78–346), the first GI Bill was passed in 1944. Besides symbolically honoring the soldiers who were defending the nation in World War II, the bill was intended to help returning veterans make a smoother transition back into civilian life. A central part of the bill was the provision of education and job-training benefits to allow veterans to attend school at government expense.[41] Subsequently, a series of laws has been passed to provide educational and training benefits to more recent veterans. Although each of these bills offers different packages of benefits and defines eligibility differently, they are often referred to generically as the GI Bill.[42]

By linking the proposal to the federal GI Bill, supporters of the GI Bill for Children put themselves in a position to counter the familiar charge that a choice plan including parochial schools would be unconstitutional. "When the GIs came home from World War II, we didn't say you could spend your GI Bill only at the University of Pennsylvania. . . . You could go to Howard University, the Jewish Theological Seminary, Southern Methodist University, Brigham Young University, or Notre Dame," President Bush and Secretary Alexander regularly pointed out in defending the proposal.[43] By using the term "scholarship," the Bush administration followed Chubb and Moe's lead in sidestepping the negative political connotations the voucher term had accumulated over the years. By making the scholarships available to public-school parents as well as those sending their children to private schools, the proposal was designed to fit within the constitutional interpretations outlined by the Supreme Court in its important *Mueller v. Allen* decision (1983).[44] By limiting the scholarships to those below the median income, the administration put itself in a position to counter charges that the proposal would benefit the wealthy.[45] Offering it as a competitive grant to state and local governments, the administration was able to avoid appearing to preempt local control, and also avoid having to address the full budget ramifications that would follow if such a model were to be enacted as a national entitlement.[46]

Redefining "Public" Schools

The reemergence of proposals for choice that would include private and parochial schools was accompanied by an attempt to redefine what is "public" and what is "private." Traditionally, we make this distinction primarily by ownership; a public school is one owned and run by government, a private school is owned and run by religious orders or private entrepreneurs. The new definition would rest more heavily on purpose and ultimate accountability. Any school that serves the broad public interest and is ultimately accountable to public authorities would be labeled "public" under this definition.

Redefining public schools in this way has an extremely important consequence. Most of the schools that we currently think of as private could claim to be public, perhaps without sacrificing anything in the way of independence and self-governance. By providing children with an education in keeping with national values, they serve a broad national purpose. And they already are accountable to public authorities in matters related to health, safety, and basic curriculum. By rhetorical sleight-of-hand, this redefinition would address long-standing concerns about the propriety of providing government support to public schools simply by declaring private schools to be public.

Under Chubb and Moe's proposal, any school that wishes to and that meets the minimal criteria "roughly corresponding to the criteria many states now employ in accrediting private schools . . . must then be chartered as a public school and granted the right to accept students and receive public money."[47] Any schools that participate, including religious schools, "will thereby become public schools, as such schools are defined under the new system."[48] It is this definitional twist that accounts for Chubb and Moe's claim that their proposals "have nothing to do with 'privatizing' the nation's schools."[49] Rather than proposing to shrink the public sector, they would have us believe that they would instead expand it substantially.

This definitional reshuffling, which Jencks first proposed about two decades earlier,[50] was adopted by the Bush administration as well. "Whether a school is organized by privately financed educators or town councils or religious orders or denominations," President Bush declared in the January 1992 Columbus speech, "any school that serves the public and is held accountable by the public authority provides public education."[51]

Without a fleshier notion of the public interest, and without a more muscular notion of governmental accountability, however, the proposed definitional criteria have little discriminatory power.[52] At the same time that Chubb and Moe suggest that simple accountability to government authority ought to suffice to make a school "public," for example, they insist that accountability to government and political processes ought to be weakened across the board. "Our guiding principle in the design of a choice system is this," they write: "public authority must be put to use in creating a system that is almost entirely beyond the reach of public authority."[53]

THE INFLUENCE OF PUBLIC IDEAS

By 1992 we had come full circle. The arguments for a market solution to problems in education, first floated by Milton Friedman in the mid-1950s, were back at the top of the political agenda. At the time, however, such ideas were launched into quite a different social context. Confidence was high in the nation, its schools, and its government. Following the Great Depression, the New Deal, and victory in World War II, people found it easy to set high public goals and natural to assign responsibility for achieving those goals to the government. In that context, "to view government expansion simply as an imposition seemed obsolete and quaint."[54]

By the mid-1980s, however, the broad privatization movement had successfully challenged the easy association between common goals and government action. The concept of "public interest" had become attenuated. The reformers who originally helped build the nation's public-school system were animated by a belief in an objective and unifying public interest, and by the notion that public schools would play a critical role in dispelling the ignorance and parochial loyalties that kept the masses from understanding what were their true interests.[55] The emergence of pluralism as the dominant intellectual force in political theory challenged the legitimacy of the very concept of a public interest, arguing that claims to act in the public interest usually mask the baser realities of a political life in which self-interested actors seek to better their position at the expense of others.[56] And the influence of public-choice theory, with the consequent infiltration of economics concepts and terminology into public-policy discourse, carried this challenge even further.[57] Rather than standing outside the game of competing self-interests, public-choice theory suggests that government should be regarded as just another player, albeit one with special advantages. The only legitimate test of governmental performance is satisfaction of the private desires of citizens qua consumers.

Proposing that we stretch the label "public" to cover largely deregulated, market-based systems of educational choice is possible only because the term *public* has been so devalued. Building on pluralist and public-choice ideas, Chubb and Moe emphatically reject the presumption that education policy can or should be directed by a common vision or social purpose. "On reflection, it should be apparent that schools have no immutable or transcendent purpose," they insisted. "What they are supposed to be doing depends on who controls them and what those controllers want them to do."[58]

In this sense, the intellectual spadework for the reemergence of a market-oriented school-choice movement was carried out in the broader arena of political thought. Without a stronger vision of collective purpose to counterbalance their deep commitment to personal freedom, Americans were left with little sense about why they wanted government at all. Although tradition and loyalty provided a residual constituency for public schools, the philosophical rationale for keeping educational decision making firmly anchored in public institutions was being forgotten.

PART THREE

REINTERPRETING THE HISTORY OF
SCHOOL CHOICE

☆

In the abstracting of an idea one may lose the very intimate
humanity of it.
(*Ben Shahn*, "The Biography of a Painting")

THE ASCENDANCY of proposals for choice on the national agenda is partly attributable to their association with familiar and respected theories of politics and economics, which has given them an intellectual clarity and persuasiveness they would otherwise lack. But Americans tend to be a pragmatic lot, slow to rally around abstract theories without some indication of how they work in practice. At least until recently, the nation's experience with choice in education has had little to do with the economic theories with which it currently is linked.

The practice of educational choice, as expressed in the operation of thousands of school districts around the United States, evolved with a dynamic of its own, shaped by pragmatic adjustment to legal, political, and administrative currents rather than the illumination of clearly defined and fully articulated theoretical models. In the three chapters that make up part 3, I consider this history of choice-in-practice and reflect on its implications for the contemporary debate over education reform. While we can learn much from history, its lessons are filled with ambiguities and misdirections. Unlike Aesop, history does not stamp each tale with a straightforward moral.

Throughout the 1950s, 1960s, and 1970s, the evolution of choice-in-practice in American education was interwoven most intimately with the thread of racial politics. In chapter 5 I review the developments in the relationship between race and school choice—an evolution that takes choice from being an anti-integration device to a prointegration device and, finally, a tool for education reform, the racial ramifications of which are considered secondary or even irrelevant. The chapter concludes with a reminder that choice can be an undiscriminating vehicle for expressing values and desires. The expression of personal desires by no means ensures a harmonious community. Whether individual choice is socially constructive or destructive depends, among other things, on the particular content of the values brought to bear and the institutional context that encourages some, discourages others, and deems still others illegitimate. What comes of choice, in other words, is not predetermined; it depends on what we make of it.

In chapter 6 I focus on the claim by proponents of choice that—when subjected to systematic techniques of policy analysis—the nation's experiences provide strong and convincing evidence that school choice works. Americans' experience with market forces in their everyday lives, I suggest, leaves them properly wary of exaggerated theoretical claims about both the wonders and the dangers of markets. In the face of skepticism about the benefits of privatization on a broad scale, those proposing to deemphasize government set about building an empirical case that market solutions are feasible and effective. This self-conscious attempt to use existing practice as a means to legitimate the claims of more abstract economic theories has played an important role in putting voucherlike choice plans back on the nation's policy agenda. But it is my contention that this evidence has been misrepresented and oversold.

My critique of the claim that school choice has been proved to work comes in two parts. The first involves basic issues of measurement and research design. My stance here is modest. I do not argue that choice never works. To the contrary, I am convinced that education policies incorporating elements of choice in some places have been associated with exciting and potentially valuable reforms. Rather than offer a blanket rejection of choice, my goal in chapter 6 is simply to highlight how little we can confidently conclude based on the evidence thus far compiled. Those who try to reassure us that the evidence is clear—that radical reconfiguration of our educational system therefore is relatively risk-free—are grossly overselling the state of our knowledge.

The second part of my critique moves from fact to interpretation. When proponents of market-based policies see signs of vitality and enthusiasm associated with school choice, they attribute them to the spontaneous eruption of healthful impulses previously buried under layers of government, regulation, and imperious professionals. This linkage seems unproblematic because the economic analogies on which they draw encourage them to mistrust government's capacity to gauge and anticipate demands or to manage supply fluidly and efficiently. Yet, even in those cases where choice may be associated with positive changes, I will argue that the lesson that market forces are responsible is strained. Rather than constituting evidence of the advantages of unrestrained choice by families pursuing private and personal goals, chapter 7 develops the thesis that, where school choice has been associated with positive change, its successes have depended on public officials exercising leadership, nurturing supportive coalitions, and authoritatively and sometimes forcefully using governmental power.

Evolving Practice

PROBLEMATIC LESSONS FROM HISTORY

WHILE CONCERNS about religious entanglement, inequality, and implementation tempered the response to Milton Friedman's economic arguments for vouchers, educational choice nevertheless was finding a niche in
American practice. At about the same time that Friedman was developing
his theoretical rationale for school vouchers, choice was being put into use
by southern school districts looking to sidestep the pressure to integrate
after the Supreme Court ruled racially separate schools to be unconstitutional in 1954. In some southern states, vouchers and tuition tax credits were
key components of this segregation effort.

Later, beginning in the 1970s, the practice of educational choice came to
be associated with efforts to *integrate* schools. Local school districts, sometimes under the direct supervision of federal courts, tried to design programs that would entice white families to enroll their children voluntarily in
schools with high minority populations. Magnet schools—schools with special programs, extra resources, or unconventional pedagogical styles—were
an important innovation in this period.

During the 1980s, the practice of educational choice underwent another
shift. A handful of innovative states and local districts began to build on the
magnet model. These initiatives—which expanded the choice alternative to
a wider range of schoolchildren and broadened the definition of the kinds of
schools eligible to take part—were not driven primarily by either a concern
with racial integration or a self-conscious effort to apply principles of political and economic theory. Instead, they emerged through a gradual and pragmatic process of administrative adjustment and the growing recognition of
choice as a politically useful tool for achieving other goals of educational
reform.

Interpretations of this history play an important role in the contemporary
debate about expanding educational choice. Opponents say that because
choice was once used to evade integration, it may be used that way again.
Many believe that bigotry and parochialism are still the driving force behind
the choice movement, explaining much of its grass-roots appeal, if not necessarily the motivations of its leaders, and that the racially divisive effects of

choice will again become apparent if choice programs are put into effect. Proponents argue that experience with magnet schools demonstrates that racial prejudice is less virulent than it used to be, that legislative and judicial protections ensure that racial discrimination will not be tolerated, and that most parents care much more about education quality than the color of their children's classmates' skins; racial bias and segregation are not a threat, they conclude, in the contemporary context. They cite the more recent innovations as proof that the goals of equality and excellence are readily wed.

Reviewing the record can help us assess how convincing each of these contrasting views is, but the point of the exercise should not be to help us land fully and assuredly on one side or the other. Both perspectives are limited by their deterministic cast. History can inform the present, but it does not dictate it. More than anything else, the record reveals an ongoing process in which conscious planning is juxtaposed with reaction and reflex; in which narrow self-interest coexists with principled assertions of a common good; in which conflicts among values and interests are sometimes resolved by compromise and conciliation and sometimes by brute political clout; and in which reasoned assessment of the lessons of experience is often clouded by overdrawn claims about proven successes and misleading interpretations of empirical findings. The lessons I attempt to draw have less to do with whether choice is inevitably destructive or inevitably benign than with how we can reasonably deliberate about public-policy decisions in an environment that is fluid, open-ended, and only partly susceptible to deliberate intervention through collective means.

FREEDOM TO CHOOSE SEGREGATION

The South Reacts to Brown v. Board of Education

In its landmark decision of May 17, 1954, in *Brown v. Board of Education*, the U.S. Supreme Court concluded that "in the field of public education the doctrine of separate but equal has no place." The following year, the Court made clearer that desegregation of southern public schools was to be initiated promptly and carried out "with all deliberate speed."[1]

Many southern leaders initially responded to the Supreme Court's rulings with outright resistance. Senator James O. Eastland of Mississippi announced that "the South will not abide by, or obey, this legislative decision by a political court."[2] Senator Harry Byrd of Virginia called for southerners to engage in "massive resistance." Georgia Democrats nominated for governor a man who campaigned on the pledge: "Come hell or high water, races will not be mixed in Georgia schools."[3] In March 1956, most of the members of Congress from the southern states issued a joint "Southern Manifesto" in which they declared the *Brown* decision "contrary to the constitution" and commended the "motives of those states which have declared an intention to resist forced integration by any lawful means."[4]

By 1957, Gary Orfield notes, "at least 136 new laws and state constitutional amendments designed to delay or prevent integration were on the lawbooks."[5] Louisiana, for example, amended its constitution in 1954 to require segregation in its schools.[6] Mississippi voters gave the state legislature authority to close the public schools if their desegregation was unavoidable. Arkansas amended its constitution in 1956 to command statewide resistance. South Carolina passed legislation that cut off funding to any integrated public school. Virginia passed legislation requiring that any school that accepted a child of a different race be closed and removed from the public-school system.[7]

Freedom of Choice

When direct resistance failed, freedom of choice was the fallback position. Southern officials took steps to comply minimally with the Supreme Court's ruling by eliminating the formal requirements for a dual school system. If schools remained racially segregated after formal segregation ended, they argued, this would simply reflect the fact that both whites and blacks preferred to attend schools with "their own kind." At the same time—and in the name of free choice—they took formal and informal steps to make it easier for white students to stay in completely segregated settings, either within the public-school system or, if that failed, in a reconstituted private-school system subsidized by public funds.

One popular technique for maintaining segregation in the public schools was the "minority-to-majority transfer" arrangement. "After formally desegregating, a Southern school district would grant to any students who constituted a racial minority in their new school the option of transferring back to their old school in which their race was a majority."[8] In practice, this ensured that the formal desegregation process would be little more than a ritual dance, with little or no impact on the racial composition of schools as the students actually experienced them. Freedom of choice in Alabama translated into an explicit legislative deferral to racial prejudice; the state passed a law that said "any other provisions of law notwithstanding, no child shall be compelled to attend any school in which the races are commingled when a written objection of the parent or guardian has been filed with the board of education."[9]

103

While nominally available to all, however, the freedom to choose within the public-school system was in fact unequally distributed. Blacks with the temerity to request transfers risked harassment from organizations like the KKK, and local school boards frequently overturned such requests, in any event, on the ground that the children could be better served in their own schools.[10] In 1963 the Supreme Court struck down minority-to-majority transfer plans as in violation of *Brown*: "Here the right of transfer, which operates solely on the basis of a racial classification, is a one-way ticket leading to but one destination, i.e. the majority race of the transferee and continued segregation."[11] Nonetheless, Orfield reports that as late as 1965, "in more than 100 districts with approved freedom-of-choice plans, community attitudes were so strong that not a single Negro student chose to enroll in any white school. In hundreds of other districts only an insignificant fraction of Negro pupils challenged the system of racial separation. The fear and apathy pervading Negro communities in areas with a poor racial climate transformed the freedom-of-choice plan from a mechanism for integration to a means of legalizing segregation."[12]

Government Support for Segregation Academies

A more extreme technique, also defended in terms of freedom of choice, involved private schools. To make it easier for white parents to escape the public system if integration did occur, several states enacted tuition grants to help defray the costs of nonsectarian private schools. Georgia, for example, amended its constitution to permit the state to provide tuition grants that would support a nominally "private" school system.[13] Mississippi, Alabama, Louisiana, and Virginia also enacted such plans.

The Virginia legislature initially approved a tuition-grant plan in September 1956. A more elaborate plan, passed in 1960, guaranteed a "scholarship" roughly equal to the per-pupil public-school cost to any student who chose to attend a qualified nonsectarian school in preference to the public school of his or her district. Funding for the program was split between state and local jurisdictions. By 1962, more than eighty-five hundred children were receiving such scholarships, at a total cost to government of over two million dollars.[14] The number of students involved, and the cost of the program, continued to escalate over the next several years, as federal pressure to integrate increased.

In Prince Edward County, Virginia, freedom of choice took an extreme form, one that colors not only the concept of choice but that of tuition vouchers as well. White citizens in Prince Edward County—one of the districts involved in the initial *Brown* case—publicly declared their refusal to operate public schools "wherein white and colored children are taught together." In 1959, when all other legal avenues were closed off, Prince Edward County officials simply stopped raising money to fund the public system. The public schools closed and remained closed for four years, leaving many black students no real option for education,[15] while white parents sent their children to a newly established private academy that did not accept any blacks. In 1960, the state and county began providing tuition grants (as well as property tax credits up to 25 percent) to those white parents. The grants of up to $225 for elementary students were the major source of financial support for the Prince Edward School Foundation, the private organization that was established to build and operate alternative schools for the county's white students.[16] Although $225 may not sound like much today, the combination of state and local grants meant that parents only needed to come up with about $15 per year out of their own pockets to meet tuition charges.[17] By 1967, there were about seven thousand Virginia students enrolled in more than twenty-five "segregation academies" across the state.[18]

The federal courts eventually invalidated state tuition-grant programs, like that in Virginia, that were so clearly tied to the desperate effort to avoid integration. Writing for the majority in the case of *Griffin v. County School Board of Prince Edward County*, Justice Black concluded that "the record in the present case could not be clearer that Prince Edward's public schools were closed and private schools operated in their place with state and county assistance, for one reason, and one reason only: to ensure, through measures taken by the county and the state, that white and colored children in Prince Edward County would not, under any circumstances, go to the same school."[19]

Ultimately, too, the Supreme Court offered a broad ruling that no version of freedom-of-choice plans was sufficient to relieve local authorities of the responsibility to undo the effects of unconstitutional segregation. The specific case involved New Kent County, a rural area in eastern Virginia with a population approximately evenly divided between whites and blacks. During the first three years in which New Kent County's freedom-of-choice plan was in effect, not a single white child chose to attend the all-black Watkins School; 85 percent of the black students remained at Watkins. This segregation of the schools was not based on residential segregation. Blacks and whites were each spread throughout the whole county, and the school buses serving the white and black schools served overlapping routes. In *Green v. County School Board*, Justice William Brennan wrote for the majority that, while freedom of choice might under some circumstances be a part of a legal and effective approach, "the general experience under 'freedom of choice' to date has been such as to indicate its ineffectiveness as a tool of desegregation."[20]

In determining the relevance of this history to contemporary debates over educational policy, a number of points need to be considered. First, the key federal court decisions overruling freedom-of-choice and tuition-grant plans took place in a particular historical context, and the courts were quite explicit in relating their decisions to that context. It was crucial that the jurisdictions involved had engaged in de jure segregation. Educational choice was found to be unconstitutional because it deliberately was used to avoid taking steps to undo the damage that formal segregation had caused. Second, as it became clear that racial motivation was to be an important criterion in the courts' deliberations, actors at the state and local levels learned to become more circumspect in the manner in which they publicly framed the issues; open admissions of racial intent became progressively more rare and justifications in the name of educational quality and local control became more common. Third, in the face of deliberate obfuscation about motivation, the courts concluded that motivation behind choice and tuition-grant schemes sometimes could legitimately be inferred from the sequence of events that led up to their adoption and implementation. Discussing Louisiana's tuition-grant program, for example, the federal district court concluded that "as certainly as '12' is the next number of a series starting 2,4,6,8,10, [the state's tuition-grant legislation] fitted into the long series of statutes the Louisiana legislature enacted for over a hundred years to maintain segregated schools for white children."[21]

The historical association of educational choice with local efforts to maintain racial separation remains an important backdrop to the contemporary movement for market-based school-choice reforms. The threat of legal challenge, combined with what seems to be a general wariness among the American people of actions that might reopen old racial wounds, makes it politically necessary for proponents of choice to offer reassurances that choice and integration are not contradictions in terms. Here, the nation's experience with magnet schools plays a prominent role.

MAGNET SCHOOLS: CHOICE AS A VEHICLE FOR MANAGING INTEGRATION

The previous year, she had been 345th in the line of over 1,500, but still had gone away empty-handed. So this year she showed up three days early and camped out in line in her Mercury Cougar. Some of the 182 people ahead of her had been waiting for three days already. One took a week's vacation from a job as a mail carrier and rented a mobile home to live in while she held her spot in line.[22] They were waiting to sign their children up for a public magnet school in Maryland's Prince George's County.

When hundreds of teenagers camp out overnight to get the best tickets for a Bruce Springsteen or Grateful Dead concert, hardly anyone is surprised. When hundreds of parents camp out for as much as a whole week to make certain their children get into the public school of their choice, the media comes out in force and people take notice. The evidence of long lines—as well as improved test scores—is what brought President Reagan to Prince George's County in 1988, when he declared the county's magnet schools "one of the great successes of the educational reform movement," and offered it as a model for schools around the nation to emulate.[23]

To President Reagan and other advocates of market-based choice schemes for educational reform, magnet schools held a number of special attractions. Because they were restricted to public schools, magnets were a step toward educational choice that would not stir up the same constitutional and political hornets' nests that continuously had bedeviled voucher proposals. Because they already were up and running in a number of large school districts, magnet schools did not raise the same fears about administrative impracticality as did more abstract calls for educational choice. And because they were linked with racial integration historically and in people's minds, magnet schools seemed effectively immunized against the charge that educational choice would exacerbate inequalities.

What Are Magnet Schools?

Magnet schools traditionally have involved the assignment of extra resources, attractive programs, or special teaching approaches to schools in high-minority neighborhoods in order to stimulate voluntary integration and moderate the conflict and white flight that might otherwise be generated in response to mandatory desegregation initiatives. By providing selected schools with additional resources and attractive programs, magnets were intended to entice parents voluntarily to transfer their children among schools in a direction that would improve racial balance.

The list of special programs to which districts have turned in order to give their magnets real drawing power includes some fairly exotic examples. Cincinnati, for example, featured one program emphasizing woodworking, and another, offered at the city zoo, concentrating on the care and feeding of animals.[24] St. Louis planned to open a magnet that would focus on individual sports called "Olympic Skills" (later renamed the "Athletic and Academic

Academy" by officials who recognized that the original title would not present the image they desired).[25]

Most magnets, however, have been built on variations on a fairly short list of areas of specialization. At the elementary level these have included programs focusing on basic skills, individualized learning, math/science concentrations, gifted and talented programs, language immersion, and the arts. At the high school level it also is common to find magnet programs offering more vocationally oriented training.[26] Sometimes magnet programs are schoolwide; sometimes they are available only for a subset of eligible students within a school. Sometimes magnet specializations are integrated throughout the entire curriculum; sometimes they are limited to special classes for which eligible students are pulled out of their normal classrooms on a daily or more occasional basis.

The Widespread Adoption of Magnets

The use of magnets to facilitate integration expanded dramatically throughout the 1970s and into the 1980s. A 1977 article noted that, while "five years ago the term 'magnet school' was virtually unknown," hundreds of school districts sent representatives to a national conference on magnet schools held in Houston in 1976.[27] By 1981–82, there were over a thousand magnet schools in the United States.[28] Most of this expansion took place with little national fanfare. Efforts were shaped at the local level and, although the leaders knew of and learned from efforts in other jurisdictions, specific programs generated were considered to be homegrown products.

One reason that magnet schools spread so widely and rapidly involved the role of the federal courts. The idea of giving a few public schools special educational missions that would draw students from throughout the district was not new. Special public schools like Bronx High School of Science in New York City, Lowell in San Francisco, Lane Tech in Chicago, and Boston's Latin School existed for years before the term "magnet" was coined. Walnut Hills High School, in Cincinnati, was created in 1918 for academically gifted, college-bound students.[29] The emphasis on "alternative" education that arose in the 1960s led some districts to experiment further with the idea of introducing diversity into public-school offerings. These remained idiosyncratic and peripheral initiatives, however, until "they acquired powerful allies: federal judges."[30]

The popularity of magnet schools was boosted because federal judges demonstrated a willingness to accept local integration plans that incorporated magnet schools as a way to minimize the extent of mandatory busing.

For all the resistance to desegregation that erupted in the rural south, when federal courts turned toward northern and big-city school districts in the early 1970s they found them in some ways an even a more difficult nut to crack. Part of the problem was the political volatility of the big-city environment, where black and white ethnic communities were more equally matched in levels of political mobilization and where they confronted one another in a more dense arena, in which memories of racial riots were strong. Part of the problem was simply that desegregating northern and big-city districts posed greater administrative and technical challenges. In many southern districts, desegregation actually reduced the need for busing, but this was not the case in big-city districts, where patterns of residential segregation were sharper and traffic congestion was more severe.[31] The promise of inducing voluntary movement of white students into more integrated schools made magnets attractive to federal judges and to local officials seeking to craft plans that would satisfy the courts with a minimum of disruption and controversy.

Magnets constituted key parts of court-ordered desegregation plans in places like Boston, Buffalo, Houston, Milwaukee, St. Louis, and Prince George's County. In Boston, perhaps the most visible case of court-ordered desegregation because of the intense resistance it sparked, the experts appointed by the federal judge to help devise a desegregation plan developed a citywide magnet plan that built on a network of magnetlike schools that were already in place. These included selective public schools such as Boston Technical High School, alternative schools created as part of the counterculture movement of the 1960s, and "schools with already established reputations for being magnetic educationally."[32] Similarly, the Prince George's County's magnet schools that Reagan lauded in 1988 were the result of more than a decade of legal suits brought by black parents.[33]

Whereas the possibility of judicial intervention and mandatory busing provided the stick that helped induce local districts to adopt magnets, the proffering of external grant support provided an important carrot. Superintendents of large cities that undertook major desegregation efforts incorporating magnet schools found that "school desegregation plans are expensive and cannot be implemented effectively without help from sources outside the district."[34] Besides paying for basic start-up costs that might otherwise be out of the reach of local treasuries, the availability of external funds helped promote magnet programs in two ways. First, it neutralized the concerns of local citizens who feared that magnet initiatives would require large tax increases. Second, it provided school officials with the flexibility to shape magnet proposals so they would provide attractive benefits to groups of educators and parents. Building a coalition to support reform of any kind is made much easier when one has material incentives that can selectively be distributed to those who support one's cause.[35]

In some cases external support for magnet initiatives came from private foundations,[36] but federal money has been the biggest factor. In 1976 Congress passed an amendment to the Emergency School Aid Act (ESAA) that initiated special competitive grants for local districts that instituted magnet schools as "part of an approved desegregation plan and that are designed to bring students from different social, economic, ethnic and racial backgrounds together." Only fourteen districts applied for the grants that year; just four years later, more than one hundred applied, with sixty-five receiving funding.[37]

BEYOND MAGNETS: RECENT STATE AND LOCAL INITIATIVES FOR CHOICE

Beyond the magnet-school experience, claims that educational choice is a proven success rest on various state and local choice initiatives that have expanded the scope of parental choice. A small number of local school districts extended the magnet model from its original conception—as a small number of strategically located schools—to one in which every school becomes a magnet. Led by Minnesota, some states extended the model by introducing the possibility for students to cross the boundaries of local districts in exercising their choice of schools. And, in an initiative that comes closer than any other to approximating the voucher model that Friedman envisioned, Wisconsin in 1990 began a program to allow low-income Milwaukee residents to attend private schools with tuition assistance from the government.

Magnetized Districts

As originally conceived, magnet schools necessarily were to constitute only a small, carefully selected subset of any district's total number of public schools. This was not an accommodation to fiscal or administrative realities, but an integral aspect of the theory behind them. Given racial segregation in neighborhood housing patterns, and given the wariness among majority parents of sending their children to racially and economically diverse schools in more distant neighborhoods, it was reasoned that parental choice could complement school integration only if some schools in minority areas were made uniquely attractive.

Against this background, the experiences of the few districts that have expanded the magnet model to all of their schools are instructive. Cambridge, Massachusetts, and Montclair, New Jersey, are relatively small and relatively advantaged communities that have moved decisively away from the traditional model of neighborhood-based schools.[38] Both districts have attempted to assign each school some distinguishing program features, and each has eliminated attendance zones entirely. Cambridge put its citywide choice plan into full effect in 1981, Montclair in 1985. Parents are not only allowed to exercise choice, they are required to. Approval of transfer requests depends on the availability of space and the potential impact on the racial composition of the sending and receiving schools. Because choice is sublimated to these overriding criteria, proponents have given systems of this kind the label "controlled choice." While controlled choice means that parents are not guaranteed that their children will be admitted to their first choice of schools, most families in both districts appear to gain entry to one of their top three ranked alternatives.

Unlike Cambridge and Montclair, District No. 4 in New York City's East Harlem is home to a desperately disadvantaged population. District No. 4 is one of thirty-two community school districts in the city.[39] Its rate of welfare dependency is twice that for the city as a whole, and nearly three times that for New York state. Approximately two-thirds of its residents are Hispanic and one-third black; there are almost no non-Hispanic whites living within the district's normal attendance boundaries.[40] District No. 4's choice system owes less to the model of magnet schools as a tool for integration than it does to pragmatic efforts by local leaders to improve already-segregated schools for the benefit of the minority children who attend them. The first three alternative schools were opened in 1974; three more were added in 1975, two in 1976; two in 1978, and so on. By 1985, twenty-three programs had been established. In 1982 attendance zones were eliminated and all junior high school students were required to apply for any of the available programs. Among the options available are the Isaac Newton School for Science and Mathematics, the Jose Feliciano Performing Arts School, and the East Harlem Maritime School. One of the most interesting innovations in District No. 4 involves its breaking way from the conventional assumption that each school has its own building. In order to diversify options more quickly and completely, and in order to obtain some of the advantages that smaller schools are presumed to have in reducing student alienation and increasing teachers' sense of teamwork and professionalism, District No. 4 established multiple schools within single buildings. Each school retains a distinct administrative structure and pedagogical style, even though it may occupy a single floor in a structure that houses one or more other "schools."

Cambridge, Montclair, and East Harlem are each frequently cited by advocates of market models to illustrate the workability of expanded educational-choice systems. District No. 4 has been labeled "the most celebrated example of choice in the country."[41]

The Minnesota Model

If East Harlem is the most talked-about choice-based system at the local level, Minnesota's is the nation's most visible statewide effort. With prodding from two business-based organizations,[42] and public-sector leadership from Governor Rudy Perpich and the state legislative majority leader, Connie Levi, Minnesota began putting together the pieces of its pioneering program in 1985.[43] The first piece consisted of a postsecondary enrollment option, which gave eleventh and twelfth graders the option to take courses at public or private colleges and universities. Credits earned were counted toward high school degree requirements, and the cost of tuition was met by the state. In 1987, the state gave school districts the option of participating in an open-enrollment program for all elementary and secondary students. In 1988 the program became mandatory for large districts (over a thousand students), and in the fall of 1990 it became mandatory for the entire state.

Under Minnesota's open-enrollment program, students may ask to be transferred to public schools in other districts. The state funds normally allocated for those who transfer travel with them to the receiving school. No district can refuse to allow a student to leave, unless the transfer would negatively affect desegregation guidelines.[44] Districts are allowed to refuse to accept incoming transfers, but they are not allowed to pick and choose among nonresident applicants based on their individual characteristics. They can reject applicants either by deciding not to participate in the program at all (as is the case with the wealthy suburb of Edina), or by selectively refusing transfers when they would result in overcrowding or racial imbalance. "They may not reject students on the basis of academic achievement, athletic or other extra-curricular interest, handicapping condition, proficiency in the English language, or previous disciplinary proceedings."[45] Parents are responsible for providing transportation to the boundary of the receiving district.[46]

Often citing Minnesota as their model, other states—including Iowa, Arkansas, Nebraska, Ohio, Utah, Colorado, Idaho, and Massachusetts—have undertaken some measures of their own for choice. Iowa and Utah began, in the 1990–91 school year, programs closely modeled on that of Minnesota. Colorado's program goes further than Minnesota's in one respect: it gives students the right to transfer to other schools in their own district, space permitting.[47] And Wisconsin, in potentially the most radical action, passed legislation in early 1990 intended to allow as many as a thousand Milwaukee public-school students to transfer to private schools, with the state footing the bill.

Crossing the Public/Private Line:
The Milwaukee Experiment

Under the Milwaukee Parental Choice Program, the approximately twenty-five hundred dollars of state funds per student that would normally go to the Milwaukee public-school system can be diverted to private schools in lieu of tuition.[48] Only lower-income students are eligible, and participants may number no more than one percent of the Milwaukee public schools' total enrollment.[49] The participating private schools must be nonsectarian, and must not discriminate in their admission practices; if more students apply than the school has vacancies for, the school must allocate spots through random selection procedures. Choice students may not exceed 49 percent of the private school's enrollment. Although not literally a voucher program, since the state aid is sent directly to the schools, it functions like a voucher program and is frequently referred to by that label by supporters and opponents alike. *Newsweek* magazine, for instance, called the Milwaukee experiment "A Real Test for Vouchers."[50]

The coalition responsible for enacting the choice legislation was a strange one. Strong support for the bill came from Republican Governor Tommy Thompson. Thompson has been a national leader among those pushing for welfare reforms intended to reinforce socially desirable norms by making rewards and punishments contingent on proper behavior. The bill's prime legislative sponsor was State Representative Annette "Polly" Williams, a black, single parent of four children, who twice chaired Jesse Jackson's presidential campaign operations in the state, and who is a member of the city's Black Panther Militia.

Williams's background gave the Milwaukee choice program a political credibility that market-oriented advocates immediately recognized. As with District No. 4 in East Harlem, the setting for the Milwaukee plan immunizes it against the charge that it primarily will benefit white children of the middle and upper classes. Williams has been lauded by the *Wall Street Journal*, called "a courageous leader" by President Bush, and introduced to a gathering of Republican notables as "an American hero" by the director of the conservative Landmark Center for Civil Rights.[51]

But the Milwaukee program also has been the subject of intense legal scrutiny. In November 1990, the Wisconsin State Court of Appeals ruled it unconstitutional on procedural grounds, and more substantive challenges remain to be resolved. While courtroom battles go on, however, students have been taking advantage of the program. In September 1990, 341 participated; the following year enrollment rose to 562.[52]

A TOOL FOR ALL REASONS

The practice of school choice, this overview suggests, has been shaped by many hands and reflects no single rationale or guiding force. Its evolution seems best understood as reflecting conflict and accommodation among shifting and competing goals. It is not the working out of a teleological march toward enlightened acceptance of market ideals. Abstract theories about the benefits of market forces undoubtedly played a role in animating some of the major actors, but compared to other considerations their role appears peripheral and indirect.

Clearly, racial animosities and fears provided the soil in which many of the earliest proposals for vouchers and school choice took root. It would be comforting to believe that we have severed our ties to this unflattering past, but it probably would be naive as well. Jennifer L. Hochschild characterizes as the "anomaly thesis" the optimistic view that racism is a bad phase in American history, one which we can be expected to grow out of, just as rebellious teenagers mature into sensible and responsible adults.[53] Her review of the history of efforts to desegregate schools convinced her that this thesis understates the depth and intensity of racial fears and antipathies. Incremental policies, intended to introduce change gradually in doses timed to coincide with gradually liberalizing racial attitudes, have not succeeded. Popular movements, presumably reflecting the values of the citizenry, more often have taken reactionary stances than progressive ones on issues related to racial change. The anomaly thesis, she is drawn somewhat reluctantly to conclude, "simply cannot explain why racial isolation and its effects persist even after our extended and heroic efforts to desegregate schools."[54] It seems prudent to take note of the experience in Eastern Europe. While

114

under the Soviet sphere of influence, ancient ethnic hostilities had been displaced or transcended by more modern loyalties to nation, state, and unifying ideologies. Subsequent events remind us that parochial and unreasonable hatreds, while they may be unfashionable, are not outdated in our enlightened age. That school choice might be used as a vehicle for redrawing racial lines is a possibility that ought not be lightly put aside.

Portraying the evolution of school choice as a movement away from considerations of racial composition and toward considerations of educational quality may be overly simple and misleading in this respect. To at least some degree, the purging of race from the public dialogue about educational reform reflects rhetorical adaptations to the rules of evidence imposed by an aggressive judiciary and the rules of civility enforced less formally by people's changing sense of what kinds of sentiments are better left unsaid. Moreover, there is an unacknowledged irony in the attempt by conservative supporters of school vouchers to use support in the minority community as evidence that school choice transcends racial boundaries. While data sensitive to differences within the African-American community is generally lacking, it appears to be the case that acceptance of school choice is strongest among those living in inner-city, low-income communities where racial frustrations and resentments run high.[55] The appeal of choice to Polly Williams and her Milwaukee followers is rooted in racial experience and racial identity. "I am not an integrationist," she told one newspaper. "I don't chase after white people."[56]

To note the continuing relevance of race is not to deny that the context and motivations surrounding school choice have changed. That Minnesota is a leader in the contemporary choice movement is indicative in this regard. The minority enrollment in Minnesota's public schools is smaller than in all but five other states.[57] If the desire for racial exclusion was the driving force, this would not be the environment in which we would expect school-choice initiatives to thrive. Similarly, on the national level, the expansion of school-choice initiatives has taken place during a period in which conservative appointments to the U.S. Supreme Court reduced the threat that local districts would find their policies under scrutiny on grounds of racial discrimination. Reduced judicial oversight might, on the one hand, help explain the initial momentum, since it makes it less likely that choice proposals will be directly overturned. On the other hand, if support for choice had been buoyed primarily by the need to craft plans that masked racially exclusionary motivations, we should expect the movement to lose momentum in the face of dwindling judicial interest. That this has not, at least as yet, occurred is another indication that other forces are at work.

115

This reading of the history of school choice in practice denies us the easy ways out. Choice is not the deus ex machina, sent by the gods of market forces to rescue a people in distress. Nor is it a Trojan horse for racial bigotry. It seems most appropriate to view school choice as something malleable. Its benefits, if real, are not intrinsic. Like other tools, it can be used wisely and to good effect, or it can be applied ineptly and with ill intent. Economic models conventionally emphasize efficiency in pursuing privately held interests; they focus attention on the choice of means and regard the determination of ultimate ends to be unproblematic or externally derived. The story of choice-in-practice, however, reminds us that the conflicts that are most compelling and difficult to resolve revolve around questions about the kind of society we wish to become.

Uses of Evidence

THE EMPIRICAL CASE THAT "CHOICE WORKS"

Almost without exception, wherever choice has been attempted, choice has worked," President Bush told a 1989 White House education conference.[1] Such claims of empirical proof for the feasibility and efficacy of choice proposals have played an important role in eroding the wariness toward market-based reform that consigned Milton Friedman's original voucher proposal to the status of "nice idea that goes nowhere."

In general, however, the empirical record is much murkier than such claims suggest. Part of this murkiness is due to the methodological limitations that plague almost all policy-evaluation research: imperfect data and lack of adequate controls. But my point is not simply that existing studies are flawed, for indeed not even the most carefully designed and implemented analysis can provide the kind of definitive answers that we might crave. It is not just that we do not know everything about the likely consequences of school choice. A careful effort to separate anecdote from evidence suggests that we know very little at all.

Declaring Success

The claim that school choice is a proven success is based on the apparent consequences of choice as it has been experienced in five situations: (1) the federal GI Bill; (2) the Alum Rock experiment; (3) magnet schools, (4) the more recent state and local choice-based initiatives; and (5) the relative performance of public versus private schools.

The GI Bill

In labeling its 1990 school choice proposal a "GI Bill for Children," the Bush administration was not tilling new ground. Rather, it was attempting to exploit even more directly an analogy that others had worked to good effect before.

The federal GI Bill is the focal point of the longest running claims that school choice has been proved to work. As early as 1958, Virgil Blum made extensive reference to the GI Bill to support his contention that public funds could legally and successfully be provided, through a voucher mechanism, to parochial schools.[2] Milton Friedman, in first introducing his voucher proposal, noted it would "follow in its broad outlines the arrangements adopted in the United States after World War II for financing the education of veterans."[3] Christopher Jencks, in the early 1970s, drew the analogy in explaining the plans of the Office of Economic Opportunity (OEO) for a voucher experiment.[4] John Coons and Stephen Sugarman, making the case for the regulated-choice proposal they sought to have enacted in California, noted that "the G.I. Bill is a much larger national program of a similar sort."[5]

Many of the early citations of the GI Bill seem to have been made primarily to establish the political, legal, and administrative feasibility of a voucher-like mechanism. Blum, Friedman, and Jencks, for example, noted that veterans used GI Bill support to attend parochial schools, and that this practice had not stirred public outrage or judicial intervention. They did not argue that the GI Bill had made U.S. colleges better or more efficient, or that it represented a pure example of the benefits of unleashed market forces. Indeed, they often acknowledged that the results of the GI Bill were mixed, with one primary lesson being the importance of government regulation. The federal OEO, in citing the GI Bill as a model, acknowledged that some veterans "enrolled in 'fly-by-night' institutions which took their money and taught them little or nothing." Such fraud had been reduced to negligible levels, Jencks concluded, "whenever serious regulatory efforts were instituted."[6] Coons and Sugarman drew a similar conclusion about the importance of government regulation and oversight. They noted that, through administering the GI Bill and related programs, the federal government "has learned some things about consumer (and Treasury) protection efforts that seem appropriately to go along with choice plans. Some of this is represented in recent regulations requiring certain disclosures and, in some instances, tuition refunds from private providers."[7]

More recent proponents, however, make stronger claims about the implications of the GI Bill and the lessons we should draw about the benefits of market forces. Jeanne Allen of the Heritage Foundation, for example, asserts that the GI Bill (along with Pell grants) proved that the charge that voucher aid to private and parochial elementary and secondary schools may be unconstitutional "simply is wrong." An assistant secretary in the Department of Education, writing about the Bush proposal, claimed that it would open new educational opportunities and transform America's schools "much like the original G.I. Bill that expanded educational opportunities for veterans and gave them consumer power to help create the best colleges and universities in the world." Similarly, more recent proponents sometimes seem less sensitive to problems of fraud and abuse that were evident to those monitoring the GI Bill experience in its early years. David Kirkpatrick, writing in support of tuition vouchers in 1990, offered a generally glowing assessment of the GI Bill experience, but without the warning about the need for regulation and oversight. While conceding that some fraud and abuse had occurred, he wrote simply that it was "on a relatively minor scale."[8]

Results at Alum Rock

Proponents of educational choice within the federal Office of Economic Opportunity, in the early 1970s, did not consider the GI Bill experience sufficiently relevant to resolve questions about the likely effects of choice at the elementary and secondary level. That is why they sought to sponsor the systematic experiment that ended up being carried out in Alum Rock, California.

The Alum Rock experiment in 1978 was called "one of the longest lived, largest, and certainly best documented family choice systems that has ever been implemented,"[9] and this judgment still stands as accurate. Begun in 1972, the experiment lasted five years. Data collection included panel surveys of parents from participating schools, surveys of a control group comprising parents from the ten Alum Rock schools that did not participate, classroom observations, teacher interviews, and assessments of student performance.

Early reports from Alum Rock were positive. A 1973 *New York Times* article, for example, proclaimed: "School Voucher Experiment Rates an 'A' in Coast District." Some proponents of vouchers seized on these early assessments to rebut critics' fears that choice would cripple public schools. Robert L. Bish and Vincent Ostrom, for example, wrote in 1973 that "preliminary indications are that public schools *can* respond to provide innovative and interesting programs for students, if the appropriate incentives exist."[10]

Ultimately, the findings from Alum Rock proved to be something of a mixed bag: some conclusions were unfavorable to vouchers, others favorable. For example, while the study found that many parents had low levels of information about the alternatives available to them—and that this especially was true of minorities and less-advantaged socioeconomic groups—it also suggested that, over time: (1) information levels improved; (2) the information gap between advantaged and disadvantaged narrowed; and (3) program-specific criteria became more relevant to parental decisions.[11]

The primary lesson that proponents of educational choice have drawn from Alum Rock, however, has less to do with the data collected than with the resistance that forced the OEO to soften the market-based components of the experiment. The OEO had envisioned testing a voucher plan that included private (nonparochial) schools, but the California state legislature balked at passing the legislation required to permit this. As a result the Alum Rock experiment was restricted to public schools. The experimenters sought to ameliorate this restriction on the supply side by encouraging teachers to form minischools, offering distinct curriculums, within public-school buildings. More than fifty alternatives for parents were generated this way, but there is no question that the integrity of the original design suffered. Similarly, the kind of market model that advocates envisioned depended on there being a threat to poorly performing teachers and schools as a catalyst for reform. But local principals and the school board vitiated this by restricting information about school performance, by taking measures that effectively ensured that even weak schools would retain enough students to survive, and by guaranteeing teachers that no one would lose a job.

As a result, most contemporary proponents of choice have disavowed the fundamental relevance of the experimental design, arguing that, as implemented, what took place in Alum Rock had little to do with "real" market-based choice at all. Denis P. Doyle, for example, calls it "a hot house demonstration that has produced some marvelous anecdotes, but it does not permit drawing broad generalizations."[12] Chubb and Moe conclude that it "cannot meaningfully be considered a test of anything."[13]

Instead of a test of the potential of choice and school competition to improve education, Alum Rock has been portrayed primarily as emblematic of the tight stranglehold that the education establishment exercises, and as a demonstration of the impossibility of bringing about reform through conventional political and bureaucratic channels. Milton Friedman and Rose Friedman, for example, limit their discussion of Alum Rock to their argument that the "perceived self-interest of the educational bureaucracy is the key obstacle to the introduction of market competition in schooling."[14]

Claims for Magnets' Success

The claim of empirical support that has played the greatest role in the recent resurgence of interest in school choice involves the magnet schools. The GI Bill, after all, involved adults and higher education; its direct relevance to elementary and secondary schools has always been problematic. The OEO's attempt to test market-based choice under experimental conditions was inconclusive; even if its results had been more positive and sharply defined, moreover, questions would remain about the extent to which lessons learned from such an artificially designed undertaking would apply in less contrived settings. The widespread adoption of magnet schools from the mid-1970s through the mid-1980s provides something akin to a natural laboratory for policy analysts interested in finding out whether choice-in-practice provides the many benefits that are attributed to it in economic theory.

Considering that there are more than a thousand magnet schools in the United States, the actual number of studies that approach even modest levels of methodological rigor is disappointing. But those that are available generally support the claim that choice can be harnessed to the goal of racial integration. As attention began to shift from racial equality to academic excellence, a few researchers made systematic efforts to determine whether magnet schools also improved students' performance. These, too, had encouraging results.

Most claims that magnet schools facilitate integration are based on case studies of individual school districts. One celebrated "success story" is Milwaukee, where magnet schools (or "specialty schools") were a centerpiece in a comprehensive desegregation plan put into place in the mid-1970s, after a federal judge ruled that the school board had engaged in a series of actions that illegally contributed to the segregation of the public schools.[15] Writing in 1990, David A. Bennett noted that "beginning in 1977 and for each subsequent year, the Milwaukee Public Schools exceeded the requirements of the court order through their magnet school and controlled choice assignment process." Even after the court order expired, the district maintained a racial distribution in which about 85 percent of students attended racially balanced schools.[16]

Another frequently cited success story is that of Buffalo, New York.[17] Like Milwaukee, Buffalo implemented its desegregation plan under a court order. Beginning in 1976, magnet schools were gradually increased, as part of a broader effort that included boundary changes, school closings, and school pairings. Between 1975 and 1986 racial imbalance in the Buffalo schools declined nearly 44 percent.[18] This occurred, moreover, with relatively little white flight or public controversy. And, while the federal court insisted that mandatory elements be instituted to supplement magnets and other voluntary measures, Christine H. Rossell argues that these simply accelerated by a year or two progress that already was assured.[19]

These and other case studies of desegregation success through magnets are given greater credibility by complementary findings in several multicity analyses.[20] The single most extensive study of magnet schools was funded by the U.S. Department of Education in 1981.[21] The study focused on 15 school districts selected to be broadly representative of the 138 urban districts that operated one or more magnet schools in January 1982. Teams of researchers visited 45 magnet schools in the sample cities, collecting a wide range of statistics but also engaging in careful observation of classroom behavior by students and teachers. The research team of Rolf K. Blank, Robert A. Dentler, D. Catherine Baltzell, and Kent Chabotar concluded that magnet schools advance "positive racial integration"; "help reduce real and potential community conflict concerning desegregation"; and "have a positive effect on holding students in public schools and reducing 'white flight.'"[22]

Another important multicity study focused on the comparison between voluntary and mandatory integration, rather than on magnet schools per se.[23] Christine Rossell and Ruth C. Clarke looked at twenty large school districts, all of which used magnet schools to some degree. In eleven of the districts, magnets were part of an approach that on balance emphasized mandatory steps for achieving integration; in nine they were part of a comprehensive, yet primarily voluntary, desegregation effort.[24] Rossell and Clarke examined the effect on interracial exposure,[25] and especially emphasized the importance of distinguishing short-term from long-term effects. They concluded that "the mandatory plans do better in the implementation year and for a few years after, but the districts with voluntary plans surpass them within two to four years and the gap increases over time."[26]

The *Survey of Magnet Schools* goes beyond desegregation to consider the impact of magnets on educational quality. In addition to reading and math achievement, as measured by standardized tests, Blank and his colleagues used their observation of classroom activity to score schools on such matters as the extent to which students are "on task," the difficulty of course loads, the teachers' effort, the teachers' availability after class, the extent to which students were recognized for improvement, the use of parents and volunteers, and student satisfaction. Most of the magnets did better than other schools in their district on standardized tests, and some did much better.[27] One-third of the magnets scored high on all dimensions of the study's qualitative assessment of classroom activity.

Other assessments of the educational impact of magnets focus only on single districts, and these almost exclusively are studies carried out by the districts themselves. Their research designs, measurements, and criteria for success vary markedly; so do the characteristics of the magnet programs they evaluate. Rolf Blank systematically reviewed twelve of these studies in order to see whether their findings cohere to form a clear picture.[28] He found that "virtually all the studies reviewed showed that average test scores of students in magnet schools are higher than scores for non-magnet schools."[29] This is tempered somewhat by the weakness of the research designs employed in nearly every case, but some evidence for a positive impact exists even in the three or four studies with more complex research designs.[30]

Impact of Recent State and Local Initiatives

In spite of their more recent vintage, claims regarding the proven success of school-choice efforts such as those in Cambridge, Montclair, East Harlem, Minnesota, and Milwaukee have been nearly as confident and enthusiastic as those presented for magnet schools. As with less-comprehensive magnet initiatives, the claims of success relate both to racial integration and to student performance.

Cambridge probably has been the most carefully studied system. According to Michael J. Alves and Charles V. Willie, since implementation the Cambridge public schools "have achieved more voluntary desegregation than any other school system in Massachusetts history and perhaps even more than any other school system in the United States." Their review of the evidence suggests that the voluntary system has led to better racial balance than before, that no school has drifted toward resegregation, and that the proportion of school-age students attending public over private schools has increased. Moreover, they indicate that "by eighth grade, minority students are outperforming white students in math and reading citywide in 60% of the public schools, and similar academic gains have been reported for low income students in 50% of the schools."[31]

Christine Rossell and Charles L. Glenn also reviewed the Cambridge experience. They conclude that the percentage of students passing the district's basic-skills test increased from 72.8 to 87 over the first four years of the controlled-choice program.[32] A more recent review concludes that scores continued to increase through 1988, although Cambridge students still fare less well than do Massachusetts students as a whole.[33]

The Montclair choice system was evaluated by Beatriz C. Clewell and Myra F. Joy of the Educational Testing Service.[34] They found schools in Montclair to be incredibly well balanced racially. In 1988, when the system as a whole had 48 percent minority students, not one of the six elementary and two middle schools had more than 52 percent or less than 46 percent minority enrollment. Using eligibility for the free and reduced-price school lunch program as an indicator of need, they found the schools to be relatively well balanced socioeconomically as well; all but two of the schools were within six percentage points of the district average. Interviews and observation led them to conclude that racial integration extended to the classroom level (except for honors and advanced classes, where minorities were underenrolled), and that the general racial climate was good. As in Cambridge, student performance also improved. Clewell and Joy note that "performance in reading and math as measured by Iowa Test of Basic Skills (ITBS) scores has improved since implementation of the magnet schools in 1977."[35]

The claim that choice has succeeded in East Harlem's District No. 4 is strategically important to the pro-choice case. Cambridge and Montclair, after all, are small, suburban, relatively privileged communities. Advocates of educational restructuring claim that market-based choice initiatives will be especially beneficial to disadvantaged groups; middle- and upper-class families, they argue, already have the option to choose their schools, either by paying tuition to private schools or relocating to another school district. East Harlem—predominantly Hispanic, overwhelmingly minority, largely poor—is a critical test case. "When people ask me if choice systems can help poor inner-city students, I refer them to New York City's District No. 4," one supporter notes.[36]

Claims of dramatic academic gains in East Harlem have been made over and over again by proponents of choice. In 1973, East Harlem ranked thirty-second out of thirty-two community school districts in New York City; by the mid-1980s it was in the middle of the pack.[37] The percentage of students reading at or above grade level, according to several reports, increased from 16 percent in 1973 to almost 63 percent in 1987.[38] Many students from East Harlem schools now perform successfully in the city's special selective high schools,[39] and at least one report suggested the graduation rate had risen from 7 percent to 90 percent in just fifteen years.[40] Little wonder, then, William Bennet, then the secretary of education, could assert, "I don't suppose anyone could be unmoved by the story of District 4."[41]

Because they are even more recent in origin, the Minnesota and Milwaukee choice programs have less of a track record. But they also have nonetheless been cited as examples of proven success. In May 1988, for example, the *Wall Street Journal* reported in glowing terms that "in Minnesota, bad schools must either get better or wither, and possibly die."[42] The article quotes Governor Rudy Perpich to the same effect: "The market forces are at work already," he asserted. "You have better programs, and more districts cooperating to offer better programs."

Even before the Milwaukee program had begun, the *Wall Street Journal* editorialized that opponents were teacher unions interested solely in preserving the status quo. "The real objection to vouchers is the fear that they will work and expose the loss of faith in the public schools system," it was asserted. If the opponents win, "the losers will be hundreds of inner-city children who expect to attend a school of their own choosing in September."[43] After just one semester, the *New York Times* reported that "the parents speak in jubilant tones about their children's progress, directors of the six participating private schools describe a relatively smooth transition, and [one student] says that for the first time he looks forward to school."[44] Jeanne Allen of the Heritage Foundation noted that Milwaukee parents "sent their children to institutions such as the highly respected Urban Day School, which boasts a 98 percent graduation rate."[45]

Comparing Public and Private Schools

A quite different kind of evidence cited in support of market-based educational choice involves comparing the educational effectiveness of private versus public schools. Beginning with a major analysis by James Coleman and his associates, and continuing with the more recent work by John Chubb and Terry Moe, some large-scale, quantitative assessments of student performance have concluded that private schools simply do a better job. To advocates of educational choice, these studies confirm the beneficial effects of competition.

The primary battleground in the public-versus-private-school debate has been waged with a single set of data, based on a sample of just over a thousand public and private high schools, known as the "High School and Beyond" (HS&B) study. HS&B was sponsored by the National Center for Education Statistics of the U.S. Department of Education. In addition to obtaining general information about the schools' funding, staffing, and programs, researchers interviewed thirty-six sophomores and thirty-six seniors, randomly selected, from each of the schools. The students were interviewed to obtain information about such factors as their parents' income, race, and educational attainment; family structure; parental support and oversight regarding school matters; their own educational aspirations; the types of programs and courses in which they were enrolled; and their involvement in extracurricular activities. Each respondent's school records and results on six standardized exams also were collected. In 1982, two years after the first wave of data collection, the original group was tracked down and reinterviewed, and, in the case of the 1980 sophomores, retested.

The first studies using the 1980 HS&B data began generating results in the early 1980s. Coleman and his colleagues found that students attending private schools performed better than those attending public schools. They also found that children in private schools were more likely to come from families with higher incomes and educational levels, less family instability, and higher expectations that their children will attend college. Most significantly, they concluded that these family characteristics did not, in themselves, account for the differences in student performance. Something about the private schools—not just the type of people they tended to attract— seemed to be associated with higher student test scores. They speculated that the safer, more caring, and more disciplined environment in private schools might account for the difference. Students in private schools reported fewer absences, more homework, fewer fights, more demanding courses, and greater teacher interest and concern than did public-school students.[46] Coleman's prestige, and the unusual breadth and detail of the HS&B data, ensured that this finding would get considerable attention. The Coleman study was "already being used as political ammunition" by those favoring vouchers and tuition tax credits early in 1981, when only preliminary reports of the results had been published.[47]

After the 1980 sophomores were retested in 1982, a second round of studies tried to figure out what accounted for differences in how much students learned (or failed to learn) over the two-year period. Looking at individual student gains provided a methodological advantage over the first round of studies, which were necessarily cross-sectional in design. One of the criticisms of all efforts to judge the effectiveness of private versus public schools by comparing the performance of their students is the likelihood that the two groups may differ in important ways that have little to do with the quality of the education they receive—ways relating to parental support, motivation, and basic ability that measures of family socioeconomic status control for imperfectly at best. Looking at student gains, rather than total scores, presumably made some of these other differences less relevant.[48]

Comparing gain scores seemingly confirmed the relative performance advantage of private schools. For example, out of 125 questions dealing with vocabulary, reading, mathematics, science, writing, and civics, public-school students improved by about 7.16 items (from 67.07 as sophomores to 74.23 as seniors), while Catholic-school students improved by 8.98 items and other private-school students improved by 8.83.[49] When various background factors are taken into account, the private school retained advantages in reading, vocabulary, writing, and math, although not in science or civics.[50]

The most recent wave of studies combines the HS&B data with additional information obtained from a 1984 Administrative and Teacher Survey (ATS) sent to about half of the schools that originally took part in the HS&B study. The ATS provides much more information than was previously available about the characteristics of the schools and their programs, including teachers' and principals' assessments of the school organization, curriculum requirements, faculty morale, leadership, disciplinary and homework policies, and the like.[51]

It is this combined HS&B/ATS data set that provides the empirical grist for the arguments presented in Chubb and Moe's highly cited and controversial work, *Politics, Markets, and America's Schools*. Chubb and Moe use the ATS data to develop an indicator of the degree to which teachers and principals find their autonomy and discretion limited by mandates and oversight from central administrators. They find an association between decision-making autonomy and the kinds of school-level leadership, professionalism, and teamwork that distinguish good schools from bad ones. They also find that private schools are much more likely to grant schools administrative autonomy than are public schools.[52]

While Chubb and Moe agree with Coleman and his colleagues that private schools outperform public schools, their explanation for this differs in a way that has potentially critical policy implications. Coleman's analysis emphasizes advantages that may be particular to private schools with religious orientations. Indeed, his findings suggest that the non-Catholic schools in his sample have few, if any, advantages over public schools; non-Catholic private schools "appear not to provide special benefits beyond the public school, except possibly in verbal cognitive skills, a result that is offset by their relatively high dropout rates and their weakness in mathematics and sciences."[53]

Coleman attributes the high performance of Catholic schools to their character as a "functional community," in which social norms are broadly shared and consistently reinforced among students, parents, teachers, and school authorities. Such functional communities may depend on a certain degree of family choice in order to survive, but that is not the same thing as suggesting that simply expanding choice will allow them to replicate themselves and flourish. Coleman and Hoffer worry, in fact, that the market forces associated with market-based choice reforms, such as vouchers, could unleash individualistic impulses that would undermine and erode value-based communities.[54]

Chubb and Moe, for their part, disregard the distinction between religious and nonreligious private schools. Their emphasis is on institutions, not values. They anchor their explanation in the generic market forces that presumably weed out, through competitive pressures, schools that fail to provide the requisite autonomy.[55] This helps account for the broader impact of their work on public-policy debate. By framing the advantages of private schools in terms of institutional differences, they open up the possibility that those advantages can be made universal through institutional reform. Changing institutions seems much more within our grasp, and much less politically volatile an undertaking, than changing people's fundamental beliefs, their orientation to religion, and the social forums in which they choose to express and shelter their personal values.

Uncertain Evidence

That citations of evidence and empirical proof play an important role in establishing the credibility of school-choice plans can be seen as a positive development. Three and four decades ago, proponents of a more objective and systematic approach to public policy analysis felt themselves to be voices in a wilderness where policy options were adopted, without self-consciousness, based on intuition, idiosyncratic preferences, and partisan strategy. After years of making steady inroads into the academic and policy-making arenas—years in which university programs in policy analysis grew rapidly, and in which governments and private organizations increasingly looked to hire experts in policy-analysis techniques—it seems that the movement for systematic policy analysis to some extent has infiltrated the terms of public deliberation as well.

While it is now de rigueur to cite relevant evidence in staking a policy position, however, the terms in which such evidence is presented in the unspecialized media and in the broad realm of public discourse are unsophisticated, and the standards by which credibility is assessed remain untutored and lax. One study is as good as another, and the weight of the evidence is determined by counting the studies on opposing sides. In the instance of educational choice, closer examination reveals that the claims of proven success are often based on a rather wobbly foundation.

Casual Claims

Proponents of choice who cite the GI Bill as a model for vouchers, for example, almost invariably rest their case on conventional wisdom rather than empirical analysis. In my review of the literature, I did not find a single case in which allusions to the GI Bill as a model for school choice were backed up by references to systematic studies. If success is defined by how widely a benefit is used, the GI Bill has indeed been a dramatic success.[56] Over 51 percent of the nearly thirty-five million veterans took advantage of GI Bill support to attend college, to attend other schools, or to obtain on-the-job training between June 1944 and September 1989.[57] But veterans' eagerness to take advantage of a generous benefit tells us almost nothing about whether the program was worth its substantial cost. Through 1989, total expenditures for veterans' education and training under the various GI Bills was about sixty billion dollars.[58]

Proponents of school choice have not felt compelled to provide data about the characteristics of the programs GI Bill recipients attended, the quality of the educational product they were provided, whether recipients would have pursued similar education and training anyway, or the impact of their added education on subsequent earnings and satisfaction. The sketchy information that is available provides something of a mixed picture. A 1979 survey of recipients under the post–Korean conflict version of the GI Bill found that the majority were "fully satisfied" with the accuracy (66.8 percent) and time-liness (57.3 percent) of the checks they received, but only 12.6 percent were fully satisfied with the career counseling and information they received.[59] The same survey found that about 60 percent reported that they had completed the training they initiated, or reached an intermediate goal; those seeking high school educations had the lowest completion rates (50 percent), and black recipients had lower completion rates than whites.[60]

A 1988 cost-benefit analysis carried out by the staff of the Joint Economic Committee of Congress appears to have been the one serious effort to quantify the program's effectiveness.[61] It concluded that the "government's investment in the education of veterans at the end of World War II had an extraordinarily large payoff for the nation." For each dollar invested, the study determined, the nation gained somewhere between 5 and 12.5 dollars in economic benefits.

Because detailed data on actual GI Bill participants, their experiences, and their subsequent work histories simply is not available, that study necessarily depended on a series of rough indicators based on problematic assumptions.[62] Its primary author indicates it was done rather quickly as "kind of an in-the-dark type thing."[63] It made no effort to assess the role of fraud and abuse by fly-by-night institutions, and based its assessment of national economic gain solely on the estimated increase in income associated with the added years of education that the bill presumably allowed. While a clever and helpful rough gauge, the series of assumptions underlying the estimate makes it one that must be treated with a high degree of caution. The report repeatedly emphasizes that it has made the most conservative assumptions, and in many cases that is true. But in at least two important instances, it seems likely that the authors of the report made methodologi-

129

cal decisions that may grossly overestimate the benefits associated with the GI Bill.[64]

Although there have been some solid studies on the impact of magnet schools, magnetized districts, and public versus private schools, the claims of proven success, in those instances too, are offered with greater certainty than the data warrant. As the sections to follow will illustrate, some of the evidence is decidedly premature, some of the measures are far from complete, and some elements of the research designs are distressingly weak.

Acknowledging the weaknesses of these studies does not mean that we should dismiss them or deny that they may shed some light on the choices policymakers face. It is an easy matter to probe for and uncover technical flaws, and the cynical use of methodological imperfections as an excuse selectively to disregard evidence has contributed to the immaturity of political discourse. What I hope to do in this section is simply to underscore the uncertainty and tentativeness of our knowledge in this area. Following that, I will argue that what we do know is being systematically misinterpreted.

Premature Assessments

Policymakers do not have the luxury of deferring decisions until the research community can declare with confidence which programs work. Systematic policy analysis has a long turnaround time; studies considered models in many ways—such as the New Jersey Negative Income Tax Experiment,[65] or the Kansas City Preventive Patrol Experiment,[66] or the Experimental Housing Allowance Program[67]—may take more than a year before data collection even begins, and five to ten years of data-gathering and analysis before researchers feel comfortable extracting recommendations from their analyses. Public officials, forced by two- to six-year election cycles to adopt a shorter time horizon, have little patience for the notion that it is worth the wait.[68]

In the case of school choice, the recent rhetoric of crisis increases the pressure to act quickly. The rush to legislate, as a result, has outrun the evidence from the start. Rather than acknowledging uncertainty and tentativeness, however, advocates of choice often have preferred to present anecdotes and initial bursts of enthusiasm as sufficient documentation of their claim that "choice works."

In May 1988, when the *Wall Street Journal* was praising the positive effects of open enrollment in Minnesota, the program itself had barely begun. In 1987 fewer than 140 students took part; the next year it rose to 435. The *Wall Street Journal* gave the impression that much more action was occurring. It used the figure of 5,600 transfers, nearly all of whom were taking advantage of the postsecondary option, not the open-enrollment plan.[69] By 1990–91, when the open-enrollment program became mandatory for all districts, the number of participants increased to 6,134. Yet even this indicated that about 992 of every 1,000 students were choosing not to exercise their choice.[70]

Shortly after the *New York Times* reported about "jubilant" parents in Milwaukee, one of the seven participating private schools suddenly closed, forcing most of the 63 students whose tuitions were being paid by the state to return to the public schools. Although the problems were not readily apparent to outside observers, it now appears that "the school was in turmoil from the beginning" of the program.[71]

One risk of the rush to judgment is that citizens and policymakers in other jurisdictions will base their deliberations on information that is partial, misleading, or even false. In the discussion about educational choice, early reports on the "evidence" have overstated the immediacy and size of the benefits likely to materialize. Boston citizens closely following the debate about whether to introduce a controlled-choice plan in their troubled school system, for example, were told by an article in the *Boston Globe* about the dramatic turnaround in Cambridge: "Since the city started its program seven years ago, the proportion of kids going to public school instead of parochial or private school has risen from 70 percent to 90 percent."[72] Yet, according to a more careful assessment, the actual figures suggest a considerably less remarkable (but nonetheless positive) outcome: from 1978 to 1987, the proportion of students opting for public over private school rose from 80 percent to 85 percent.[73]

Similarly, reports of the success of the East Harlem program have offered wildly different figures. One account holds that the choice options have "attracted more than 2,000 white students from other parts of the city—some of them having turned down acceptances from private schools to attend."[74] Another offers the more modest figure of 1,500 transfers from the outside, without distinguishing how many of those are nonminority.[75] Another, even more recent, cites the director of alternative programs as saying only 800 in total come from outside.[76] There is more agreement on the claimed size of the increase in students reading at or above grade level: several reports present this as having increased from about 16 percent in 1973 to almost 63 percent in 1987.[77] But another authoritative report offers the more modest, and seemingly inconsistent, estimate of an increase from 27.3 percent in 1978 to 41.5 percent in 1989.[78]

A case study may make it clearer how early reports can get distorted. William Raspberry, in a June 12, 1989, editorial in the *Washington Post*, reported that the high school graduation rate for East Harlem had risen, in the previous fifteen years, from a dismal 7 percent to an astounding 90 percent.[79] His source apparently is an article by Sy Fliegel, formerly the deputy superintendent in District No. 4, and the most visible spokesperson for the East Harlem "miracle."[80] Fliegel does indeed use the 7 percent and 90 percent figures, but in neither case do they refer to a high school graduation rate for all, or even most, East Harlem students. The 7 percent figure he offers is for Benjamin Franklin High School, which Fliegel notes that "only a handful" of District No. 4 students attended.[81] The 90 percent figure is based on the first graduating class of the Manhattan Center for Science and Mathematics, a new school that replaced the closed Franklin High School in 1982. This was a very special and attractive program, and could hardly be taken to represent the norm.

Early judgment also can exaggerate success by mistaking as permanent initial gains attributable to the enthusiasm for change. The Rand Corporation study of the Alum Rock experiment, for example, concluded that "in general, parents' satisfaction with the schools increases substantially at the outset of an innovation and then falls when the innovation does not live up to expectations."[82] It is possible that something similar is going on in Milwaukee. In spite of surveys indicating high levels of parent satisfaction, 35 percent of the first year's class of choice students apparently decided not to return for the second year.[83] Moreover, it is a commonplace with policy innovations that, in spite of rave reviews, they often do not travel well to other jurisdictions.

One explanation for such a pattern involves the special role of the policy innovator, whose enthusiasm, confidence, and intensity can create a contagious atmosphere of excitement that is not readily transferable and that may not be easily sustained. Another focuses less on personality and attitude and more on the resource base from which early reforms are launched. Successful innovations often are launched in times of fiscal abundance, or rely on external funding from federal demonstration grants, foundations, or the like. In the case of school choice, such a resource base may be needed to improve enrollment planning and projection capacity, to generate attractive magnet programs, and to ensure that parents are sufficiently informed about the options available to them. In Kansas City, for example, "substantial resegregation" occurred at some magnet schools after support from Federal Emergency School Assistance funds declined.[84] Access to start-up funds and general fiscal conditions can change. And, even in good economic times, political demands can erode the resource base as other groups and other programs make the case that it is now their turn to have their needs addressed.

Finally, early judgments often fail to take into account undesirable results that were not anticipated and that may not at first be recognized. "No

one would defend magnet schools as a major policy alternative if they provided better education for the most privileged students and did even more
damage to those who were doing worst and being offered the least stimulating curriculum," Gary Orfield notes.[85] But the first waves of assessments
have told us virtually nothing about whether or not magnets drain resources,
the best students, the best teachers, and the most supportive parents. Blank
found that none of twelve case studies he reviewed considered whether
purported gains in magnet schools came at the expense of other schools
within those districts.[86]

There are at least some indications that negative consequences of educational choice do exist. Many of those in favor of choice link their argument
to the problems of central city (inner-city) schools; often they suggest that
choice will promote smaller schools offering more intimate and supportive
environments, extend to city dwellers some of the privileges that suburban
youth already enjoy, and spontaneously complement integration goals. But
some early indications are that choice may undermine smaller, more rural
schools, while buffering central city districts from competitive pressures.
Motley, Minnesota, for example, lost half of its five hundred students to the
larger nearby town of Staples.[87] And, because of desegregation rules, Minneapolis has had to deny transfers to 88 percent of white students seeking to
leave.[88] Even where provisions to maintain racial balance are on the books,
some studies indicate that choice plans have the potential to lead to racial
and economic resegregation over time.[89] Three years after Iowa instituted a
choice program similar to Minnesota's, controversy flared when the Des
Moines school board voted to reject all of the requests by white students to
transfer to suburban districts. In the first two years of the program, 402
white students had transfered out, compared to only 11 minority students.[90]

Inadequate Measures

Most of the evaluations of existing choice practices have been ex post facto
studies, forced to rely, for the most part, on whatever statistics are collected
by federal, state, or local agencies as a matter of course. As a result, neither
the measures of racial integration nor those of academic performance are
particularly strong.

With few exceptions, the major assessments of the racial impact of educational choice rely on school-level, not classroom-level, data. This is a serious
limitation in light of the clear indications that magnets are sometimes turned
to as a way to hold white families in integrated schools by buffering their
children in special subschool programs or tracks in which their regular exposure to minority children is quite limited.[91] The study by Blank and his

133

colleagues of fifteen cities, and the Clewell and Joy study of Montclair, did attempt to observe racial composition in the classroom; both found some evidence that racially balanced schools may harbor racially imbalanced classrooms.[92]

Measures of educational impact are even more problematic. That most standardized exams fail to assess the kinds of intellectual skills and richness of knowledge that we are most interested in is widely acknowledged. So are concerns about racial and class biases. It is somewhat less widely recognized that jurisdictions that stick with a given form of standardized test almost always show "improvement" over time. This is attributable partly to the fact that teachers consciously or unconsciously learn to "teach to the test." It can also be because the norms for some standardized tests are updated only on an occasional basis. This means that, when school districts report that their students are performing better than the national norm, the actual comparison group may be a sample of students who took the test more than five years before, not a contemporaneous sample, as might naturally be assumed. Toch estimates that the major standardized tests are renormed about once every seven years. He warns that some districts continue to use old tests even after new ones are made available. "As late as 1989–90," he writes, "Maryland was administering a version of the CAT [California Achievement Test] normed in 1977, permitting the state's teachers to teach to the same test for twelve years, as well as have their students' performance measured against that of students in norming groups that lacked such advantages."[93]

Figure 6.1 illustrates this vividly, and underscores another reason that claims of success attributable to school-choice initiatives should be regarded warily. The figure is based on information collected in a survey of the forty-five members of the Council of Great City Schools.[94] These are the large central city districts that are foremost in the minds of most Americans when they think about education problems. Yet, based on standardized test results for elementary-level students, most report scores at or above the national average and nearly three-quarters cite evidence that things are getting better. The report by Blank and his colleagues is the only major study to make a genuine effort to get beyond reliance on standardized testing by observing teachers and classrooms directly in order to assess the educational process itself.

In at least one important case, substantive claims of improvement attributed to choice appear to be based on improperly comparing performances on different standardized tests. The sharp gains claimed in for East Harlem students in the percentage of students reading at grade level (from 16 percent to almost 63 percent; see above) appears to be based on a pupil-achieve-

Relation to National Norm

	Above	At	Mixed*	Below
Increasing	Boston Dade County Dallas Houston Jacksonville Nashville New Orleans Pittsburgh Portland Rochester San Diego St. Louis St. Paul	Atlanta Baton Rouge Fresno Washington	Baltimore Buffalo El Paso Indianapolis Memphis New York City Norfolk Oakland San Francisco	Chicago Cincinnati Dayton Los Angeles Milwaukee Philadelphia
Stable	Anchorage Omaha Seattle Tulsa	Minneapolis Tucson	Cleveland Columbus Denver Detroit Long Beach Toledo	None
Decreasing	None	None	None	None

* "Mixed" category means some grades are above national norm, some are below.

FIG. 6.1 Elementary achievement in reading and math, 1985–1990. *Source*: Council of Great City Schools, *Results 2000* (Washington, D.C.: Council of Great City Schools, 1990).

ment report by the New York City Board of Education.[95] These figures do not take into account at least one change in the testing instrument, in 1986, which may account for as much as 14 points of the jump.[96]

Just as significant are several limitations specifically of the HS&B measures used as the foundation of all the important studies comparing public to private schools. First, as others have detailed, the actual degree of student gain between sophomore and senior years proves to be so small that assessments of variation are of doubtful substantive significance.[97] For example, 1980 sophomores averaged 61.32 correct answers out of the 115 items used to assess knowledge in reading, vocabulary, math, writing, and science on the exam; as seniors, those same students answered only 6.17 additional items correctly.

Chubb and Moe turn this limitation to their advantage. Following Coleman's lead, they convert small gains in the number of items correct into estimations of "gains measured in years." Thus an average gain of 2.35 items correct on the quantitative sections between sophomore and senior year is translated into a *two-year* gain; the gain of 9.97 items by the highest quartile is translated to *eight and one-half years*.[98] As Witte notes, "this has the effect of getting the reader into the habit of thinking in terms of years of learning; years that nevertheless represent only a fraction of a percent of the test variance and a very modest percent of what could be learned."[99]

Nor does it really make sense to look for the impact of private schools and competition so late in students' academic careers. Nearly everything we know about education suggests that the most critical experiences come at an early age. Analysts have tried an array of techniques to attempt to estimate and account for the extent to which prior advantages might account for why some high school students do better than others, but these attempts are necessarily artificial. If we are interested in determining the independent effect of private schools, we would be much better off looking at changes in performance across the earlier grades.

The HS&B data, moreover, simply were not designed for the purpose of telling us much about private schools, their independent effect, or choice per se. The number of private schools included was small and the sample was not designed to allow reliable estimates of the performance of different types of private schools; only 111 private schools were included, all but 27 of them Catholic schools.[100] The data do not make any distinction among public-school districts reflecting the amount of choice they provide parents through magnet schools or relaxed transfer provisions.

What this means is that the connection between choice and the HS&B and ATS data sets is based entirely on inference. Neither the HS&B data nor Chubb and Moe's ATS data contain any direct measure of students' exercise of choice or the extent to which schools are forced to respond to market demands. It is assumed that all private schools are forced to compete for student-customers, even though some elite private schools have long waiting lists and some parochial institutions charge tuitions so low that they may lose money for each additional student they accept. It is assumed that all public schools are shielded from competitive pressures, although administrators in some districts may feel that opportunities for career advancement and additional resources are related to their ability to keep parents content.

Lack of Controls (Internal Validity)

Even when early and roughly measured improvements appear to be associated with choice-oriented policies, the link between cause and effect is often obscure. Improvements in student performance following the introduction of magnet schools, controlled choice, or open-enrollment plans may be due to a host of other factors. Just a few of the possible rival explanations for improvement are: (1) the continuation of trends already underway before the policy was put in place; (2) independent changes in the demographic composition of the student body; (3) self-selection processes that bring to the choice schools and programs motivated students who would be likely to succeed no matter where they were educated; (4) other new education-related policies undertaken more or less simultaneously at the school, district, state, or federal level; (5) other policies or events not related to education (such as expanded nutritional programs or expanded job opportunities) that may have an important indirect influence on students' readiness to learn; (6) artifacts of the testing strategy, including the tendency of scores on standardized tests to improve as teachers learn how to teach to the test. Similarly, real differences in performance between students at private and public schools might be attributable to differences in the characteristics of families attracted to and able to afford private schools, the criteria for admission that private schools apply, or the greater freedom of private schools to expel difficult students.

Social policy, as has frequently been noted, never takes place in a tightly controlled laboratory. Scientists testing whether a drug causes cancer in mice can compare those injected with the drug to a control group that does not systematically differ from the subjects except in that it receives only a placebo. When differences in cancer rates result under such circumstances, the inference of causality is unproblematic. The appeal of unambiguous information is powerful, and some policy analysts have dedicated themselves to trying to replicate, as closely as possible, such an experimental approach. Political, administrative, legal, and ethical barriers, however, create substantial obstacles that either deter such efforts altogether or force methodological adaptations and compromises that weaken the design in nontrivial ways.[101]

To the untutored, the naive, the cynical, and the mischievous this absence of definitive controls may suggest either of two extreme conclusions. To some it suggests that careful empirical analysis has nothing of value to add to our deliberations about policy options. To others it suggests that one study is as good as any other. Both inferences are wrong. It is true that, absent more perfect controls, inferences about the causal effects of policies require judgment and interpretation. But it also is true that well-designed studies can narrow the scope within which judgment must take over and make it possible for interpretations to be more, rather than less, informed.

Policy analysts have a full bag of tricks to help them sift through rival explanations and determine how credible the conclusion is that this or that change is attributable to a specific policy, such as educational choice.[102] For the most part, they build on two simple points. One has to do with comparison over time; the other involves comparison across groups. Rather than a simple before-and-after comparison, it is better when possible to base inferences about policy effects on a historical series of observations, since this makes it possible to distinguish real changes from those that are either continuations of trends, episodes in a normally unstable and erratic pattern, or recoveries from an extreme. Rather than looking only at changes within the group that is the intended target of the policy, it is better to juxtapose the experiences of that group to coincident changes in roughly comparable groups that are not exposed to the policy, since this makes it easier to distinguish changes attributable to the policy from changes due to other policies or societal events that would have brought about the observed changes even in the absence of the policy in question.

With relatively few exceptions, assessments of initiatives for educational choice lack any but the most basic kinds of controls. The fifteen-city study of magnets by Blank and his associates offered unusually rich measures and a strong design, yet for some reason the Department of Education specifications for the study directly ruled out the inclusion of a comparison group of nonmagnet schools.[103] Of the twelve single-city studies of educational effects of magnet schools that Blank subsequently reviewed, only ten compared magnet students' performance to that of nonmagnet students or district norms, only eight analyzed outcomes over time by tracking individual students, and only six did both.[104] Only four studies attempted to control for student background, ability level, or criteria for magnet selection. And only one of the twelve tried to control for student and parental motivation by comparing students who transferred into a magnet program to a control group of nontransfer students within the magnet schools.[105]

The study with the most advanced design, according to Blank's criteria, was an assessment of magnet-school performance in Montgomery County, Maryland. The study resulted in a rather mixed picture of magnet-school results, which highlights the importance of such controls. Among sixth graders, magnet transferees and magnet nontransferees both showed gains in reading performance when compared to students in nonmagnet programs; transferees showed a slightly greater rate of increase, perhaps reflecting the greater motivation implicit in their decision to relocate. Among third graders the pattern was quite different. Magnet transfer students had significantly outscored the nonmagnet controls at the end of first grade; they maintained an advantage when tested again in the spring of their third-grade experience, but their margin of advantage was slightly decreased. Magnet students who did not have to transfer in order to attend the schools had scored slightly better than nonmagnet students at the end of first grade, but they "progressed slower so that by the end of the third grade they were behind the nonmagnet group in reading by a small but statistically significant margin."[106] This pattern is consistent with the inference that self-selection, rather than the quality of the program delivered, may account for the magnet transferees' gains.

The existing studies of fully magnetized districts, such as Cambridge, Montclair, and East Harlem, also have serious control limitations. For Cambridge and Montclair, there is better time-series data for assessing desegregation outcomes than for assessing educational outcomes. Rossell and Glenn's assessment of educational gains in Cambridge offers a simple before-and-after design, comparing the percent passing the city's basic-skills test in 1981–82, when its choice plan was fully implemented, to scores in 1985–86. Because the test was developed by Cambridge itself, it was not possible to compare changes to norms from other districts, the state, or the nation. And because only two time points are presented, it is not possible to determine whether the improvement that most schools registered is a continuation of a longer-term trend.

Tan updates Rossell and Glenn's analysis after Cambridge switched to a state-developed test in 1986. This allows a comparison to performance in other jurisdictions, but for some reason Tan does not present these comparisons in a systematic way. What is apparent is that Cambridge students, in 1987, were still scoring well below the state averages—for example, 82 percent of third graders passed the reading test, versus 93 percent for the state; 78 percent passed math, versus 93 percent for the state; 79 percent passed the writing test, versus 91 percent for the state.[107]

Clewell and Joy present a series of graphs showing that the percentage of Montclair students scoring below grade level in math and reading declined markedly between 1974 and 1986. These graphs present only the two time points, and they leave the impression of sharp improvements following the institution of the full-choice program in 1985. Looking at year-by-year changes (Figure 6–2), however, shows how problematic it is to attribute the improvement to educational choice per se (see fig. 6.2). While there is certainly a long-term trend in a favorable direction, one would be hard-pressed to identify a consistent pattern of improvement tied to a particular year. What is clear is that most of the improvement substantially predates the initiation of the full-choice system in 1985. The improvement may be partially explained by choice, but other explanations (such as teaching to the test) are just as likely. The most striking increases coincide with the earlier

139

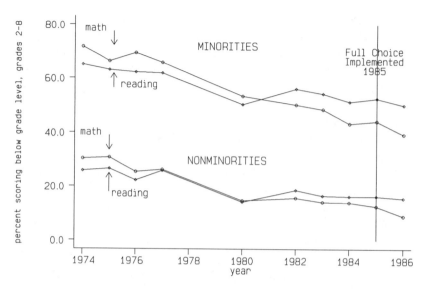

FIG. 6.2 Academic achievement: Montclair public schools, 1974–1986. *Source*: Compiled from Beatriz C. Clewell and Myra F. Joy, *Choice in Montclair, New Jersey* (Princeton, N.J.: Educational Testing Service, 1990), appendix, tables 3 and 4.

period (1977–82), in which a few magnet schools were instituted along with more affirmative government actions to mandate racial integration, such as redrawing some attendance-zone boundaries and closing several schools.

Even the more detailed data generally available on changes in racial balance leave some questions as to whether improvements can appropriately be attributed to choice, as opposed to other policy actions taken around the same time. For racial balance as well as test performance, the most dramatic improvements in Montclair coincided with the period in which more affirmative government steps were being undertaken (see fig. 6.3).[108] While the data for the post–1985 full-choice period is limited, it shows evidence of possible slippage.

Similarly, Alves and Willie conclude that "a key lesson to be learned from Cambridge is that under the correct conditions 'controlled choice' can achieve more effective desegregation outcomes than conventional voluntary and mandatory methods of assignments."[109] But, while their interpretation is suitably qualified, it may be that an even more modest conclusion—that controlled choice can allow for *sustaining* desegregation progress begun using more authoritative governmental means—is more appropriate. Figure 6.4 presents two measures of desegregation in Cambridge schools.[110] It suggests that the sharpest decline in racial imbalance occurred during the pe-

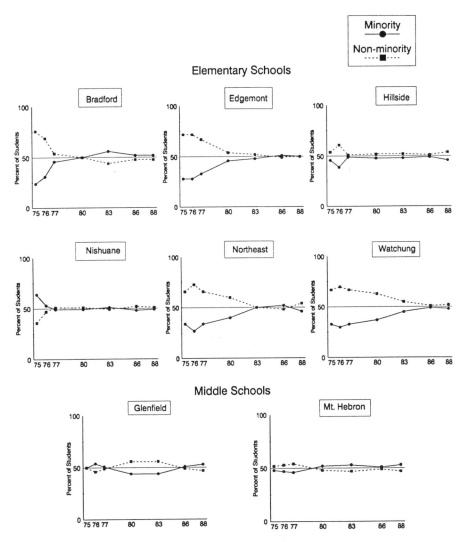

FIG. 6.3 Changes in the racial composition of Montclair's schools, 1977–1988. *Source*: *Choice in Montclair, New Jersey* by Beatriz C. Clewell and Myra F. Joy. Policy Information Paper, Policy Information Center, Educational Testing Service, January 1990. Reproduced with the permission of the Policy Information Center, ETS.

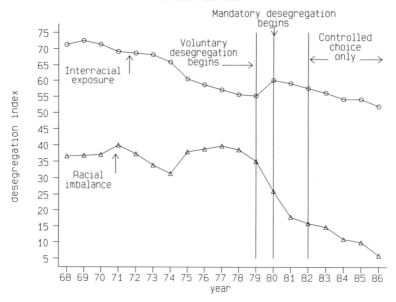

FIG. 6.4 Desegregation indices for Cambridge, 1968–1986. *Source*: Compiled from figures presented in Christine H. Rossell and Charles L. Glenn, "The Cambridge Controlled Choice Plan," *Urban Review* 20, no. 2 (1988), table 5.

riod from 1979 to 1981, a period marked by a series of strong government actions. In 1979, in response to pressure from the state, Cambridge tightened its controls on transfer requests and strengthened magnet-school programs and recruitment efforts. In 1980, one school was closed, all attendance zones were redrawn, and several special programs were relocated.

Despite such ambiguities, the research designs applied to programs of choice in Cambridge and Montclair are far more ambitious than those on which proponents of choice base claims of success in East Harlem. Indeed, it would hardly be an exaggeration to assert that the East Harlem experience has escaped any serious effort at controlled analysis. This is all the more significant—and surprising—in light of the special role that East Harlem has played in countering charges that the benefits of choice programs will not accrue to minorities and the poor.

The frequently cited statistics on East Harlem's improvements are aggregate figures that do not distinguish improvements due to better education from those attributable to the attraction of students from outside the district, whose ability to perform well on standardized tests may reflect better socioeconomic circumstances.[111] Indeed, in some of the most popular and prestigious schools in District No. 4, high scores on standardized tests probably reflect little more than that school officials have the luxury of picking and

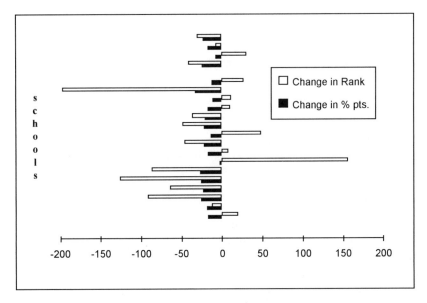

FIG. 6.5 District No. 4, East Harlem, New York: Changes, 1988–1991. *Source*: Compiled from figures presented in the *New York Times*, February 23, 1988, and March 25, 1992.

choosing among competing candidates. Schools such as Manhattan East, New York Prep, and the Talented and Gifted School have many more applicants than openings, and David L. Kirp reports that some schools aggressively recruit students they know are likely to succeed. "It is largely because of this hidden selection process—which screens both for levels of skill and for traits of character," he argues, "that some very good schools have been created in East Harlem."[112]

While the uncertainties caused by the absence of control do not mean that the cited improvements are not real or that claims of great successes are fraudulent, they do underscore how little we really know for sure. It seems apparent that some genuine improvements have been taking place in District No. 4, but as Richard F. Elmore observes, "the data do not support any specific conclusions about the role that choice has played in that improvement."[113]

Moreover, it now appears to be the case that District No. 4's progress leveled off substantially. In 1991, 50.6 percent of New York City students read at or above grade level. But only three of East Harlem's sixteen elementary schools, and only one of its four junior highs, reached even this modest goal.[114] Figure 6.5 graphs changes in academic performance in East Harlem between 1988 and 1991. For each of District No. 4's schools, the graph indicates the change in rank among all the city's schools and the change in the percent of students on grade level. All the schools had a lower percentage at or above grade level in 1991 than 1988, and for most the drop was sharper than that experienced by other schools in the system.[115] In 1992, District No. 4 slipped even further; aggregate figures for the entire district showed just 38.3 percent of students reading at or above grade level, compared to a citywide average of 46.4 percent.[116]

The studies comparing the performance of public and private schools offer more sophisticated controls. The unusually rich HS&B data includes detailed information about each student's family situation, making it possible statistically to control for many differences that the children carry with them into the schools. The analyses by Coleman and others confirm that private-school students do have many advantages. The median income of Catholic-school families was 121.5 percent that for public schools, and that for other private schools was 130 percent that for public schools. Parental education also differs markedly; only 12 percent of public-school children have mothers who have completed at least a four-year college degree, versus 24 percent for Catholic schools and 36 percent for other private schools.[117] Findings about the superior performance of private-school students are so impressive because a performance edge exists even when statistical controls for family background are introduced.

But the private-school edge, once background is controlled for, is small, and it may yet reflect family and student differences that the HS&B data cannot take into account, such as the differences in motivation that may distinguish those lower-income families that make heroic financial sacrifices in order to send their children to private schools, and behavioral tendencies resulting from the fact that private schools can screen out individual students who are disruptive or difficult to educate. As Karl L. Alexander and Aaron M. Pallas remark, "when good students go to good schools, how are we to know which is responsible for the good performance that is likely to be observed?"[118]

John Witte presents strong evidence, from the ATS survey, that Catholic schools do, indeed, screen admissions in a manner that would tend to filter out probable poor performers. For example, 55.5 percent of Catholic-school principals indicated that prior academic record was an important factor affecting their admissions, while only 8.4 percent of public-school principals did so; 51.0 percent versus 4.7 percent indicated that test scores were important; 71.3 percent versus 4.7 percent indicated that disciplinary records were important.[119] "Statistically, what this implies," he concludes, "is that with this magnitude of screening going on in private schools, statistical controls for selectivity probably do not capture the true differences in student populations."[120]

A systematic study of the Milwaukee choice program eventually may provide the best evidence about the independent effect of private schools. Witte has begun a foundation-supported assessment of the program and its consequences. The preliminary results confirm the importance of developing precise modes of control. Although program requirements ensure that participants are poor, the self-selection bias may still be a factor: parents of choice students were substantially lower in income and more likely to be on welfare than the average Milwaukee public-school parent, but they (especially mothers) also were substantially more likely to have had some college-level education. They were more likely to have participated in school activities, even before entering the choice program, and were much more likely to have supported educational activities in their homes.[121]

The early results suggest that families that have taken advantage of Milwaukee's voucher program are very satisfied with their children's experiences in their new schools. Whether that satisfaction will be reflected in the students' educational performance remains uncertain, however. Even with the advantage of supportive families and after a year attending private school, Milwaukee's choice participants still did not fare well on standardized tests. Choice students improved on standardized reading tests (from the thirtieth to the thirty-fourth percentile nationally) but declined on mathematics (from the thirty-third to the thirtieth percentile).

ARE MORE STUDIES THE ANSWER?

The evidence regarding the consequences of school choice is mixed and uncertain. In spite of confident assertions to the contrary, there has been little in the way of careful and systematic empirical assessment of choice-in-practice. Most of the claims that "choice works" are anecdotal and impressionistic. Even where more sophisticated analyses have been conducted, the clarity and force of their findings are blunted by reliance on inadequate measures of success and the lack of more than rudimentary controls. That high-powered techniques of data manipulation have been applied sometimes mask this basic fact. The High School and Beyond survey, for instance, is a rich source of information that can tell us a lot about the characteristics of students and schools. It is fully appropriate that researchers like Coleman, Chubb and Moe, and others take advantage of its availability to shed what light they can on the contemporary debate over school choice. The large

145

sample size and the variety of indicators collected make it possible to apply more sophisticated statistical techniques such as regression analysis. Such "bells and whistles" can generate a gratuitous air of certainty and exactitude. They help to account for Chubb and Moe's analysis being so widely cited and so apparently influential. But there is no denying that the data were not gathered to address the issue of school choice, and are of limited utility in doing so. There is a certain irony—if not tragedy—in that the study that has lent the greatest credence to the claim that "choice works" does not include any direct indicators of choice at all.

That proponents have oversold the definitiveness of the existing evidence is, to some extent, undoubtedly intentional and politically motivated. But less important ultimately than the question of whether some educational reformers are insincere is the question of why such a perspective seems to resonate so strongly in the sound chamber of public opinion. Part of the explanation seems to lie in Americans' complex attitude toward systematic social science and its capacity to provide firm guidance to policymakers. On the one hand, pragmatic orientation, respect for scientific expertise, and desire for reassurance combine to form an audience that insists that political platforms come festooned with scholarly declarations of "proof." On the other hand, unsophisticated expectations about the certainty that analysis can provide, and an untutored capacity to make distinctions among studies based on their relative strength in measurement and design, leave an audience prone to manipulation in the short term, and radical skepticism in the long term.

Does it make any sense, in this context, to hold out the hope that further studies will shed greater light on the matters at hand? Or will they simply add new echoes of confusion and contradiction, and further fuel the impression that social science—like legal experts at a courtroom trial—can be counted on to neutralize its own impact by taking both sides of conflicting issues with equal fervor and aplomb?

My own conclusion is nuanced. It depends on distinguishing between more studies and better studies. And it depends on shedding the false hope of certainty for a more modest aspiration. In the rush to claim the mantle of proof, proponents of school choice have been indiscriminate in grounding their claims. But the beauty of social science, properly understood, is that it includes skepticism among its most central values. Critical scrutiny, replication, reanalysis, and reinterpretation are part of the basic enterprise. So, for that matter, can be obfuscation, unthinking reaffirmation of conventional wisdom, and political opportunism. But the latter cluster of attributes represent a corruption of basic ideals, and this, I think, makes a difference in the long run. The process tends to have self-policing elements, which is not to say it necessarily is self-correcting.[122] Not all misinformation is excised, but conclusions based on methodologically suspect analyses are likely to enjoy a shorter shelf-life than those which can better sustain evenhanded scrutiny.

Carried out in good faith, this suggests that future analyses of the school-choice issue can sharpen our understanding. Sensitive reconsiderations of the existing studies have the potential to sort through and reinterpret conclusions without dismissing them outright; it is possible, in other words, to learn something of value even from studies that are flawed. The passage of time will make it possible to consider the longer-term effects of innovations like those in Cambridge, Minnesota, East Harlem, and Milwaukee. Studies employing more careful designs can be undertaken; a few already are in place.

But this optimistic view needs to be tempered in at least three respects. First, it understates the extent to which social science relies on an infrastructure that must be deliberately maintained. Good indicators of educational quality cannot be spontaneously generated. Assessments across communities and over time depend on coordinated and sustained efforts to test children using consistent instruments. The best research designs are not necessarily the most expensive, but carrying out studies that will be deemed to have general implications often requires large samples and multiple settings, and these invariably impose costs. The best research designs, moreover, require policymakers to cooperate with evaluators in determining how and when a policy is introduced. Historically, the federal government has played an important role in supporting these conditions for good research, as well as in funding the research directly. My recommendations for future policy, offered in the concluding chapter, recognize the need for an active role for the government.

This optimistic view of the potential for further study to provide valuable information needs to be tempered also by an acknowledgment that policymakers do not have the luxury of waiting patiently until social scientists are ready to speak confidently and in unison. I have argued that the sense of crisis has been artificially inflated. But this is not an excuse for inaction. There are pressing social problems, and if improvements in America's schools can play a remedial role, citizens are right to demand immediate action and public officials have a responsibility to respond. Given the high levels of tentativeness and uncertainty about the evidence that "choice works," it takes some combination of daring, hubris, and foolhardiness to take giant or irreversible steps. But social science condemns itself to the periphery unless it can help policymakers even when information is partial, ambiguous, and conflicting.

Finally, it is important to recognize the limits of social-science techniques. No matter how many the studies or how sophisticated their design, experience indicates that evidence about the likely effects of public policies rarely is definitive. The step from evidence to policy is always a problematic one. The uncertainty of social-science techniques means that important decisions about what should be done inevitably requires that decisions be made in the face of incomplete and conflicting evidence, competing values, unselfconscious assumptions, and shifting contexts.[123] Ultimately, we must rely on interpretation and judgment—the evidence can inform, but it cannot define our move. This is where the world of ideas and theories comes back into play. And, as I argue in the next chapter, it is the area where we are in greatest danger of drawing the wrong lessons from our experience with school choice so far.

Reinterpreting the Lessons of Experience

THE EMPIRICAL CASE for market-based school choice rests on two legs. The first leg is the claim that there is systematic evidence that "choice works." The second leg consists of an interpretation about why choice works.

The favored interpretation is that past successes—with the GI Bill, magnet schools, and the like—are attributable to economic forces of supply and demand. "Magnet schools, open enrollment, and controlled choice have proven effective in improving education," one proponent explains, "by injecting an invigorating dose of competition into the public school system."[1] This interpretation sets the stage for the transition from evidence to policy recommendation. If past successes associated with school choice are attributable to market forces, further injection of such forces would appear to be the logical course of action.

I already have made the case that the first leg is shaky. That the evidence of the success of choice-based schemes is more mixed and uncertain than has been claimed should be taken as an argument for cautious moderation, not an argument against choice nor an argument for doing nothing. More and better studies gradually can help sharpen the picture; if the weight of the evidence tilts strongly in favor of choice, then aggressive steps will be more clearly justified.

In this chapter, I offer another argument for wariness, which focuses on the second leg of the empirical claims made on behalf of choice. This argument is both more innovative and more radical. Rather than simply propelling us to move more quickly than caution dictates, it suggests that the siren call for restructuring along a market-based choice model may pull us in exactly the wrong direction. The problem is not choice per se, but the particular approach to choice that poses it as an alternative to public governance rather than as a tool of public governance.

A NOTE ON METAPHOR AND INTERPRETATION

Advocates of extreme school-choice schemes present individual freedom and market forces as alternatives to, and improvements on, reliance on government authority and intervention. Through their recitation of the history of choice, their recounting of successful cases, and their citation of supportive studies, they give their claims a credibility that abstract theories of market behavior lack on their own. But the edifice of evidence rests on softer ground: on the power of the market metaphor to bridge the gap from evidence to prescription.

On the surface, metaphors "simply draw a comparison between one thing and another," as Deborah Stone observes. But "in a more subtle way they usually imply a whole narrative story and a prescription for action."[2] Lacking any working examples of a truly market-based school-choice system, as noted in chapter 1, proponents have had no choice but to base their claim to empirical support on a buried metaphor. Magnets, districtwide choice systems, and state open-enrollment options are *like* free markets, only just a little less so. It is the metaphor, not the weight of the evidence, that sustains the interpretive leap from the finding that these practices have experienced some success to the recommendation that the role of government should be substantially scaled back.

Policy analysts like to believe that the tools of their trade are more precise and hard-edged than this, but metaphor plays a necessary role in broadening the range of experiences to which we can turn in looking for guidance. The specific array of problems we face as citizens and policymakers is in constant flux. So too are the many contextual factors that will determine the consequences of our actions—the responsiveness and capacity of our governing institutions, the strength and resilience of our economy, the inclinations and impulses of our fellow citizens. Heraclitus, who lived around 500 B.C.E., observed that you cannot step into the same river twice, since other waters are continually flowing in. To insist on basing contemporary decisions on the results from identical actions taken in identical circumstances, therefore, would be to consign ourselves to immobility. Instead we rely on analogy and metaphor. We look for historical situations and actions that were *like* the current ones in what we judge to be important respects, and attempt to learn from them.

Accepting the principle that metaphor plays a legitimate role in thinking about public policy does not, however, mean that all metaphors are equally apropos. The criteria for assessing the reliability and validity of evidence, as employed in the previous chapter, are relatively well defined and straightforward. The standards for assessing interpretive metaphors are more elusive. This chapter reconsiders the history of school choice through a different interpretive filter. I suggest that the expanded use of magnet schools and other choice options is better understood as having arisen from collective negotiation, public leadership, and authoritative government, rather than from an unleashing of individual interests and market forces. Moreover, while claims about the success and failures of these various choice schemes necessarily are tentative,[3] it appears that the jurisdictions most frequently cited as models are marked by strong democratic cultures, fiscal commitments to public education, traditions of public leadership, and acceptance of the legitimacy of public law and regulation.

RECONSIDERING THE EXPANSION OF INITIATIVES FOR CHOICE

What accounts for the broad adoption of initiatives for choice, and what general lessons should we learn from this history? Contemporary school-choice reformers draw one set of lessons. Proponents of market approaches argue that the nation's experience with magnet schools demonstrates the power of market-based approaches to solve social problems. Magnet schools represent a precursor of more completely market-oriented systems because they rely on individual choice instead of government coercion to attain integration, and because they introduce an element of competitive pressure into the public-school monopoly. By successfully attracting white children to predominantly black schools, magnets have reduced the fear that freedom of choice necessarily will undermine the national commitment to racial integration. By spreading so wide and so rapidly, they prove that altering the traditional mandatory assignment to neighborhood schools is administratively feasible and politically popular. That students attending many magnet schools perform better and seem more satisfied than other children is an indication that competition for students heightens schools' sensitivity to their clients' needs and desires.

But the analogy between magnet schools and market solutions is dangerously unsophisticated. Magnets evolved as an effort by public officials to use government authority and resources to structure a system within which individual choices would promote a social goal: racial integration. As related below, the expansion and success of magnets depended on decisive action by public authorities. Intervention, or the threat of intervention, by federal courts was integral in getting local governments to adopt magnet programs. External financial support from state and federal governments was critical in making programs substantial enough to work. Strong local leadership made the difference between magnet plans that were superficial and those that represented genuine reforms. Where it was not simply imposed by government through the courts, the adoption of choice represented a pragmatic adjustment in which key values and ideas were often in tension with one another and unarticulated, in which indigenous plans evolved out of an accumulation of compromises and ad hoc decisions, in which local officials played an intermediary role between courts willing to impose mandatory solutions and mobilized citizens preferring to forestall any change at all.[4]

Decisive Action by Public Authorities

In light of the conservative argument that choice can be used as an alternative to authoritative government action, it is important to acknowledge that it was largely the threat of strong action by the federal government (backed up by a demonstrated willingness and capacity to carry through on threatened intervention) that fueled the adoption of magnet alternatives—either directly, by mandate, or indirectly, by altering the political environment to make it more feasible for receptive local interests to build support for the potentially disruptive and costly changes that would be involved.

As indicated in chapter 5, the promise of inducing a voluntary movement of white students into more integrated schools made magnets attractive to federal judges and to local officials seeking to craft plans that would satisfy the courts with a minimum of disruption and controversy. Some northern cities turned to magnets without direct intervention, but even in these instances the desire to forestall judicial intervention was often the precipitating factor. Among districts in which magnets were implemented as part of a school board–initiated (rather than court-initiated) effort to desegregate the public schools are Cincinnati; Montclair, New Jersey; Portland, Oregon; Tacoma, Washington; St. Paul; Seattle; and Montgomery County, Maryland.[5] In some of these cases, local officials found it useful to manipulate the threat of direct federal intervention in order to defuse likely sources of opposition within the local community and gain acquiescence in carrying out reforms that might otherwise be stymied by various "veto groups."

As Daniel J. Monti notes, based on his study of the politics of desegregation in St. Louis, "school administrators know that under the best of circumstances it is difficult to close schools, fire staff, or increase the amount of funds for education from local sources. Such things may be more feasible if they are called for under a court order."[6] Magnet schools "made good educational sense" to St. Louis school officials, but they had "lacked either the funds or the political will" to initiate them prior to the involvement of the federal court. "It would be fair to say, in fact, that officials seized the opportunity presented by the consent decree in order to propose a whole series of magnets."[7]

In Seattle, the mayor used the threat of intervention by the federal court (coupled with the implied threat of racial disorder) to convince the business community to give public support to a magnet proposal.[8] Seattle's experience is somewhat typical of those cities in which magnet plans evolved as a compromise among pragmatic and politically centrist groups seeking to forestall external intervention and restrain internal polarization. There, the NAACP first filed suit against the schools in 1962. The district initially sought to respond voluntarily by allowing students to switch schools when the transfer improved racial balance, but this strategy did not make much more headway in actually desegregating schools than had the freedom-of-choice plans in the South. In the spring of 1977, the school board approved a magnet plan proposed by the superintendent. The NAACP's first reaction was to file a complaint with the U.S. Office of Civil Rights, charging that the magnet proposal was just a continuation of voluntary efforts "which have a history of failure whenever and wherever used."[9] The willingness and ability of the city's political and business elite to pursue the magnet plan aggressively helped temper that response. According to Ann LaGrelius Siqueland, a clear background factor was the presumption by many in the predominantly white establishment that, if the magnet plan was not given substantial resources to make the magnet schools distinctively attractive, the result would be a court order, which might impose a more extreme and disruptive desegregation formula.[10]

The Power of Public Dollars

With few exceptions, advocates of market-oriented school choice have emphasized its potential to increase performance without increasing cost.[11] Yet the availability of external financial support played a critical role in accounting for the expansion of magnet schools throughout the United States. Advocates portray external support as an initial catalyst needed to meet special start-up costs. But there is evidence that, at least in some cases, the infusion of external funds is necessary on a continuing basis for magnet programs to retain their viability.

Kansas City used federal money, made available specifically to districts using magnet schools to support desegregation, in order to combine three adjacent elementary schools into a science- and math-oriented magnet—the Southwest Cluster Elementary Magnet School. The magnet was later found to have helped maintain racial desegregation at two of the schools, but "substantial resegregation" began immediately at the third and continued for at least the next eight years. "In addition, district evaluation reports also identified problems which occurred in implementing the Cluster's original magnet program, particularly after federal funding diminished."[12] Similarly, at the Swinney/Volker Applied Learning Magnet, enrollment of nonminorities began to decline in 1980, and the decline accelerated in 1984 and 1985; by September 1985 only sixty-six nonminority students were at the school, many of those concentrated in the two classes for gifted and talented students.[13]

Blank and his colleagues noted that federal funds spent on magnets and other Emergency School Aid Act programs dropped from a high of nearly four hundred million in 1979 to just over twenty-five million in 1982. Based on their survey of a representative sample of school districts offering magnet programs in 1981, they concluded that "this drop in federal aid has shivered the timbers of many magnet schools and programs but has not resulted in their destruction. . . . Few new magnets are being created, meanwhile, and some districts have been debating the issue of terminating their magnets for the last two years."[14]

Constructing Coalitions: The Local Political Context

It would be a mistake to overemphasize the independent force of external actors such as the federal judiciary and grants from the Department of Education. Courts cannot enforce their decisions directly, and competitive categorical grants go only to jurisdictions with the will and capacity to pursue them. Both require the cooperation of other branches and other levels of government before their pronouncements of principle and stated objectives can be translated into meaningful change. The ability of local political actors to mobilize such cooperation had a profound effect on the particular mixture of mandatory and voluntary elements in the desegregation plans that evolved. And this ability to mobilize cooperation, in turn, depended on such factors as public leadership, coalition building, and broader perceptions of the legitimacy of government institutions.

In spite of the positive connotations attached to the abstract concept of choice, left to their own devices most local communities historically have resisted the idea of deliberately fostering differentiation in funding and curriculum among their public schools, and have tended to favor the maintenance of neighborhood schools over strategies that allow a broad freedom to transfer. Resistance to magnet schools was based on more than parochial self-interest, and support on more than an intellectual commitment to market ideals.

Some groups potentially did have a direct interest in resisting magnet plans. These included: (1) local school bureaucracies, with an incentive to protect their professional sphere of influence and familiar and comfortable ways of going about their business; (2) parents who preferred their children to attend their own neighborhood schools with other children from the neighborhood; (3) civil-rights groups, who perceived magnets and other choice components as diluting more direct and substantial efforts to reduce racial and economic disparities; and (4) taxpayers who feared the burden of financing magnet plans and associated transportation costs.

Besides these groups with direct interests, certain broad principles also potentially clashed with the magnet approach. Magnet schools seemingly were at odds with deeply held values regarding equal treatment and socialization into a common culture. The idea of differentiating the curriculum among public schools was regarded warily among those who hold to the notion of public schools as the key tool for making America a "melting pot" that would meld various ethnic and religious strands into a single national culture. Denis P. Doyle and Marsha Levine note that "from the beginning the charge of elitism has plagued selective schools and by extension, magnet schools." Three selective academic high schools in New York City, for example, "found that they needed special legislation to protect them from bureaucratic intervention and even extinction."[15] One study of the introduction of magnet schools into a midwestern city found that, while rhetoric emphasizing the educational superiority of the magnets helped defuse political resistance in the short run, "in the long run it sparked controversy because it undermined the formal claim that the schools of the city were all equal."[16] In Seattle, the Church Council for Greater Seattle opposed reliance on magnets because "magnet schools are elitist and serve families with parents who are sophisticated enough to take advantage of them" and "rob resources from other programs and thus give other children an inferior education."[17] And a survey of magnet schools in a number of cities found evidence of resentment, in about half the cases, among parents, teachers, and administrators associated with neighborhood schools, who "had the view that magnets attract the best students and staff members from other district schools."[18]

In this environment, local leaders who spoke out for magnet schools risked political isolation. The disadvantages of magnets were more immediately apparent and more assured than were their potential benefits, and they fell on more readily mobilized groups. Appeals to market ideals would not suffice to rally support for magnets; the principles of laissez-faire were claimed by those who opposed a governmental role of any kind.

The attractiveness of magnet schools in the local political context often depended on the public's desire to forestall more radical changes, not on a broad constituency motivated by a shared positive vision of the role of choice in education. The school district in Buffalo, New York, for example, "waved its court order at anyone who stood in the way of its drastic reforms—a tightfisted city council as well as recalcitrant parents."[19] Milwaukee is often cited as an example of an enlightened district that smoothly instituted a large magnet-based system, and thereby avoided the violence and disruption that characterized desegregation in Boston. But Milwaukee residents made both their collective and their individual educational choices with the threat of mandatory busing very much in mind.[20] Just as it was clear to Milwaukee that it had the power to shape its own destiny through its choices, "it was equally clear to the community that a mandatory student-assignment backup provision would immediately be invoked."[21]

In some cases, local citizens and policymakers were pulled to the magnet solution kicking and screaming all the way. Blank and his colleagues discuss five cities in their sample where magnets were adopted as reluctant compromises. In one, "Steeltown," the magnet plan was clearly adopted as a way of forestalling a more extreme mandatory busing plan; "the leadership of one of the region's most virulent Ku Klux Klan klaverns literally stood behind the seated members of the Steeltown Board of Education as they deliberated the magnet compromise."[22]

But subsequent studies have shown that integration went most smoothly in northern districts in which local leaders played a more affirmative role.[23] Besides political courage, such local leaders exhibited an ability to stitch together a coalition of support from disparate elements. Some supporters were rallied by a moral vision of progressive government committed to racial integration. Others were attracted by less elevated concerns: desire to put the issue behind them, fear that the alternatives would be more disruptive, attraction to specific elements of a magnet plan that would benefit them directly.

The constituency for choice, in other words, was not ready-made. It had to be constructed deliberately. This required public leadership. Special responsibility lay on elected officials to provide this leadership, but they were not the only candidates. Business and community leaders and parents also played a role in many cities. While they acted as individuals—motivated to be sure by personal values and with private interests in mind—what counted most was that their actions took place in the open, public arena in which the pros and cons were debated, reconsidered, and ultimately weighed. The formal processes and effective criteria for decision making in this public arena differ from those that we apply in private and on our own.

Choice as Pragmatic Adjustment: An Illustrative Case

The adoption and implementation of magnet schools in Montgomery County, Maryland, in several senses challenges the historical view preferred by those who portray market-based choice as resulting from the eruption of a long-frustrated popular movement. The story suggests that public leadership, rather than a victory of grass-roots sentiment over recalcitrant bureaucrats, played an integral role. The story reveals how choice-based schemes draw much of their support from individuals and groups motivated by values quite distinct from those emphasized by economic theory. Indeed, rather than representing the application of any clearly defined set of values and principles, the Montgomery County case illustrates how the installation of a system of educational choice typically has depended on what Charles Lindblom colorfully labeled "the science of muddling through."[24]

The Montgomery County Public Schools (MCPS) are located in a large suburban district, with a predominantly white, well-educated population. Beginning in the 1960s, the county began to experience an influx of black and Latino families, many moving in from the District of Columbia, which borders Montgomery County on the south.[25] Montgomery County had voluntarily abolished its dual school system by 1958, and has never been faced with a court order to integrate its schools further.

The origin of the magnet idea in MCPS had nothing at all to do with economic theories about the advantages of markets over the governmental process. The initial impetus came from the superintendent of schools, who saw it as a tool through which the public sector could take affirmative action to preempt the pattern of white flight that occurred in some areas when schools made no constructive response to the onset of rapid demographic change. Homer O. Elseroad was committed to the idea that public schools should be an institution in which children of all races and backgrounds interacted on relatively equal terms; the threat, as he saw it, lay in market forces and individual choices that, unconstrained, would turn the initial inroads by upwardly mobile minorities into an escalating cycle of racial turnover, ending, eventually, in segregated neighborhoods and segregated schools. In the spring of 1972, he announced plans to convert Rosemary Hills, the elementary school undergoing the most rapid racial transition, into the county's first magnet school.

Support for the magnet proposal within the education community was not based solely on the principle of progressively managed racial change. The magnet idea appealed for quite independent reasons to a small group of teachers who had been meeting together to discuss their frustration with conventional teaching techniques and their common interest in experiment-

157

ing with more individualized modes of instruction, an alternative approach referred to at the time as "open" education. They wanted a chance to try out their ideas of open education, and Rosemary Hills could become their laboratory. The idea also appealed to key members of the school board, the administration, and the teachers' organization, who saw this as an opportunity to put into practice their own ideas about encouraging teacher-initiated innovations as a way to build professionalism and improve morale.

The district's initial proposal for a magnet at Rosemary Hills was defeated by community opposition, but the plan was reformulated and put into effect in a different school. Five years later the single magnet was expanded to include seven elementary schools; today there are nineteen magnet programs, including two at intermediate schools and one at the high school level. Both the initial resistance and the subsequent adoption and expansion are instructive.

Resistance to the magnet proposal did not come from the predominantly white neighborhood schools to which the minority students of Rosemary Hill would have been transferred. It came, instead, from the black and white parents of students at Rosemary Hills, who argued that the plan infringed on their right to maintain a community-oriented, multiracial school. In order to ensure that there was space to accommodate white children transferring in from outside the neighborhood, many of the children in the community would have to be barred from attending the school. Increasing choices for some families, in other words, inevitably impinged on the choices of others.

Faced with intense and multiracial opposition, school officials at the last moment agreed to relocate the program to North Chevy Chase Elementary, where a group of parents saw the planned open-education magnet as a quick fix to their dissatisfaction with their principal and teaching staff. In accommodating their original proposal to fit this new location, officials pared down their aspirations for racial integration and for expanded parental choice. Parents at North Chevy Chase insisted that the school retain its character as a neighborhood school, even after the individualized-education program was put in place. No families would be unwillingly reassigned; transfers from outside the neighborhood would be accepted only if space was available. Unlike Rosemary Hills, North Chevy Chase was predominantly white, and the magnet itself would do nothing to change that. There were twenty-two black children in the school the year prior to the initiation of the program and twenty-two black children when the program began.

In a similar fashion, the eventual expansion of the magnet effort represented a pragmatic accommodation of competing interests and values worked out through negotiation, compromise, and incremental adjustment rather than through the imposition of a comprehensive, theory-based model for educational reform. The proportion of minorities in the school system continued to grow; at the same time, the total number of school children dipped, creating pressure on officials to close some schools. Closing schools is almost always a controversial process, but it was made even more volatile by the context of racial change. Boundaries would have to be redrawn, the racial balance of remaining schools necessarily would change, and some children who previously walked to neighborhood schools would now be forced to ride a bus.

From the first, some members of the school board saw alternative programs and parental choice as ways to reduce resistance to school closures. Neighborhoods facing the loss of a school might be appeased by the opportunity to have special magnet programs established nearby. The promise of greater parental choice might ease the concerns of parents whose neighborhood schools would have influxes of minorities as a result of boundary changes. After a tumultuous process, a cluster of seven magnet elementary schools was designed for an area in the southern section of the county that had high proportions of minority residents.

Neither the original magnet proposal for Rosemary Hills, nor the subsequent expansion of the program in the context of school closings, was based on a clear blueprint for magnet development or a careful consideration of system goals. In neither case was the introduction of market forces a major consideration. The Rosemary Hills proposal was launched from the top down, the superintendent and a few top officials rapidly framing a professional response to demographic changes they feared would be destabilizing. The expansion to a cluster of magnets, in contrast, evolved in a context of negotiation and compromise. Officials primarily were concerned about closing schools while minimizing conflict and racial imbalance; residents, for their part, hoped to preempt more rigid approaches and to obtain a commitment from the school system for additional resources and innovative educational approaches. Both groups were willing to tolerate ambiguity about long-term objectives rather than risk the consequences if no agreement could be reached.

Activist Government

Such a trial-and-error, muddling-through approach—in which actors with multiple and sometimes conflicting goals came temporarily to be joined in a loose and expedient coalition—has characterized the evolution of choice-based initiatives in a number of jurisdictions. Leila Sussmann, for example, relates the story of one suburban middle-class district's attempt to innovate educationally. As in Montgomery County, the desire of teachers to experiment with open education was critical at the start. When some parents complained about their children being subjected to this nontraditional style of teaching, the principal agreed to allow them to opt out of open classrooms and to choose a more traditional setting for their children. Choice, in this case, was an ad hoc policy intended to ease parental distress, not at all an end in itself.[26] In Richmond, Virginia, in the late 1960s, adoption of a magnet plan was part of an effort by conservatives to minimize the scope of integration without attracting judicial attention.[27] In Berkeley, California, the combination of a local cash crisis and the availability of federal funds to support experimental schools led to one of the nation's first efforts at using choice to attain integration, but given the configuration of local interests, by the mid-1970s, "experimentation and not integration became the goal of the policy."[28]

In some cases, state and local government adopted a reactive stance; the catalyst for action was external pressure (usually from the courts), and the operant objective was to do just enough to reduce the pressure for additional change. In other cases, such as Montgomery County, state or local officials were more active. External pressure was still an important background factor in these jurisdictions, but rather than serving as the sole driving force it provided an opportunity for local actors to articulate and mobilize support for positive visions of educational change. Needless to say, there was no guarantee that a local consensus would coalesce around a particular vision. But in some jurisdictions, public officials or other political activists were able to capitalize on the opportunity to build enough of a coalition to bring about and sustain change. Whether reactive or activist, in all cases the process of experimentation has been public and political—mediated through collective institutions and made to work through the application of authoritative government action.

It is significant that the most highly celebrated examples of school-choice initiatives are associated with states or localities with traditions of strong, affirmative, and innovative public-sector action. Massachusetts, which prodded and supported the Cambridge experiment (at one point providing about nine hundred thousand dollars per year),[29] and which continues to be in the forefront of efforts to implement "controlled" public-school choice,[30] was the national leader in developing the common, public-school model earlier in this century. But it also has a tradition of being a leader in the application of public resources to social needs. Among the fifty states, it ranked second on the index of state policy innovation compiled by Jack Walker,[31] third on that compiled by Virginia Gray,[32] fifth in welfare expenditure as a percentage of general expenditure,[33] and fifth in spending on public elementary and secondary education.[34] The same can be said of Minnesota and Wisconsin, long noted for their "moralistic" political cultures and traditions of Progressive politics.[35] Minnesota and Wisconsin ranked twelfth and tenth, respectively, on the Walker index, nineteenth and fifth on the Gray index, third and first on an index of the adequacy of AFDC grants,[36] and third and first among the twelve midwestern states in public-school expenditures.[37]

Measuring policy innovation and government commitment to social welfare is more complicated at the local level, but there probably is no jurisdiction more closely identified with public spending and the expansion of public responsibility than New York City, where the East Harlem experiment with choice has taken root.[38] New York's high expenditures reflect more than its large size; they also reflect that the city provides its citizens a broad range of services in the areas of health, welfare, housing, and higher education that other cities simply do not offer.[39] Montclair's governmental apparatus does not compare, of course. Yet, among New Jersey's thirty-eight municipalities with populations of twenty-five thousand or more, this small township ranks fifth in city employees per resident.[40]

Rather than representing a break with this these traditions, moreover, the choice initiatives in places like Cambridge, Montclair, East Harlem, Minnesota, and Milwaukee appear to build directly on the institutional practices, popular expectations, and political coalitions that gradually evolved through this history of progressive government action. In Cambridge and Montclair, controlled-choice plans rose from the ashes of failed efforts to integrate with more modest, more voluntary efforts; the shared learning process experienced by public officials and citizens broadened the base of political support beyond that which would have existed otherwise.

In East Harlem, the roots of choice lay not in market theory, but in the efforts by a handful of school officials and local citizens to make government work better. The first alternative schools in District No. 4 date back to 1974, and were oriented toward meeting the special needs of problem students. The current arrangement, one participant notes, "developed organically"; it gradually built community support, after initiation by a dedicated and activist staff.[41] The East Harlem experiment represented the kind of renegade, activist, antiestablishment effort that conservatives identify with the worst excesses of New York City's liberal political culture. It was only years later, around the mid-1980s, that this radical experiment in teacher-initiated reform became identified as a prototype for market-based choice schemes.

Minnesota's 1985 leadership in school-choice legislation can also be traced to both strong leadership in the public sector and a political constituency that developed gradually. In accounting for the 1985 legislation, Mazzoni emphasizes the authoritative action by Governor Perpich: "Public-school choice became the focal issue because the governor wanted it that way, not because external pressures had inexorably pushed the reform to the top of the legislative agenda."[42] But the existence of a cadre of parents in the Twin Cities area who had positive experiences with alternative education undoubtedly made for a more receptive climate as well. In the early 1970s, when federal officials had such a hard time finding sites in which to assess voucher plans, Minneapolis and St. Paul were two of a small number of cities that were experimenting with school choice on their own initiative. As in Montgomery County and East Harlem, the intellectual and cultural roots of that experimentation had more to do with 1960s philosophies of alternative education than with market theories about the benefits of choice.[43] Indeed, Minneapolis gave all parents in one section of the district the choice among three types of schools offering three different educational styles after explicitly rejecting a more market-oriented voucher experiment in 1970.[44]

Similarly, the 1990 Milwaukee choice experiment built on an existing base. The Wisconsin state legislature undoubtedly found it easier to enact the Milwaukee choice program because it had used the basic approach—the redirecting of state aid—before. In April 1976, the state passed Chapter 220, which was intended to provide a financial incentive for intra- and interdistrict transfers that furthered racial integration. Suburban schools that accepted a black student transfer from Milwaukee would receive the usual per-pupil state allocation, and transportation costs would be covered by the state as well.[45] Although it was not perceived in those terms at the time, Chapter 220 provided the model for the mechanism that substitutes for a literal voucher in the Milwaukee choice plan.

ACCOUNTING FOR EDUCATIONAL SUCCESS

The same types of community support that relate to desegregation success also appear to be critical in determining whether magnets succeed in promoting educational effectiveness. The generally positive endorsement that emerged from Blank and his colleagues' review of magnets in twelve communities was tempered by the recognition that, in some of the districts, magnets were little more than symbolic efforts, lacking in substance and genuine innovation. "Magnet development," they concluded, "will not produce either instructional quality or racial/ethnic integration in some mechanical way."[46] What distinguishes the successful from the unsuccessful cases, again, is political leadership and community will. Failure to use magnets successfully to integrate results from indifference or deliberate policy, "sometimes because racial inequities are still cherished by white decision-makers and sometimes because competing ideals outweigh the goal of integration." Failure to use magnets to improve educational quality "were characterized by weak district leadership of the program, low policy commitment to magnet schools, and little planning and program development in the schools."[47] An important background factor was the development of a base of community support. "Magnets can succeed educationally in the absence of a deep policy consensus about their deliverability, but each departure from the consensus will jeopardize the magnet program's observable outcomes of quality, integration, or cost-effectiveness."[48]

Political will and government capacity are important because the framework to sustain choice requires the dedication of additional resources, the definition and enforcement of regulations and rules, the reallocation of opportunities, and ongoing monitoring and remediation through public intervention. Rather than being self-sustaining, functioning choice programs must be affirmatively protected from atrophy and cannibalism, to which they are quite vulnerable.

Fiscal Commitment

It is somewhat surprising how little systematic attention has been devoted to determining the fiscal implications of sustaining a choice-based approach. Market theory equates competition with efficiency, and for true believers that may suffice to sustain a faith that choice initiatives can pay for themselves. But the programs that advocates have adopted as models are far from cost-neutral.

Again, the information about magnet schools is most detailed, not least because court oversight often has mandated a careful accounting. Advisors to Kansas City school officials projected the need for about fifteen million dollars per year for 1989–90 and 1990–91 to fund adequately just the magnet component of that city's court-ordered integration plan. In addition to direct program costs, their estimate of what was needed included "a recruiter who will actively recruit principals nationally and within the District and Kansas City area"; at least one additional transportation officer and appropriate technical and staff support; an ombudsman "responsible for reviewing and resolving complaints, monitoring the implementation of procedures, rumor control, early warning of Central staff of emerging problems, and representing parent and student interests in policy formulation by the office"; grant and program-area specialists; directors for elementary schools, middle schools, and high school magnets; a "marketing program that is managed from each magnet site and is supported by the central public information department and private sector firms."[49] Blank and his colleagues found that magnet schools, in general, cost about 8 percent more to operate than nonmagnet schools, with high school magnets costing the most.[50] Transportation costs for magnet schools were substantially higher, averaging 27 percent more than for nonmagnet schools.

Few of the published reports about more recent choice initiatives have included careful assessments of costs, but it is clear that the costs can be substantial. Cambridge had considerable federal support during the start-up period of its choice program. During the mid-1980s the state provided nearly half a million dollars per year to support desegregation, the parent information office, and some of the staff and program expenses. In addition, the state reimbursed the city for 90 percent of the principal and interest incurred when the city substantially renovated some schools to equalize facilities.[51] East Harlem's District No. 4 at one time received more federal aid per student than anywhere else in nation. It also exceeded its budget by 3.5 percent annually for many years, while it was developing its special choice offerings.[52]

Some of the ironies in using existing choice plans to build a case for greater reliance on markets over government became apparent when Lauro Cavazos, then the secretary of education, visited East Harlem in the fall of 1989. The visit was part of the Bush administration's campaign to promote educational choice. But Cavazos was confronted by angry parents, who complained that federal government was threatening their program by rejecting their application for renewal of a $1.4 million grant.[53]

Regulating Choice

Advocates of market-based educational choice point to the experience with magnets and controlled-choice plans as evidence that individual choice will not lead to resegregation, as critics have charged. The lesson they draw is that family preferences and needs for different types of schools are distributed among the population in a pattern that is racially neutral. In its simplest version, this racial-neutrality thesis assumes that such preferences and needs are distributed more or less randomly, or according to idiosyncratic principles that elude generalization. Allowing school enrollment to be dictated by choice, rather than by the racially segregated pattern of where people live, thus will result in "natural" integration.

Government intervention, according to this perspective, has exacerbated racial segregation. By artificially elevating residential location into the position of being the primary determinant of school assignment, it has prevented families from sorting out into school communities based on common values. By imposing a bureaucratic sameness across the curriculums of the public schools, it has left the class and racial composition of the student body as the major factor that differentiates among schools in popular perception. And, through heavy-handed efforts to mandate equality within school districts, it has reinforced the tendency of many Americans to flee central cities and withdraw for protection behind the buffer of suburban jurisdictional boundaries. Critical to this formulation is a presumption that direct preferences regarding the racial composition of schools are of minor importance. Once schools offer educationally meaningful diversity, racial criteria will diminish in influence.

Yet the evidence existing so far can be read to support quite a different interpretation. Successful choice plans have required rules designed to ensure that individual options do not lead to racial resegregation—rules that mean that some children are denied the opportunity to transfer to schools they would prefer.[54]

An analysis of the 450 requests to transfer into Montgomery County's magnet schools in 1985, for example, found that white parents tended to request transfer into schools with fewer minority students.[55] Minority parents tended to request transfer into schools with fewer white students. Moreover, as table 7.1 indicates, the racial and ethnic composition of the student body was a better predictor of transfer requests than were other characteristics of the schools, including indicators of school resources, special programs offered, school performance on standardized tests, or the degree of satisfaction expressed by parents with children already at the school.

The school district's regulations regarding transfer requests to magnet schools called for approval unless they would result in a racial imbalance, overcrowding, or substantial underutilization in the sending or receiving school. It was the county's rules prohibiting transfers that hurt racial balance at either the sending or the receiving school, not freely exercised choices, that kept racial imbalance within acceptable bounds. Only by directly constraining the choice of some parents—by rejecting about 15 percent of requests for transfer on grounds that they will worsen racial unbalance, and by discouraging applications that would likely be disapproved—have Montgomery County officials been able to keep the magnet program from exacerbating segregation.

165

TABLE 7.1

Requests to Transfer into Montgomery County Magnet Schools,
by Race (Simple Correlations)

	White	Minority
Race and Class		
% minority in school	−.57	.26
% black in school	−.31	.22
% Hispanic in school	−.59	.13
% Asian in school	−.43	.17
% professional staff white	−.14	−.46
% minority in census tract	−.27	.35
% poor in tract	−.37	.29
Median income in tract	.05	−.53
Resources and Demands		
Total enrollment	.33	.14
Student turnover	−.11	−.13
Overcrowding	−.37	.11
Student/professional ratio	.34	.52
Student/teacher ratio	.02	.07
Teacher/aide ratio	.27	.60
% with 16+ years experience	−.65	−.58
Age of school structure	.08	.22
Program/Structure		
Grade level	−.12	−.37
Kindergarten present	.24	.57
All-day kindergarten	−.25	.08
Whole school magnet	−.42	−.14
Foreign language focus	.58	.64
Gifted and talented focus	−.05	−.45
Math/science/computer focus	−.22	−.06
Performance		
Mean CAT score[a]	−.27	−.45
Parent satisfaction[b]	−.19	.06
Parent satisfaction (white)	.15	.01
Parent satisfaction (minority)	−.42	.06

Source: Jeffrey R. Henig, "Choice in Public Schools: An Analysis of Transfer Requests among Magnet Schools," *Social Science Quarterly* 71, no. 1 (March 1990): 76.

[a] Schoolwide average on California Achievement Tests.

[b] Based on a survey conducted by the school system's Department of Educational Accountability in the spring of 1985. A total of 575 parents of children attending the fourteen magnet schools were asked to give their school a grade (A, B, C, D, or F) for several distinct areas of performance. The score presented here represents the "grade point average" (GPA) obtained in response to the summary question: "If you could give your school just one grade for everything, what grade would you give it?"

Reallocating Opportunities

In adopting the language of microeconomic theory, many advocates of choice also have adopted a naive vision of choice as benefiting all and harming none; this is the appeal of perfectly functioning markets—that they may harmonize competing individual interests through uncoordinated bargaining in a context of expanding productivity. But, in practice, expanding choice for some has meant restraining choice for others. Converting schools into magnets, for example, often has meant limiting access to children from the surrounding area into what otherwise would be their neighborhood schools. As we have seen, too, existing magnet and citywide choice plans have often worked hand in hand with mandatory public-sector actions. As Mary Metz found in the large midwestern city she labels "Heartland," choice-based policies can be given credit for accomplishments that they do not necessarily deserve: "Despite publicity to the contrary, Heartland did not desegregate a large city without mandatory reassignment by instituting magnet schools, but by closing and reducing enrollment in central city schools and busing black children to neighborhood white schools. . . . The magnet schools played a part in desegregating Heartland's system only by effecting a small amount of reciprocal movement of whites and by distracting the city from the fact that desegregation was occurring."[56]

Often making choice work has meant crimping the perceived freedom of more politically powerful and mobilized groups in order to extend options to those traditionally lacking in political clout. And, when that is the case, even the most progressive public officials may fail to follow through on steps that would be needed to make "free" choice a reality. State officials in Minnesota, for example, have been very wary about requiring suburban school districts to accept inner-city students. This is one reason why the actual exercise of the transfer option has lagged behind the expectations that the legislation raised. That the officials have been able and willing to move at all to challenge the normally sacrosanct local prerogatives is probably due to an unusual tradition of regional cooperation as well as to unusually daring political leadership.[57]

Monitoring and Response

Where choice initiatives have worked well, besides making an initial financial investment, government has had the capacity to monitor performance and the political will to take remedial steps when performance lagged. *Not one* of the existing school-choice schemes invites public officials to allow

167

schools that do not attract students simply to close their doors.[58] When a school fails to attract students, it has been up to the public authorities to shift programs, alter grade structures, change principals, provide special resources, or undertake other aggressive actions to turn that school around.

In distinguishing successful magnets from those that have been less successful, Blank and his colleagues note the need for "maintaining the special rules, procedures and support that make magnet schools unique."[59] The superintendent of the Montclair public schools observes that the district has had to "do a lot of incremental adding to the magnets" in order to make sure that they not draw disproportionately from one part of the city. "These things take a lot of constant attention," she suggests.[60] Putting a magnet in place did not suffice to attract white students to New Hampshire Estates Elementary School in Montgomery County. By 1986 there were only 14 white students in the school, out of a total enrollment of 232. That year, fewer than 10 students from outside its normal attendance area asked to transfer to the school, and all but 2 of the 10 were minorities. Among other steps taken by the school board to improve the situation were moving the school into a brand-new facility, pairing it with another elementary school that had a larger white population, and approving a special "enhancement project" including additional funds for instruction training and the media collection.[61]

Besides ensuring that lagging schools are able to attract and hold students, officials overseeing choice programs have had to act aggressively to disseminate information and to overcome the patterns uncovered in the Alum Rock experiment for wealthier, better-educated, and majority-group families to gain an information advantage. Even in a relatively small district like Cambridge, with a generally well-educated population, ensuring that parents have the information necessary to make good decisions required "a lot of hoopla."[62] For example, Cambridge works with the local public-access cable television station to present daily messages and run videos highlighting activities and events at individual schools; videos showing some schools in action also are available at parent information centers.[63]

Laura Salganik and Rebecca Carver have been undertaking an analysis of the content, format, and distribution of information made available to parents in states and districts offering major choice plans.[64] Their preliminary findings emphasize that the flow of good information requires attention and commitment. While they "found a great deal of creativity and commitment of both energy and resources being invested in providing information to families,"[65] such attention was not universal, and some of the most valuable kinds of information are not generally available. In Minneapolis, the school system produced *A Guide to High School Programs* and individual brochures for each school. But in several other districts, the predominant form of information is flyers and brochures produced by the individual schools, many of which are vague and self-promotional. Some use terms that many parents are unfamiliar with, and many provide a narrow range of information, often targeting a single aspect of the program they offer. Some districts work hard to make materials available in languages other than English. Cambridge provides interpreters at information meetings to translate into Portuguese, Spanish, Haitian, and Chinese. Boston offers an information booklet in Cambodian, Chinese, French, Greek, Italian, Laotian, Portuguese, Spanish, and Vietnamese.[66] But not all districts are so aggressive. And almost none offer the kind of quantitative assessments of student performance that an informed consumer might seek. "Average test scores, grade retention rates, graduation rates, and college attendance rates—these are all missing from the information we collected from schools of choice around the country."[67]

Sustaining Successful Initiatives for Choice

Finally, there is the difficult problem of protecting the conditions that make choice work from erosion due to fiscal and political pressures. As already noted, external sources of funding have been an important precondition for the launching of many choice initiatives, and strong political leadership has been important in building the coalitions to get educational choice into place. But the need for money and leadership does not end once a program is put on the books. Moreover, the threats to choice initiatives may emerge from their success.

Once enacted, policies must be implemented and sustained, and there is ample verification within the field of political science of the many obstacles to implementation that generally exist. In the specific case of school-choice initiatives, maintaining the viability and effectiveness of choice has meant denying some schools special programs, facilities, or techniques because their spread would undermine the distinctiveness on which other schools rely in order to attract a racially and economically diverse student body.[68] And it has meant withstanding pressures from taxpayers to trim budgets supporting choice programs, especially as state and local governments have come under increasing fiscal pressures in recent years.

PART FOUR

CHOOSING OUR FUTURE

☆

A REVIEW of the evidence has suggested that educational-choice schemes, where they have worked relatively well, have depended on public officials deliberately building supportive coalitions and on government institutions acting with authority. Unmoderated either by government or communal values, individual choice is often a destabilizing force. Yet public debate has been preoccupied with vague symbols and exciting anecdotes; it has not taken seriously the question of what is needed in order to nurture and sustain a political and institutional milieu within which individual choices will bring about the imagined social gains.

The market metaphor has played a role in confusing the terms of debate through its evocation of the invisible hand. A market-based system of school choice would be like a child's brand-new set of electric trains. Once the track is laid and the cars are linked up, all that is left is to throw the switch, sit back, and enjoy. But making public policies work the way we want them to requires more than putting a well-designed machine into action. It is an ongoing process, requiring translation of abstract goals into working procedures, adaptation to changing circumstances, compromise among competing values, monitoring of results, and pragmatic adjustment. The two chapters that constitute this final section draw out the implications of this fact. Because meeting social goals requires continual reconsideration and exertion, we must take special care that our short-term initiatives do not undermine the institutions in which public values are most effectively articulated, negotiated, and made concrete.

Chapter 8 begins by acknowledging that educational-choice initiatives can send us down several possible paths—some potentially favorable, others potentially quite destructive. Focusing on the *implementation* of initiatives for choice, it argues that linking choice to market rationales makes the unattractive scenarios more likely. Chapter 9 takes on the task of translating the themes of this book into a positive agenda for educational reform. Choice plays a role in this agenda, but as a circumscribed tool, not a driving rationale. The agenda I offer differs from the conventional by eschewing the promotion of any specific institutional or pedagogical notion as the key to improving our nation's schools. It focuses instead on the less glamorous— but ultimately more important—questions of building government capacity and authority and, just as important, nurturing the constituency to sustain them over the long haul.

173

How Market-Based Plans Will Fail

W ORDS ARE SLIPPERY and thought is viscous," Henry Brooks Adams observed in *The Education of Henry Adams*. This is especially true of words like choice, which come fully freighted with potent connotations relating to freedom, abundance, assertion, and individuality. When an idea like school choice first slips into the realm of public discourse, those who mouth the words may be a little like strangers who speak a common language laced with differing dialects and idioms. Rapid nods of agreement may dissolve into puzzled expressions, angry confrontations may be launched over a misread nuance.

Sheltering under the broad umbrella of the word *choice* are a number of policy options that could take quite distinct concrete forms. "The variety of plans for organizing schools that can be subsumed under the title of choice is so large and so diverse in its educational, social, and political consequences," Mary Metz notes, "that to speak of them all together under the single category of schooling based on choice is to confuse far more than to communicate."[1]

While nominally recognized, these differences often are given short shrift in the contemporary debate over education policy. These are matters of detail that, it naturally is assumed, can safely be put off until later. Once we decide whether to move in the direction of choice, specifying its precise form is a simple matter. This has worked to the advantage of those who favor privatization and market-based reforms in at least two ways. It has helped inflate the movement for choice by allowing groups with different basic interests and visions temporarily to coalesce. And it has made it easier for proponents of market-based proposals to sidestep serious questions about whether the institutional and social frameworks that their models presume can be developed and sustained.

But the devil, they say, is in the details. The surface meaning of this old saying is familiar. Decisions about details matter. While some differences among school-choice plans may indeed be technical matters that could be worked out later, others have consequences potentially so great that they represent variations of the same policy in name only.

But there is devilry, too, in the way that premature attention to details can obscure important issues. Policy as implemented often differs dramatically from policy as envisioned by its sponsors and as passed by legislators; this is one of the clearest and most consistent findings in the literature on public policy. An ardent focus on the details of proposed school-choice plans is misplaced, therefore, if it distracts us from considering how such plans are likely to be reshaped and redefined in the implementation process. The real danger of the market metaphor is that it can erode the very conditions of governance and public support on which successful school reform ultimately will depend.

THE DEVIL IN THE DETAILS:
CHOOSING AMONG VARIETIES OF SCHOOL CHOICE

Contemporary debate about educational reform is muddied and misdirected because of basic confusion about what school choice would entail in specific terms. "The meaning of choice proposals," as Richard Elmore notes, "can only be understood in the context of specific alterations of institutional structures within specific constraints on organization, money, and information."[2] Given a broad commitment to the abstract notion of educational choice, it remains to be determined what decisions the nation is likely to make in order to translate that commitment into specific program alternatives. Choice programs may vary in several key ways, among them regulation, redistribution, level of support, and scope.

The Extent of Regulation

Among the specific questions about regulation that must be answered in fashioning a workable program of school choice are these:

- *Curriculum requirements*: Will participating schools be required to provide at least some base level of instruction in key subjects such as math and science? What about geography and government? How demanding and detailed will such standards be? Will any subjects or ideas be proscribed? For example, should schools be free to teach creationism as fact, to advocate racial separatism, to assign sexually suggestive literature, to include abortion counseling in health classes?
- *Teacher qualifications*: Should teachers in participating schools be required to have graduate degrees in education? take graduate-level coursework in education or the area of their teaching expertise? have

college degrees? Should they be required to pass competency tests? What about background checks for criminal records? Should any regulations regarding teacher qualification be illegal for participating schools? For example, should schools be free to require teachers to belong to a particular religion, sign a national loyalty oath, submit to mandatory drug testing, join (or not join) a union?

· *Admissions and discipline*: Should participating schools be free to accept or reject applicants according to whatever criteria they deem relevant? Should they be required to hold a certain proportion of spaces for low-income students? minorities? children from the surrounding neighborhood? Should they be prohibited from rejecting applicants based on certain criteria? For example, should they be permitted to refuse admission to students based on racial or ethnic compatibility? prior disciplinary record? prior academic record? parents' religion? parents' criminal record? parents' educational attainment or profession? older siblings' academic and disciplinary record? parents' willingness to provide a donation to the school? What about regulations regarding discipline and expulsion? Should participating schools be allowed to suspend or expel students based on their failure to "fit in," or should more precise grounds for acceptable action be legislatively specified? Should procedures for due process be defined and enforced? Should any forms of discipline be prohibited? For example, should participating schools be allowed to inflict corporal punishment? impose long-term isolation? encourage systematic hazing?

· *Health and safety*: Will participating schools be required to provide a minimal ratio of restrooms per person? Must facilities be gender-specific, with the proper ratios figured separately? What about access for the disabled? Should participating schools be required to provide lunch?[3] If so, what, if any, nutritional standards will be required? How about regulations regarding refrigeration and food handling intended to reduce the risk of disease? Will there be building-code requirements relating to fire safety, lead paint, asbestos, ventilation, and sunlight? Will access to medical services be required, and, if so, how strict will the requirements be? Should participating schools be required to acquire insurance to cover liabilities incurred due to injuries to students or staff?

· *Tuition and fees*: Should participating schools be allowed to charge as much in tuition and fees as the market will bear? Should they be required to limit tuition to the face value of publicly funded vouchers? Should they be allowed to charge different tuitions to different types of students? For example, should they be allowed to offer reduced tuition to students from low-income families? to academically talented students? to athletes? Should they be required to provide scholarships for low-income students? Should they be required to charge lower fees to neighborhood applicants? to those living within the district or state?

· *Order and stability*: Markets are dynamic. They can also be disruptive. Historically, one of the frequent catalysts for government regulation is pressure from citizens, workers, and employers to moderate harsh cycles and maintain services when market forces withdraw. Should participating schools be completely free to retract previously advertised programs, replace teachers in midyear with substitutes willing to work at lower pay, or relocate or close without considering the impact on the surrounding neighborhood? Should the state or district guarantee that no area will be left without a school within a specified distance? What about participating schools whose labor practices result in frequent or lengthy strikes? Should they be forced to refund a portion of the tuition to parents? Should they refund the value of the vouchers to the government? Should they be barred from the choice program?

· *Intrafamily disputes*: Should the right of choice be invested in the parent, or should the child at some age gain a formal role? How will disagreements be mediated? Should there be conditions under which school officials can challenge a parent's decision if they believe that it is injurious to the child's well-being?

· *Data collection and reporting*: What, if any, information will participating schools be required to collect regarding the characteristics and performance of their students? What information must they provide about their internal decisions and practices? Will they be required to collect data on race? on religion? on place of residence? Will they be required to administer standardized tests? to record graduation rates? to keep track of dropouts and transfers? to monitor the racial characteristics of disciplinary cases? What, if any, rules will govern disclosure of such information? Will it be published and disseminated through specified outlets? Will schools be required to make such data available, upon student request, to other schools or employers? What information about their revenues and expenditures will schools be required to keep and make available? What information about their teachers and administrators will they be required to keep and make available?

· *Truth in advertising*: Will advertisement practices or outlets be regulated? Will participating schools be permitted to air appeals on television or radio shows watched primarily by young children? Will they be restricted at all in the types of appeals and claims they can make? For example, will they be permitted to claim that their students are less likely to use illegal drugs, or more likely to obey their parents? that their graduates will make more money, or be happier, or live longer? What, if any, substantiation will they be required to offer?

The boundaries of regulation are set informally as well as formally. Elaborate regulations will mean little if they are disregarded and cannot be enforced. Linked to the question of the extent and specificity of regulation, then, are additional questions regarding the capacity of the public sector to monitor behavior, its political will and financial capacity to pursue enforcement, and the readiness of the judicial sector to view such regulations as acceptable exercises of the public authority.

The Commitment to Redistribution

Consider the difference between two voucher programs. One offers modest vouchers worth about fifteen hundred dollars to every child in the state. The other sets the amount of the voucher in inverse proportion to the child's educational disadvantages; low-income, homeless, or physically or emotionally disturbed children may qualify for vouchers of as much as sixty-five hundred dollars, while the majority of healthy, middle- and upper-class children receive a base level voucher worth five hundred dollars. If poorer districts cannot afford to finance these vouchers, the state supplements their revenues with taxes raised in other communities.

These two programs would be strikingly different in educational and political impact. Providing a fixed but modest universal grant to all students might be akin to offering ten free driving lessons to any teenagers purchasing a new car; those who are already advantaged are in a much better position to take full advantage of the offer. A grant of sixty-five hundred dollars might truly be sufficient to entice schools actively to pursue students who are difficult to educate, and to entice suburban districts to accept transfers from inner-city schools; a voucher of five hundred dollars most likely would not.[4]

As with regulation, the full distributory effects of choice proposals would depend on more than formal and open decisions about the size and progressivity of vouchers or "scholarships." Other key factors include whether parents are permitted to supplement vouchers with their own money,[5] whether family costs are given special tax status and whether they are treated as credits (progressive) or deductions (regressive), and whether or not free transportation is provided to children who opt for schools outside their normal attendance zone.

Footing the Bill

Proposals for school-choice can differ dramatically depending on whether they are accompanied by increased, stable, or decreased public financial support. Experience has shown that making educational choice work can be an expensive proposition. As discussed in earlier chapters, magnet schools and other initiatives for choice often have depended on substantial subsidies from external sources. In spite of hopes that such expenses could be limited to an initial start-up phase, it so far appears to be the case that continued investment usually is necessary in order to maintain meaningful distinctions among schools, to ensure a continuing flow of information to succeeding generations of families, and to counteract resegregation tendencies rooted partly in residential patterns.

The Scope of Choice

School-choice systems can differ according to the types of schools they include, the jurisdictions they include, and the students they include. One question relating to the types of schools to be included concerns grade level; should choice be offered at all grade levels, or restricted to secondary schools where students are more mature and where curricular specialization may be more appropriate? Another question concerns whether to include private schools and, if so, which ones? Should only nonprofit, secular private schools be included, or should for-profit entrepreneurial schools and parochial schools be included as well?

The most pressing question about jurisdiction is whether school-choice programs will be restricted to schools within district borders or will allow cross-district transfers. If cross-district transfers are involved, decisions must be made about whether a district's participation in the program is to be mandatory or voluntary.

School-choice programs also can differ in the breadth of the eligibility criteria applied to students. In one scenario, assignment of a student to a "home" school could be the default for those who fail to exercise their option to change. In another, designations of home schools could be eliminated, and all students required to make an affirmative choice, as is nominally the case in Cambridge. Should choice be universal, or restricted to certain categories of students—perhaps those defined by race, income, academic interest, academic ability, or the availability of adequate programs at the home school?

The scope of choice, as implemented, may be affected by informal as well as formal provisions. For example, if free transportation is not provided, the formal extension of choice across district boundaries will be relatively meaningless for many students, who will be able to afford neither the time nor the expense that would be involved in taking advantage of the theoretical possibility of transferring. The same is true if parents are not provided with adequate and understandable information about the available options and the procedures for pursuing them.

What We Want versus What We Get: The Implementation Dilemma

As this discussion makes apparent, a jurisdiction does not face a simple yes-or-no decision about whether to move in the direction of expanding educational choice. It faces, rather, a series of ongoing decisions. Being clear about the distinctions among school-choice plans can help citizens and policymakers shape a plan that meets their needs and aspirations. But getting the policies that we want is not just a question of thinking clearly. Well-intentioned and seemingly well-designed plans often go wrong. A rich and detailed literature has developed in the social sciences that centers on the tendency of social policies to founder in the implementation stage.[6] Three relevant lessons from that literature concern the limits of good intentions, the continuation of political battles past the stage at which a policy is formally agreed on, and the false hope of bypassing bureaucratic channels.

The Limits of Good Intentions

Evidence about the limits of good intentions is nearly overwhelming. This is the case even when such good intentions are held by powerful actors well situated to bring the forces of government to bear. Martha Derthick, for example, has chronicled the disappointing history of the federal "new towns in-town" program launched in the summer of 1967. The program was intended to use federally owned land in inner cities as the sites for large planned communities that would attract residents of different incomes and combine housing, social services, and amenities. Conceived by President Lyndon Johnson, the program had a lot going for it. Johnson, after all, was a strong and aggressive president, a master doer. Because the program would take advantage of land already in government hands, political and administrative hurdles would be minimized. Existing laws for disposing of surplus federal lands appeared to give the president the tools he needed to move immediately, without requiring Congress to pass new legislation. In spite of this, Derthick concluded, "the program was unequivocally a failure. Not only did it fall short of its goals; it produced few visible results of any kind."[7]

Jeffrey Pressman and Aaron Wildavsky tell a similar story about the implementation of federal Economic Development Administration (EDA) projects in Oakland at just about the same time. The projects, launched when concerns about potential riots were high, were intended to provide permanent new jobs for minorities. The federal new towns in-town project eventually foundered because of resistance at the local level, but the EDA proposal seemed to face no opposition: "all of the major participants throughout the program's history insisted that they believed in the program and that there were no fundamental disagreements among them."[8] Yet here, too, the results were crushingly disappointing. After long delays, few jobs were created, at great expense. "The hopeful 'experimental program' of 1966 had become a painful example of the problems of implementation."[9] The large number of actors whose cooperation, and even enthusiasm, is required to bring a policy to fruition means that the "cards in this world are stacked against things happening," Pressman and Wildavsky concluded. "The remarkable thing is that new programs work at all."[10]

By highlighting the tendency for national policy initiatives to be delayed, redirected, and distorted—by bureaucrats, by elected representatives at other levels of government, and by private actors whose cooperation was presumed—such studies of implementation have provided an important corrective to the traditional tendency to look at the passage (or blockage) of legislation as the final step in the political process. Such general tendencies, moreover, are likely to be especially pronounced in the area of education policy, where implementation depends on the coordination of officials at all levels of government, as well as through a loose chain of authority within the schools themselves,[11] and where "a widespread lack of confidence in the underlying cognitive theories" makes implementation of innovative policies more difficult.[12]

In this light, it is ironic that so many conservative market advocates feel secure in the premise that we can make school-choice work if we really set our minds to it. Conservative critics of the nation's various social-welfare programs have been especially vocal in drawing attention to the vagaries of policy implementation. They characterize the period of government activism spanning the 1960s and early 1970s as a typical example of the inevitable tendency of government's good intentions to go awry. If coherent and ambitious government plans are destined to fall short of our expectations, it was reasoned, perhaps we should scale down our expectations to more modest levels.

For some, the critical distinction is between government policy that requires public-sector action and responsibility (destined to fail) and government policy that substantially reduces the role and responsibility of government (likely to succeed). But this distinction resolves the apparent contradiction only for those who hold a purely laissez-faire position. As we have seen, even those who offer very strong promarket appeals for educational choice tend to reserve an important role for government in establishing and maintaining the conditions under which the program would operate.[13] For those who acknowledge that a successful school-choice plan will require wise, authoritative, and effective public action, resolving the tension between optimism about school choice and skepticism about policy implementation depends either on the belief that *this* policy action can somehow be inoculated against the diseases that normally infect the political system, or a belief that current conditions are so bad that taking a risk is justified.

The Open-ended Battle and Shifting Venues

It would not be highly significant that policy continues to be reshaped well after formal legislation is enacted if the balance of influence among competing interests were relatively stable. Recalcitrant bureaucrats and reluctant officials might dawdle and redirect, but once alerted, the coalitions that prevailed at the policy-formulation stage presumably would reassert their will. But the complications introduced at the implementation stage entail something more than a simple lag in enforcement.

The need to continue the battle over policy through the implementation stage most directly alters the balance among competing interests through the differential effects of time. Mobilizing supporters and building coalitions requires the investment of energy and other resources. Majorities that coalesce in the highly public period of legislative debate may win the sprint, but fall back, expended, in its aftermath. This gives a structural advantage at the implementation stage to interests with more permanent organizational infrastructures. Public bureaucracies have such an advantage. So do corporations, trade unions, political-action committees, and other long-lasting interest groups.[14]

But the differential effects of time on competing interests are not the only twist introduced by the implementation dilemma. Decisions made during implementation are made in different venues than those in which policy is formally declared. These venues represent distinct and semiautonomous political arenas, in which different groups may have different advantages. Implementation venues tend to be more bureaucratized, more localized, and less subject to public scrutiny. This can confer structural advantages at the implementation stage to interests with superior access to bureaucratic channels rather than legislative ones, interests that are locally powerful even if marginal on the state and national scene, and interests with a greater capacity to collect and analyze information independently.

Not all proponents of market-based school-choice schemes have overlooked the potential significance of the implementation hurdle. Chubb and Moe, for example, are greatly concerned about the potential for educational professionals and other well-organized interests gradually to erode the school-choice framework they favor after it initially is put in place. The very state legislators and executives who might have instituted their "scholarship" proposal, they warn us, "will come under pressure in the future to use their authority to control schools from above—and thus to destroy what they are trying to create."[15] Their consideration of the vagaries of implementation is selective, however. They do not consider, for example, whether well-organized suburban constituencies or coalitions of private schools would force the gradual abandonment of the equalizing elements of their framework, such as redistributive vouchers and prohibitions of parental tuition add-ons. Moreover, the solution that they offer—to buffer the initial legislative model from subsequent modification in response to political pressures—runs counter to the third lesson of implementation studies: the false hope of working outside the system.

The False Hope of Working Outside the System

The tension between optimism about school choice and skepticism about policy implementation is resolved for Chubb and Moe by imagining that school-choice policies can somehow be buffered from the forces that normally derail implementation. They propose that public authority over the schools be vested solely in state legislators and governors. Then, to reduce further the likelihood that publicly elected officials might later alter the parameters of the plan, they propose enshrining key elements with constitutional status. "The legal foundations of the new system would then be very difficult to change or violate once put into effect. And, because state constitutions are the ultimate authorities in state government, they have the power to constrain what future legislators and governors (and the political groups that pressure them) can do in controlling the schools."[16]

Chubb and Moe's identification of majoritarianism as the source of the problem is somewhat unusual. More common is the view that majorities are the source of legitimacy in democratic policies, and that the implementation process unfortunately empowers well-placed minorities to frustrate the public will. From this perspective, working outside the system means circumventing the self-protective bureaucracy and multiple layers of government that reject the original policy goals and insert their own values and interests wherever possible.

In their classic study of the failed implementation of EDA programs in Oakland, however, Pressman and Wildavsky found that efforts to bypass the existing bureaucratic channels had precisely the opposite of the intended effect. For all its flaws, they argued, bureaucracy establishes patterns of interaction and reciprocal dependence that moderate the centrifugal forces of self-serving behavior. "Many of its most criticized features, such as the requirement for multiple and advance clearances and standard operating procedures, serve to increase the ability of each participant to predict what the others will do and to smooth over differences. The costs of bureaucracy—a preference for procedure over purpose or seeking the lowest common denominator—may emerge in a different light when they are viewed as part of the price paid for predictability of agreement over time among diverse participants."[17]

An illustration may make clearer the implications in the education-reform arena. While some school principals could get away with ignoring or otherwise undermining a school-board policy on teacher discipline, for example, they often elect not to do so because they realize that they will need reciprocal support from the board on other matters at other times. That the principal intends to make a career in the system is integral to his or her calculation; in other words, the bureaucratic framework moderates the impulse to pursue short-term interests that are at variance with policy goals. Notwithstanding market theories about the constraining aspects of supply and demand, entrepreneurial educators offering a hot new curriculum taught by freelance teachers may actually be quicker than career bureaucrats to substitute their own priorities for those of their "customers."

DEALING WITH THE IMPLEMENTATION DILEMMA

Political scientists' consideration of policy implementation has come in two waves. The first wave emphasized the obstacles to successful implementation. Besides alerting us to the danger of naively equating policy-as-announced with policy-as-carried-out, this insight delivered a message that fit the ideological temper of the time. But the first wave of studies painted with too broad a brush. While policy implementation may always be problematic, it is not a black hole into which all light is equally and totally absorbed.

Some policies negotiate the obstacles of implementation more successfully than others. The second wave of implementation studies takes this variation as its starting point. Rather than assessing the naïveté of our societal ambitions, its central research questions are designed to help us improve policy. It asks: What distinguishes reforms that are successfully enacted from those that are not? Some of these second-generation studies have emphasized the role of strong, authoritative—even coercive—government action in ensuring that policies are implemented as envisioned. Some have pointed to ways that government may encourage cooperation without coercion.

Coercion and Authoritative Action

In *The Implementation of Civil Rights Policy*, Charles Bullock and Charles Lamb reviewed a range of domestic-policy initiatives. The programs could roughly be categorized into three groups, ordinally ranked. The Voting Rights Act of 1965 and the desegregation of southern schools, while not successful in all regards, were the most fully implemented. Between 1964 and 1972, the percentage of eligible blacks registered to vote in the states targeted by the voting rights legislation increased from about 29 percent to almost 57 percent.[18] Only about one out of ten southern black students attended schools with white children in 1963; ten years later the comparable figure was more than eight out of ten.[19] Equal-employment and bilingual-education policies were somewhat less fully implemented. Integration of colleges and universities, fair housing, and second-generation discrimination in the schools were the least successfully implemented of the programs Bullock and Lamb reviewed.[20]

The reforms that were most successfully implemented, Bullock and Lamb concluded, were characterized by more active involvement by federal officials; specific and preferably quantitative standards for compliance; strong commitment by the public agency assigned responsibility for enforcement; strong support from the top levels of the three branches of government; and the willingness of public officials to carry out meaningful sanctions against those who resisted.[21] Successfully putting a program into effect—at least one whose intended beneficiaries include groups, such as minorities and the poor, lacking strong political clout of their own—has tended to require strong action by central authorities, the articulation of precise standards of intended outcomes, and the willingness of government to step in when outcomes are not achieved.

Encouraging Cooperation

Robert P. Stoker emphasizes that government also has some less-coercive ways to encourage the successful implementation of its policies.[22] Forceful and authoritative actions can be costly, and difficult to sustain, leave too many loopholes, and create alienation and public backlash.[23] He argues that government can nurture implementation regimes that encourage cooperation from the public and private actors who have the potential to scuttle public policies.

An implementation regime is both a political accommodation negotiated among disparate groups and a set of rules, norms, and expectations that "identifies the values to be served during the implementation process and provides an organizational framework to promote those values."[24] Implementation regimes can counteract some of the obstacles to policy implementation by increasing the rewards for cooperation, manipulating the levels and distribution of information, and increasing the regularity and predictability of interaction among key actors.

One example that Stoker analyzes in depth is the National School Lunch Program (NSLP). Congress enacted the NSLP nearly five decades ago, with the basic goal of providing free or reduced-price meals to students from lower-income families. The program is funded jointly by the national and state governments, and key administrative responsibilities are spread across all levels of government. Stoker argues that the NSLP has gone though several broad phases of development. During the 1960s, in keeping with the more liberal social atmosphere in Washington, the program entered a progressive phase in which needy children found the opportunity to improve their daily nutrition greatly enhanced. During the 1980s, as the orientation in Washington began to focus more on fiscal constraints and deficit reduction, NSLP entered a period of tightened standards and budgetary consciousness.

What is most important is that these phases responded to changes in orientation and policy at the national level and were reflected in the actions of state and local officials, whose political leanings and financial positions otherwise might have led them in different directions. Such success in implementation would not have been predicted based on first-generation studies that emphasized only the tendency for governmental initiatives to go wrong. And the success is all the more impressive, Stoker argues, because the potential for failure was great. The NSLP "broke new ground in an environment historically hostile to federal participation—education,"[25] yet officials were able to forge a working partnership among distinct units of government and sustain that relationship through periods of readjustment and program reform.

While Stoker's primary emphasis is on the relations between the national government and other governments in the federal system, the thrust of his analysis applies to nongovernmental partners as well. Analysts increasingly have come to realize that the ultimate success or failure of most policies is jointly determined by government actions and responses by citizens acting individually and in groups.[26] No matter how diligently public sanitation agencies set about collecting the trash, if citizens litter and dispose of waste improperly streets will remain dirty and the risks of rodents and health hazards will be high. No matter how many police are patrolling a neighborhood, the ability to catch and convict criminals will vary with the willingness and capacity of citizens to report crime and present evidence. Similarly, no matter how carefully designed a school-choice initiative, its consequences will depend on citizens' cooperation as well. If parents seek to use choice to escape social responsibility—to insulate their children from those with different racial and ethnic backgrounds, to shift the burden of paying for education to others, to shield their children from exposure to ideas and values different from those they encounter at home—the chances are good that school choice will encourage social fragmentation and a further unraveling of the coalition that traditionally has supported public schools.

Bullock and Lamb, focusing on what government can do to coerce compliance, emphasized clear and consistent goals, authoritative action, and willingness to impose penalties on the recalcitrant. Stoker, focusing on how government can establish an atmosphere more conducive to voluntary compliance, emphasizes the gradual evolution of a history of cooperation and success. State and local officials were willing to curb their own short-term interests because they had learned that NSLP provided advantages as well as constraints, because they had had some discretion in the shaping of the program and therefore wished it to succeed, and because they recognized that the national government had the capacity not only to punish them for noncompliance, but to reward them for cooperation not just for the school-lunch program but in other policy areas as well. Similarly, citizens may be more likely to resist the temptation to solve their individual problems through the exit option, and instead collectively to support and improve existing schools, when they are convinced that public officials have the capacity to provide them with genuine support.[27] From the standpoint of regime analysis, what makes a government an attractive partner is its ability and willingness—evidenced over the long term—to mobilize resources, manage them effectively, and "engage in a dependable system of cooperation."[28]

Both categories of facilitating factors—coercion and cooperation—are unlikely to be associated with market-based initiatives for educational choice. The very ideas animating market theory delegitimate such an ongoing, authoritative, and often interventionist role for the government. And the individualistic and private workings of market decision making undermine the public deliberation process through which coalitions animated by social objectives can best be forged and maintained.

THE DANGER OF MARKET RHETORIC

The greatest risks associated with the movement for educational choice come not from choice itself, but from its overly close association with the market metaphor. Although economic reasoning and the language of markets are an important part of the public face of the school-choice movement, the arguments and evidence I have presented in this book challenge the appropriateness of thinking about school choice only in economic terms.

Experimentation with school choice in the United States has been rooted in practice, not theory, and has evolved through pragmatic adjustment in the context of authoritative governance and political leadership. The rejoining of this practical experience with market theory served the purposes of conservatives in and outside the Reagan and Bush administrations. Voucherlike proposals that had proven politically unworkable were revived by the association with already popular initiatives, and long-held suspicions about the risks associated with unleashed choice were moderated by the claim that there now was evidence that choice could promote educational quality without undermining racial and economic equality.

As noted in chapter 1, many of those attracted by the broad concept of expanded educational choice have been drawn by their allegiance to non-market rationales, such as individuality and personal growth, cultural diversity, community empowerment, and the opportunity to shake up lethargic public bureaucracies. For some, the association with the market metaphor may be inadvertent. Others have reasons for strategically and conditionally acquiescing in the linkage: the market overlay provides a sheen of intellectual rigor, the reflected stature of economic theory, and an opportunity to gain financial support from corporations, foundations, and grant-giving agencies that otherwise have shown indifference toward their initiatives.

Does it really make a difference if many advocates of educational choice base their stance on something other than a commitment to the market model? It is probably asking too much to expect that all (or even most) of those supporting a particular policy will do so for the same reason. As Charles Lindblom argued, sometimes the test of a good policy is simply whether various groups can agree on it, "without their agreeing that it is the most appropriate means to an agreed objective."[29]

But ideas can have consequences.[30] While the practical consequences of the differences among the diverse visions of educational choice may be latent or obscured during the period of debate and policy formulation, failure to come to grips with the latent cleavages in values within the choice movement invites four distinct risks.

Misreading the Public Will

The first risk is that public desires will be misinterpreted. The current popular appeal of educational choice is apparent, but what this popularity signifies is less clear. The elasticity of the choice label concedes to those who capture the initiative all the positive connotations that attach to the term. School-choice plans are associated with freedom of movement, freedom of thought, religious freedom, and cultural pluralism. But this association, forged in language rather than experience, muddies the ground of public debate. If reservations about specific forms of school-choice proposals are reflexively interpreted as attacks on human choice and all its associated positive connotations, legitimate concerns will be unvoiced or unheeded. A majority forged in such a context of blurred meanings and sublimated concerns lacks the standing deserved by a majority that evolves after thorough and open consideration of competing values.

A careful consideration of public-opinion polls confirms that Americans' support for the abstract concept of "choice" does not translate directly into a mandate for markets over government. As I argued in chapter 3, Americans' views about the limits and potential for government intervention are fluid and uncertain. Nearly two out of three Americans, in 1991, indicated they favored public-school choice.[31] Asked whether they supported a voucher system that would include public, private, and parochial schools, 50 percent indicated they were in favor, versus 39 percent who were opposed.[32] At the same time, however, respondents indicated support for a range of other policy responses that would call for a *more* activist government. And expressions of support for vouchers proved to be highly dependent on the wording of the question.

Free-market theory tends to link solutions to less government; where government is necessary, it favors decentralized units over national government.[33] By this standard, the same public-opinion polls that demonstrate support for choice and vouchers show that Americans continue to reject reliance on market forces to achieve public ends. When problems emerge, people look to government for solutions. And when problems are national in scope, they expect the national government to play a leading role.

At the same time that they responded positively to calls for reducing the role of government and reducing public spending, Americans indicated they want to protect the basic core of existing programs; in one poll, they strongly opposed eliminating all extracurricular activities (62 percent to 32 percent), strongly opposed reducing the number of teachers (78 percent to 19 percent), strongly opposed increases in class size (72 percent to 21 percent), and narrowly opposed freezing salaries (47 percent to 46 percent) and reducing support staff, such as janitors, secretaries, nurses, and the like (47 percent to 45 percent).

Even in these financially hard-pressed times, moreover, there was solid support for having the government move aggressively into a new area of education responsibility; by 55 percent to 40 percent, respondents favored expanding publicly funded, publicly implemented educational programs to preschoolers.[34] A solid majority was willing to accept higher sales taxes dedicated to support public education (55 percent to 40 percent); a smaller majority (50 percent to 44 percent) favored a dedicated income tax; slightly fewer (49 percent to 44 percent) favored relying on users' fees, the revenue-raising mechanism of choice for those interested in bringing market forces to bear.[35] In spite of conservatives' traditional insistence that the national government's role be strictly limited, 81 percent of Americans favored requiring local public schools to conform to national achievement standards and goals; 77 percent favored requiring local public schools to use standardized national tests; 75 percent indicated support for a nationwide system of public-school "report cards" that would monitor each school's and each district's progress toward attaining "national education goals"; and 68 percent favored requiring local public schools to use a standardized national curriculum.[36]

190

Undermining Competing Values

While the practical distinctions among the different rationales for choice may seem minor at the preimplementation stage in which issues are argued in the abstract, the commitments to differing underlying visions are likely to become more evident and important once implementation begins to force ongoing adaptations to unanticipated feedback, and to necessitate tough choices in which legitimate values are in tension.

Maximizing personal freedom and development, for example, can erode the ties that bind traditional communities. Ethnic and religious groups that favor choice because they see it as a way to sustain schools promoting their way of life may want to limit students' own freedom to explore; the only choice programs they will support may be the ones that vest the right to choose in the parents. Building community power may conflict with free-market principles; parents in poor inner-city communities who see choice as a way to build more locally oriented institutions may demand public protection and subsidization of such institutions if they prove economically fragile. Those whose attraction to choice is contingent on its presumed link to organizational forms promoting more orderly environments and higher academic demands may show little patience for choice if it sprouts alternative schools based on experiential learning, open classrooms, and countercultural ideals.

Blurring distinctions among the rationales for choice at the stage of policy adoption simply may delay conflict until the implementation stage, when the stakes may be higher because the consequences are more direct and immediate, when the degrees of freedom may be smaller because available funds have already been committed, and where the prospects for compromise may be diminished as a result. Moreover, groups that play an influential role in pushing a policy onto the public agenda may find that they lose the ability to monitor and shape the policy once it is put into effect. Those who join the school-choice coalition as fellow travelers, rather than as converts to market theories, cannot necessarily count on being able to assert their own visions later on.

Restricting Choice in the Name of Choice

The rhetoric of educational choice emphasizes individual liberty, breaking down the walls that constrain us. One man's liberty, however, can be another man's corral. When we move from abstraction to policy, it becomes apparent that almost every workable plan entails, first of all, a *redistribution* of choice.

The redistribution of choice may be from one family to another. Such is the case, for example, when my neighbor's choice to throw noisy parties conflicts with my choice to read quietly in my own backyard. Or the redistribution may be from one group to another. Regulations in my community, for example, limit on-the-street parking for cars without resident stickers; this opens up choices to me and my neighbors by restricting those of commuters, who would like to park here and walk to the train station nearby. Choice, also, can be redistributed from one broad level of society to another, as when individuals acquire increased discretion (for example, to avoid exposure to others whose values and traditions seem different) only as the broader collectivities to which they belong acquire less (for example, to sustain public institutions where people from different backgrounds learn to interact on relatively equal terms).

Our experience with educational choice to date confirms that the label "choice" does not ensure that an initiative will not impose substantial constraints. Converting a school to a magnet school, for example, increases the choices for students outside the immediate neighborhood; to ensure that there is room for these transfer students, however, school districts often must bar children who live in the immediate neighborhood. School-choice plans implemented with guidelines to promote racial balance can require discouraging or refusing transfer requests from black parents who wish to move their children from overwhelmingly white schools to those where they might not be racially isolated. Proposals that would allow inner-city students to attend suburban schools would impinge on the ability of families to exercise the choice to follow a particularly potent American dream: to scrimp and save to buy a house in the suburbs precisely for the purpose of leaving the problems of the inner city behind.

The winners and losers are not preordained. Lower-income groups currently locked in ghetto public schools would benefit under some conceivable choice schemes; under other arrangements the principal beneficiaries would be middle- and upper-income families given the freedom to redirect personal funds now dedicated to private-school tuition. Given economic and educational disparities, both among families and across school districts, there is a serious risk, of course, that choice-in-practice will expand the opportunities of those already advantaged, at the ultimate cost of limiting opportunities for those in greatest need.

Market theory systematically distracts attention from such trade-offs. It accepts—as an article of faith or as a consequence of definition—the notion that giving individual consumers the freedom to shop around determines the aggregate level of societal choice. And it is fundamentally indifferent to existing inequalities in market power and the ways they shape people's actual ability to choose. The model can accommodate redistributory adjuncts (like proposals that vouchers or "scholarships" should be larger for the educationally disadvantaged), but it treats them as peripheral concerns dictated by political expediency and taste.

Undermining Collective Values and Institutional Capacity

Least recognized, but ultimately most important, is the risk that the market rationale associated with educational-choice proposals will undermine the social and political institutions that are prerequisites to achieving genuine reform. Granting individuals greater choice to pursue their interests does not automatically establish a course toward social betterment, through the benign mechanism of an invisible hand. Rather, the consequences of choice depend on the institutional and legal framework and the nature of the particular values that individuals and groups bring to bear. Unconstrained by moderating values, school choice can erode collective ideals, as the historical reliance on freedom of choice as a means of evading racial integration reveals. Where school choice has appeared most successful—as in some of the many experiments with magnets, magnetized districts, and statewide open enrollment—it has been at the instigation and under the direction of strong and affirmative government action.

At least as conventionally articulated, market theory questions the basic meaning of collective values and challenges the legitimacy and utility of government action beyond a minimalist menu of necessary functions.[37] To put into place a system of educational choice that does not exacerbate fragmentation and inequality is possible, but not easy. Advocates of market models for education rely on several forms of intellectual sleight of hand to hide this difficulty. They imply that racial bigotry is largely a thing of the past. They presume the willingness of suburban residents to accept and even help to fund lower-income, minority students who might exercise their choice to leave the inner city to attend their schools. They rely on government, as a deus ex machina, to monitor the implementation of educational choice and to intervene authoritatively when circumstances demand. Yet they deny the corrosive effect that market premises might have on the social goodwill and governmental power that they assume at the start.

The problem is not choice per se. Properly conceived and properly implemented, the introduction of elements of parental choice can refresh and revitalize public-school districts that too often seem stodgy and tired.

The danger comes, rather, from the ideological rationale on which market-based conceptions of educational choice are based. Many of the individuals and groups that favor educational choice are attracted by values and ideas that have little to do with market theory; indeed, under many foreseeable conditions, free-market forces are as likely as not to clash with personal development, communal values, community empowerment, and the maintenance of an ad hoc coalition for effective schools. While undoubtedly frustrated with bureaucracy and government inefficiency, Americans show few signs of readiness to abandon their tendency to turn governmentally funded, governmentally implemented, and governmentally enforced solutions to social problems as they arise. But the logical coherence, academic legitimacy, and conservative appeal of conventional economic theory results in the market rationale dominating the choice movement in public, even if nonmarket rationales account for most of the enthusiasm and support.

Individual choice is a spirited and mischievous puppy. Treated respectfully, regarded cautiously, and disciplined appropriately, it can be a delight. Give it free rein and leave it untended, and you will wake in the morning to find your sofa cushions in shreds.

Those among its supporters who recognize that the consequences of educational choice will depend on the specifics of its design and the institutional and cultural milieu into which it is introduced may hope to assert their own views of choice in due time. But their opportunity to do so is predicated on their capacity to mobilize sufficient political strength to win—and to protect against subsequent erosion—the eligibility, regulatory, redistributory, and financial provisions they prefer. Whether they will be able to do so is unclear. While almost certainly outnumbering the free-market enthusiasts among them, those attracted to school choice by nonmarket values are a diverse lot, lacking a unifying intellectual vision vivid enough to challenge the market ideal. What is more, it is by no means certain that once put into effect, a market-based system of school choice will provide the institutional channels through which collective demands for corrective measures could readily be directed. Taken in its pure form—as an alternative to majoritarian processes and public control—the market model has the potential to erode democratic institutions and buffer implementation in a way that may make collective deliberation and control less practical than many on the school-choice bandwagon anticipate.

In the final chapter, I provide the outline for an alternative concept of school choice, one that takes as its starting point the recognition that the consequences of individual choice are determined by social and institutional context. This view of "encapsulated" choice brings into the foreground the factors—some directly manipulable through government policy, others not—that will determine whether initiatives for educational choice do good or do harm. It leads to a much more modest assertion of the potential benefits of expanding educational choice, one that sees choice as just one tool among many in what must be a sustained and collective effort at institutional reform. At the same time, it builds on a more generous vision of education as a force for influencing interests, interpretations, and ideas rather than as a consumer good to be packaged and marketed to meet a demand.

Putting Educational Choice in Its Place

A BRIGHT LIGHT can blind, and so can an immodest promise. Out of zealous self-certainty or in a calculated effort to appeal, advocates of market solutions have exaggerated the power of school choice to solve the problems of education. Choice, say Chubb and Moe, should be thought of as a panacea. It is "a self-contained reform," they suggest, with "the capacity *all by itself* to bring about the kind of transformation that, for years, reformers have been seeking to engineer in myriad other ways."[1]

Such optimism is supported neither by the historical record nor by the evaluative studies carried out to date. It ignores that initiatives launched in the name of choice can affect existing choices by individuals, groups, or the society at large. And it fails to come to grips with findings from studies of policy implementation that cast doubt on the prospect that choice as implemented would retain the ameliorative features that characterize choice as imagined, without the strong and authoritative government role that market theories may serve to undermine.

But where does that leave us? Useful as it is to underscore the need for wary caution in evaluating the pro-choice claims, it is not particularly satisfying. It is not satisfying because it is too easily read as a rationale for inaction. Although I have argued that the crisis label has been applied too uncritically, I believe that we have many serious problems, that many of these problems can be addressed through public action, and that schools are an especially significant lever for intervention. It is not satisfying because it is too easily mistaken for a generic prescription for incrementalism. There are situations in which boldness is called for. Although I take issue with this particular call for a radical restructuring of American education, I reserve most of my wariness for the proposed direction of change, rather than its degree. And it is not satisfying, finally, because it does not in itself offer concerned citizens something to be *for*.[2]

Accordingly, in this chapter I take on the task of outlining a positive agenda for educational reform. School choice has a role to play in this agenda, but it is a role shaped by and subordinated to broader values and concerns. My criticisms have been aimed at market-based conceptions of choice, not at the concept of choice per se. Charles Glenn has written an essay titled "Putting Choice in Place."[3] Glenn is an enthusiastic proselytizer for choice, but his long experience in the Massachusetts educational bureaucracy has made him more sensitive than many to the ways in which the consequences of choice utterly depend on the context of scope, regulations, financing, redistribution, and information that must be established and sustained through government action. The title of this chapter—"Putting Educational Choice In *Its* Place"—is meant to point even more emphatically to the importance of the societal context (nongovernmental as well as governmental) in shaping market dynamics and outcomes.

Putting choice in its proper place means several things. Because the effects of individual choice are contextually defined, it means recognizing that relying on market forces is appropriate only in some times and some places. Because individual choice can be socially destructive unless set in a collectively endorsed framework, it means nurturing the democratic processes of decision making and building a constituency for reform that goes beyond mobilization around a "hot" idea. Because government is the mechanism through which democratically defined objectives can be self-consciously pursued, it means fighting against the tendency to let frustration with public bureaucracies further sap governmental capacity and authority. Finally, because doing all this will depend in the long run on citizens more attentive, analytic, patient, broad-minded, and full of foresight than we are accustomed to, it means recognizing that schools have a role to play as shapers of minds and values, not just as reflectors of consumer demands.

Laying the Groundwork

Like Archimedes, who speculated about moving the earth with a lever, we first need a place to stand. The broad agenda outlined in this chapter builds on a reconceptualization of the nature of social learning, public institutions, and schools. To some extent, this reconceptualization can be said to emerge from the analysis that has come before. But it would claim too much to present the basic ideas as conclusions drawn from that analysis, as if they followed from it necessarily and unambiguously. It is best to think of them as core premises, held with some conviction but open to reconsideration and refinement over time. They provide an interpretive framework that is an alternative to the market metaphor, and like the market metaphor they help bridge the gap between interpretation and recommendation.

Rethinking the Concept of Social Learning

The hope that we might bring the clarity, precision, rigor, and certainty associated with the techniques of the physical sciences to the task of solving social problems has been an important theme in the twentieth century. "Mankind in a test-tube is the hope and aim of social science," wrote one enthusiast during the 1930s.[4] The dream helped fuel a tremendous explosion in the field of public-policy analysis—the initiation of academic departments and professional policy-analysis degrees, the vast increase in government spending on applied social-science research, the emergence of a cottage industry of private firms offering skills in policy analysis as their product. Emphasizing rigorous designs for data collection, sophisticated quantitative techniques, formal deductive models, and the application of cost-benefit analysis, the quest for a new science of public policy proposed to take the guesswork, the ideology, the personal preference, and the appeal to vague moral imperatives out of the social decision-making process once and for all.[5]

This model for social learning informed a related view of the proper structuring of the public decision-making process. In emphasizing the application of sophisticated techniques, not readily understandable by the average citizen, it seemed to carve out a special role for those with a claim to expertise. Giving a special role to experts was not seen as contrary to democratic principle because—paralleling the sharp distinction it drew between facts and values—this model of social learning differentiated the political arena (which set broad priorities and in which the average citizen was encouraged to play a full role) from the administrative arena (which focused on questions of means rather than ends, and which could best be left in the hands of those with special expertise).

To acknowledge that social learning is a more open-ended and inconclusive process than the scientific model suggests is not to say that the techniques of systematic analysis are irrelevant. A small boat cannot guarantee safety in a storm, but that is hardly an argument for diving overboard; we always operate in an environment of imperfect information, but this makes improvements in our techniques of analysis more important, not less. What it does mean, however, is that we cannot escape the necessity of applying interpretation and judgment to the products of systematic analysis. Moreover, it implies that we must resolve ourselves to do so continuously, with little likelihood of reaching a resting point at which we could utter the satisfying claim, "Now we've finally got it." This suggests the importance of structuring our public decision-making processes so as not to favor premature closure. It is an argument for elevating the importance of open debate, critical thought, intellectual integration, and policy experimentation, and for providing special protection to the institutions that make these most possible.

In this ongoing enterprise of interpretation and judgment, moreover, scientists have only a weak claim to special expertise. As Lindblom argues, the knowledge that social scientists bring to bear is not different in kind from the common sense applied by the average citizen.[6] This, then, is an argument in favor of broadening the range of participants invited to partake in serious policy debate as well as broadening the range of the kinds of evidence we are willing to accept as worthy of consideration. But legitimating a grass-roots, pluralistic form of policy deliberation should not mean elevating anecdotes and gut feelings over careful consideration of the available evidence and the development of coherent arguments.

This underscores the long-range importance of cultivating a better-informed and analytically more sophisticated citizenry. Significantly, however, framing the issue in this way has implications that differ from the more conventional thinking about the importance of education as an investment in human capital. That more conventional line of thought—associated with the linkage of the education crisis to economic distress (see chapter 2) and guided in part by the market metaphor—portrays human capital in terms of the needs of our economic system. The argument suggested here calls for investing in education in order to improve the character of our collective brain as it will be applied to shared decision-making responsibilities. Where the former may justify an emphasis on basic skills, discipline, and a certain degree of specialization, the latter points toward the need for general knowledge, critical facilities, and experience in exercising responsibility.

Rethinking the Meaning of "Public" in Public-School Choice

It is because there is no single, stable, clearly defined set of societal values and understandings—recognizable by consensus, study, or special insight—that we properly give extra weight to values and understandings that have been openly articulated, subject to public challenge, collectively negotiated, and validated through democratic processes. This goes to the heart of the distinction between public and private institutions. This distinction ostensibly is at the center of the contemporary debate over school choice. But the anemic view of public schools as nothing more than one of several alternative "service providers" distracts attention from the most important considerations.

During the 1992 presidential campaign, President Bush and challenger Clinton squared off directly on the question of whether school-choice initiatives should include private schools. Bush, as noted in chapter 4, offered a voucher proposal, modeled on the GI Bill, that would incorporate parochial as well as nonreligious private schools. Bill Clinton took a stand in favor of limiting choice to public-school systems. While disagreeing on their substantive positions, however, both accepted a common frame for the debate. "Private" school choice meant including private schools; "public" school choice meant not doing so.

While the contemporary debate over choice is properly framed in terms of public versus private choice, it is mistaken when it treats that distinction as if it relates simply to the question of whether privately operated schools ought to be included. Rather than simply focusing on the strengths and weaknesses of private versus public institutions and processes as *service-delivery mechanisms*, we need to focus on the differences between private and public institutions and processes as *vehicles for deliberation, debate, and decision making*. The real danger in the market-based proposals for choice is not that they might allow some students to attend privately-run schools at public expense, but that they will erode the public forums in which decisions with societal consequences can democratically be resolved.

Recasting the issue this way has important implications for education policy. First, it opens the door for advocates of public-school choice to endorse school-choice arrangements that include private schools on a selective, pragmatic, and contingent basis, a point on which I will elaborate below. Second, recasting the issue in this manner reminds us that making public-school choice work requires more than simply barring the door against the inclusion of private schools. Plans limited to public schools can reflect either the positive or the negative aspects of market forces. When bounded by publicly defined goals and implemented authoritatively and effectively by public officials, school-choice plans have the potential to be stimulating and liberating. But when such plans are enacted hastily, when important values are neglected in the public debate, when critical choices about financing and regulation and scope are made without reflection or by default, and when public officials lack the capacity to intervene affirmatively to ensure that public goals are kept in the forefront, the result may be greater inequality, greater disillusionment with public institutions, and greater fragmentation along racial, ethnic, class, and cultural lines.

Rethinking the Socialization Function of Schools

The market orientation considers education as a *product* of public and private decisions; as such the issues involved are generic ones applicable to other domestic policies. But education also has a special status as a *producer* of the values, perspectives, knowledge, and skills that will be applied in the ongoing enterprise of collective deliberation and adjustment. This socialization function of schools at one time was widely recognized, even celebrated. But contemporary debate treats it warily if at all. Part of the explanation lies in the growing influence of economic theory and market ideas, which make the satisfaction of consumers' interests the primary evaluative criterion but which show little interest in the question of where those interests come from. Part of the explanation lies in an aversion to the concept of socialization because of its association with manipulation and authoritative regimes.

It was recognized by Horace Mann and others during the nineteenth century that universal suffrage demanded both a politically literate citizenry and one acculturated to democratic norms; this insight provided some of the impetus to expand public education in the United States. But the dominant paradigm that social scientists and citizens apply to politics today is ill suited to taking such needs into account. In adopting the language of economics, analysts working in the pluralist and public-choice traditions also have adopted the economists' lack of interest in questions regarding the origin of interests.[7] Interests are taken to be equivalent to individual preferences or tastes—and therefore idiosyncratic, changeable, and essentially beside the point.[8] Economists see no need to understand why some shoppers prefer shiny apples; they are content to know that their models let them predict, from that preference, patterns in price and supply.[9] Nor does it seem to make much sense to ask how rational economic actors "know" what their interests are. As understood by the economic metaphor, interests are felt or experienced. Preferences for lower taxes or more public parks do not need to be pondered and deciphered any more than preferences for health food or cigarettes. As a result, the economic view of interests defines as out of its range some issues central to the sustenance of democracy. It conceives of democratic institutions as instruments by which vectors of pressure are measured, rather than as a forum for debate in which interests are mediated, reinterpreted, and redefined.[10] It thinks of education policy as a dependent variable, to be shaped by—as well as evaluated in the light of—preexisting patterns of interests and values, rather than as an independent variable that plays an ongoing role in transmitting values and skills to the next generation of citizens.

In addition to the influence of economic ideas, lack of interest in the socialization function of schools also reflects the uneasiness—rooted in classical liberalism and felt viscerally by many Americans—about the damage that might be done in the name of socialization by heavy-handed bureaucrats. The power to socialize also is the power to indoctrinate, at least potentially. Religious minorities and those who hold politically marginal views have history on their side when they warn that majorities may turn the socialization function of schools to their own advantage, purging dissent under the guise of promoting consensual values.[11] Like the economic perspective, this view deemphasizes the socialization function of schools, but it does so for different reasons. Economic theory does so because it dismisses the potential for schools systematically to alter individuals' understandings of their own interests. This view sometimes does so out of fear that acknowledgment may confer legitimacy in a way that invites abuse.

But it makes no sense to lay out an agenda for education reform without recognizing directly that schools *do* affect the way children learn to interpret their environments—for good or ill. Because of its potential to influence the way future voters and political leaders will come to interpret their roles and their social environments, education policy plays a critical role in sustaining democracy. Democracy depends on its citizens to play two key roles. The first and most familiar role for a citizen is as an intelligent and informed arbiter of issues. The second role is as a protector of values. Democracy rightly is perceived as an open forum of values and ideas, but it is not true that all values and ideas are created equal. A few values are central and legitimate because they are prerequisites if democratic institutions and processes are to be sustained. These values include respect for minority opinion, a commitment to freedom of expression, and an allegiance to reason over unreason. The institutions and processes that we associate with democracy would prove to be hollow shells should a majority emerge that reneges on these values. Citizens have a responsibility not only to acknowledge these values, but to mobilize to defend them if they are under attack.[12]

Taking seriously the function schools play as producers of citizens need not, and should not, mean inviting the kinds of thought control that rightly concern those who fear the potential for governmental abuse. This is true for several reasons. First, while substantial, the socialization powers of schools should not be overstated. Schools are by no means the only place that citizens gain experience in debating issues, critically assessing information, dealing with diversity, and exploring the way their interests relate to those of others. Cumulatively more important are experiences in the family, community, and religious institutions, and through television and other media. Nor are schools particularly effective at shaping such learning according to a deliberate plan. Much of what children take away from schools has to do with subtle messages communicated through example, nuance, and peer interaction rather than formal curriculum and disciplinary policies. These cannot readily be manipulated from above, especially in a highly decentralized educational system such as ours, and efforts to impose particular values and ideas often backfire.[13]

Second, in considering the risks of abuse, the *substance* of the emphasized values and ideas makes a difference. Properly conceived, the socialization function of schools involves inculcating cooperative habits of heart and critical habits of mind, not particular doctrines. The open-ended nature of the collective learning process and the need to protect core democratic principles underscore the importance of respect for minority views, empathy, skepticism toward received wisdom, an analytic orientation, a range of experience, and a depth of knowledge. These traits, which we might like to see in the generation to which we will pass stewardship of the nation, are unlikely to emerge in authoritarian classrooms or in response to rigid and repetitive curriculums; indeed, they more likely die there.

Finally, unless we are willing to rule out the potential to use public power deliberately in such a way, schools are the best available tool. While other factors—both private and governmental—have as much or more impact in shaping tomorrow's citizenry, schools are strategically important in ways these other factors are not. Compared to other important areas influenced by government, schools reach more deeply and directly into the private realm where future citizens are socialized at an early age. While the risk of abuse must be acknowledged, public schools have another characteristic that makes this risk potentially manageable. Compared to other forces of socialization—the family, religion, the mass media—schools are more open to public scrutiny and democratic intervention.

CHOICE AS A TOOL . . . NOT A SOLUTION

Moving from a broad rethinking of the nature of social learning, public institutions, and schools to a more concrete set of proposals for education reform calls for an intermediate step. One of the most troublesome aspects of the contemporary movement for market-based school choice is the willingness of some partisans to present choice as a panacea: a solution that fits all times and places and that has the power to solve all problems completely on its own. Chubb and Moe state this position baldly: "Choice is a self-contained reform with its own rationale and justification. It has the capacity *all by itself* to bring about the kind of transformation that, for years, reformers have been seeking to engineer in myriad other ways. Indeed, if choice is to work to greatest advantage, it must be adopted *without* these other reforms, since the latter are predicated on democratic control and are implemented by bureaucratic means."[14] Such zealous presentation of choice as a universal and exclusive solution hampers clear thinking about reform in at least two ways. It encourages unreflective applications of choice, regardless of local circumstance. And it threatens to crowd off the public agenda a host of other reform possibilities—funding for preschools, smaller class sizes, extended school days—some of which, because they are more suited to local cultural, institutional, and political realities, may simply be more likely to work. Instead, choice should be regarded pragmatically as one tool among many, which citizens and officials should consider in seeking a workable education-reform strategy suited to their district's values, resources, and needs. This involves fitting choice to the context, considering opportunity costs, and appreciating modest victories.

Fitting Choice to the Context

Like the street vendor offering T-shirts with a sign claiming "one size fits all," some proponents of school choice offer legislative models as universal recipes for reform. Yet, there are dramatic differences among the more than fifteen thousand school districts in the United States. Some districts are dense, urban, and heterogeneous, while others are sparsely populated with little ethnic or racial variation. Some are compact; some cover many square miles. Some contain high proportions of students whose parents have the resources and desire to provide, at home, a supportive climate that complements the mission of the schools; others have too many children living in households so ravaged by economic hardship, drugs, and disease that learning takes second place to bare survival. Some communities have traditions of racial harmony; some bear scars of lengthy racial conflict. Some boast property wealth that provides a rich pool of resources for funding public initiatives; some are desperately underfunded. Some have well-developed public-transportation systems that make it feasible for students to move readily from home to school; others are dependent on automobiles. Some are dotted with well-regarded private schools; others have few of even minimal quality. Some districts are governed by effective leaders kept on their toes by a mobilized citizenry. In other districts, inept and part-time officials run systems in a relatively unmonitored and unaccountable fashion.

Differences such as these can have a tremendous effect on the way school choice would unfold. Considering choice as a tool, rather than a universal solution, means taking these differences into account. It means tailoring school-choice plans to meet the circumstances. In some cases it may mean delaying experimentation with choice until some of the preconditions can be put in place. School-choice plans for rural districts where students and schools are far apart, for example, might have to include quite different provisions from those for dense urban areas and those effectively served by mass transit. To the extent that viable programs require a threshold number of students, rural areas may simply be unable to accommodate the full range of choices sustainable in an urban area. For logistical reasons, choices may have to be structured as alternative programs or concentrations within schools (rather than between schools). School-choice plans in systems in which demographic changes have resulted in excess school capacity might need provisions different from those needed in growing areas where there are no empty seats in school.[15]

One Tool among Many

A hammer can be invaluable for some tasks and in some hands. But a hammer is no help in repairing a broken dish, and it can be dangerous if wielded in the dark or by a child. Those who use a tool have a responsibility to make sure that it is used when the time and the place are right. Because choice can have destructive consequences under some conditions, those who propose school choice as a policy priority have the responsibility to do the same. They also have a responsibility to consider other tools that might be available.

Choice is by no means the only weapon in the arsenal available to school officials. Those who insist on nothing short of a radical restructuring of the entire system obscure this point with their undifferentiated charges of educational breakdown. Public officials at all levels of government have undertaken a vast array of school-reform initiatives over the last ten years. These have included tougher graduation requirements, more challenging curriculums, more sophisticated measurements of student performance, teacher competency testing, longer school days, longer school years, merit pay for teachers, school-based management, and school-finance reform. The blanket charge that these have failed simply is not substantiated by the evidence. By some indicators, as noted in chapter 2, school performance has actually improved. More to the point, there have been far too few of the controlled and careful studies that might more accurately sort through the web of non-school factors that bear on performance to let us assign, with confidence, either congratulations or blame.

A pragmatic approach calls for evaluating school choice in relation to these alternatives. In some cases, the relationship may be complementary. In others, limited resources or underlying inconsistencies mean that pursuit of choice will make other options less possible. Choice can entail substantial expenses. Making transportation available to transferring students, for example, could mean having to settle for higher student/teacher ratios, or fewer advanced-placement courses, or less-competitive teacher salaries. Because different people emphasize different values, increasing the scope of parental choice may require scaling back on efforts to expose all students to a common core of knowledge or significantly encroaching on traditions of local control. After public deliberation, based on the best available evidence, we might conclude that these are opportunity costs worth taking on. But they should not be ignored.

Exploiting Existing Opportunities:
Choice as Safety Valve and Social Indicator

Finally, thinking of choice as a tool means making certain that we do not forsake small victories in pursuit of grand solutions. Individual choice already exists in education on a much broader scale than has been recognized. Families exercise choice by opting for private schools, by choosing where to live, by taking advantage of school-district policies for obtaining transfers under specific conditions, by illicitly using the addresses of relatives or friends to obtain entrance to the schools they prefer, by pressuring principals to assign their children to the particular teachers they prefer. The sub-rosa and ad hoc nature of this choice limits its availability, undermines its fairness, and keeps it from contributing as it might to our ability to identify and respond to problems. A realistic program for using choice as a tool should take better advantage of the types of choice compatible with existing values and institutional structures so as to make choice function better as a safety valve and social indicator.

Even under the best circumstances, the neighborhood public school will not adequately serve the needs of every neighborhood child. This can be due to the particular characteristics of the child, the particular limitations of the school, or a simple lack of fit between one and the other. Making it more feasible for the families of such children to choose a different school setting, with guidance and support from public officials, can serve the legitimate interests of the individual while providing a useful social safety valve.

Some children have special needs. These can include those associated with physical and learning disabilities, emotional problems, inability to speak English, and unique learning styles that may characterize the extraordinarily bright or artistically inclined. There are plenty of good reasons to mainstream such children when possible. The benefits can accrue both to the special child, who avoids stigma, and to the other children, who have the opportunity to gain a healthy perspective on the diversity that characterizes the human community. The debate about when those advantages outweigh the personal and social costs is intense and ongoing. It tends, as such debates do, to crystallize into positions framed as absolute principles. Yet it almost certainly is the case that drawing the line calls for judgment, discretion, and attention to the particulars of the case. And it almost certainly is the case that, however the line is drawn, some children will fall on the far side, where the opportunity to exit from the neighborhood school will benefit them more than it harms others.

Even well-run and generally successful schools have certain things they are not able to do as well as others. This is partly a reflection of limited resources, and the need to make calculated decisions to deemphasize some things in order to emphasize others. A school with talented Spanish and French teachers in its bilingual program, for example, cannot necessarily be expected to offer instruction in Russian, Japanese, and Vietnamese; a school that builds an extraordinary program in computer sciences around a few key instructors and an investment in up-to-date equipment in most instances will not be able to match the biology instruction provided by another school that has emphasized that component of its curriculum. Also, teachers and administrators are human beings with diverse interests, capacities, experiences, and sensitivities. The way the staff meshes, the complementarity and synergy that exist, define a collective personality that—like individual personalities—almost always couples weaknesses with strengths. Through conscious sculpting or informal processes of selective recruitment, selective retention, and strategic investment of finite resources, some schools might develop an especially good atmosphere for encouraging the brightest students to excel, for example, while others might do relatively better at encouraging less-able and less-advantaged students to reach their full potential.

Even children without special needs and schools without special limits can experience a poor fit. Sometimes a child can use a fresh start; a tough year due to problems at home, difficulty fitting in socially with other children, or simply the need for the stimulation that can come from a change in surroundings can account for this. Sometimes even a healthy institution loses its capacity to fine-tune its response to meet the needs of every changing child. When things are working well, such a lack of fit should be an extreme exception. A child needs to learn perseverance and that running away from a tough situation is not always the best solution. A good school should be slow to throw up its hands. But in a small proportion of cases, choice can serve as a mutually beneficial escape hatch.

A vision of choice-as-safety-valve has quite different implications from a vision of choice-as-solution. The former retains primary responsibility for education in the public sector, where broad strategies are subject to open debate, conflict, compromise, and the assertion of an informed majority will. Unrestrained choice, by contrast, saps the vitality of this public forum; as Hirschman explains, individual exit in many circumstances can redirect the most alert and most able citizens from investing in the exercise of a public voice.[16] Publicly derived actions cannot meet the particular needs of all individuals even under the best circumstances, however, so allowing choice as an exit option in some cases can be reasonable, prudent, and just.

In the same way that choice can be made to function better as a safety valve than it does in our current arrangement, so can it be made to function better as a source of information to public officials and concerned citizens. One of the appealing aspects of market processes is that they can often respond more speedily and certainly to problems than can government institutions that depend on electoral mechanisms or bureaucratic monitoring to perceive and identify needs.[17] That is because many social problems are manifested first as personal distress. Under the right conditions, people can respond to felt distress almost immediately through market channels; a tenant faced with a rent increase can choose to relocate, for example, or a diner subjected to indifferent service can choose to leave no tip. Converting personal distress into collective demands for government help is more problematic.[18]

That said, improving the capability of government institutions to identify problems and worrisome trends is both desirable and possible. Some harmful conditions are not readily perceptible at the individual level. They may by their nature elude the senses, as is the case with carcinogens in our food or the workplace, some airborne pollutants, ozone depletion, and the like. They may develop so gradually, or their effects may be so dispersed, that their intrusion is not easily noted or is mistakenly accepted as part of the norm.

For reasons like these, many observers have called for expanding the range and quality of social indicators available to researchers and public officials.[19] Garry D. Brewer and Peter deLeon note especially the need for better measures of social conditions at the local level. "Much social information is aggregated at the national level," they observe; "many problems are not."[20] Although not explicitly linked to a broad call for social indicators, President Bush's *America 2000* similarly emphasized the need for better measures of school performance. The absence of good indicators of school performance is one reason why, as noted in chapter 6, so many of the empirical studies of existing school-choice programs are methodologically flawed.

Properly instituted and monitored, school choice can become a valuable addition to the still fairly limited array of indicators for reliably assessing educational problems and trends. Net transfers out of a school or district are a signal that something may be wrong. Net transfers into a school or district may be a signal that a school is doing something well. To use choice in this limited way calls for instituting uniform procedures for monitoring and reporting transfers, undertaking "exit" surveys of at least a sample of those exercising choice to determine the reasons for their decision, engaging in systematic analysis to distinguish movement attributable to school failures from that due to other regional or neighborhood changes, and committing to use the signaled dissatisfaction as a spur to design and target ameliorative efforts.

MAKING CHOICE WORK: A REALISTIC PROGRAM

Rejecting the dual fictions of choice as an alternative to governance and choice as a panacea does not mean overlooking the potential of choice as a specific tool. A realistic program of school choice should take into account the open-ended nature of social learning and the importance of protecting public institutions as vehicles for deliberation and decision making, and be sensitive to the ways schools create interests as well as respond to them. It should pay attention to context, consider opportunity costs incurred by forsaking other policies, and build on, not preempt, the present roles that choice can play: safety valve for motivated families seeking immediate relief from unsatisfactory conditions, and social indicator that can help public authorities identify problems and target responses.

In this section I lay out the basic elements of an agenda for making choice work. For each objective, I attempt to provide specific steps to illustrate how citizens and policymakers might reach it. This reflects the simple rule of thumb: first things first. Before undertaking radical reform that would depend for success on broad and simultaneous changes in the cultural, institutional, and political milieus, it makes sense to make the existing apparatus of education and educational governance work better. I begin with those goals that I think present the fewest disruptions and finish with those that are more radical and more likely to encounter resistance.

Clarification of Existing Options

Where diversity and choice currently exist in public-school districts, available options and the criteria for transfer should be made more clear, consistent, and publicly known. Teachers within a single school often rely on different pedagogical styles due to differences in training, talent, or personal preference. Similarly, schools within a single district frequently differ in emphasis and style. Education bureaucracies usually deemphasize or deliberately mask these differences, in the misguided belief that public education is supposed to be uniform. Procedures for requesting different teachers or transferring among schools often are informal and ad hoc, and when they are formally defined, information about them may be scattered and difficult to obtain.

The importance of improving the information provided to parents has appropriately been underscored by those advocating systemwide magnet schools and those promoting voucher systems including private schools.[21] But even without changes in curriculum, staffing, or the types of schools included, public officials can broaden the options available to parents simply by making information more readily available. School districts should encourage schools to develop detailed mission statements, require that these be presented in terms understandable to the lay public, and undertake the responsibility to disseminate this information widely. Ideally, the dissemination should be through multiple formats, not simply written brochures, in order to mitigate the tendency for lower-income families to have more limited access to information. The parent information centers and aggressive outreach efforts apparently used to good effect in Cambridge, for example, would have payoffs in most school districts, whether or not they are associated with deliberate attempts systematically to differentiate programs between schools.

Acknowledging the meaningfulness of *within-school* diversity and choice is another important step that districts should be encouraged to undertake. Imagine a situation—hardly unrealistic—in which two third-grade teachers at the same school offer different types of teaching environments, based on differences in their training, preference, or personal style. Assume that both styles of teaching fall within the broad range of acceptable practices, that some types of children would respond better in teacher #1's classroom, and that others would thrive under teacher #2. Insisting that teachers make their products as uniform as possible leaves both less enthused and less effective than they might otherwise be; ignoring the differences in assigning the students to one classroom or the other makes it likely that some proportion of both types of learners will be misplaced. Managing within-school diversity is in some ways a bigger challenge than would be sorting out the teachers into like-minded educational communities. But within-school diversity has other advantages: it makes for an environment in which orthodoxy is less likely to go unchallenged, it reduces the disruption associated with exercising choice,[22] and it makes it easier to harmonize the goal of individual choice with other social goals, such as racial integration and community-based schools.

Fairness of Implementation

Making existing options clear and well publicized undoubtedly will put new demands on school officials to handle the logistics of transfers, to exercise discretion and judgment, and to withstand pressure to favor some requests based on family status, political clout, aggressiveness, or friendship. Conservative critics may be correct in assuming that bureaucrats' desire to avoid such demands is an obstacle. But that does not mean it cannot be done. Moreover, the ad hoc and surreptitious exercise of choice that currently takes place is exactly the kind of format likely to respond to the "squeaky wheel" and exacerbate inequities rooted in differences in parental education, income, and socioeconomic class.

But market advocates are wrong when they seek systematically to undermine or bypass the bureaucracy in response. For all its many flaws, public bureaucracy is well designed for providing uniformity and consistency of access.[23] Taking the necessary steps and carrying them out well requires a stronger, more astute, and more confident bureaucracy, not its opposite. Making sure that a strong and capable bureaucracy serves the public's interest rather than its own requires making the existing processes for exercising democratic control more open and more vital, and making the citizens more interested, responsible, and informed. Withdrawing key decisions into the private and personal arena of family choice is more likely to enervate than to energize these mechanisms for democratic control.

The first step that districts must take to ensure fair implementation of choice within and among schools is to make the criteria for accepting and rejecting transfer requests clear and public. Vaguely worded references to "maintaining racial balance," "avoiding overcrowding," and meeting children's "individualized needs" invite selective interpretation unless they are accompanied by practical definitions. Second, the rights of appeal, the acceptable grounds for appeal, and the procedures for appeal must be made clear and public. Finally, to ensure that the broader public has the opportunity to assess the consequences of choice and evaluate the terms of its implementation, it is critical that school districts make available reports that summarize the number of requests, approvals, and actual transfers, with the information disaggregated by individual schools, by neighborhood, and by parents' race and education.

Strategic Differentiation

While substantial differences currently exist among districts, schools, and classrooms, the differences are largely unpatterned and idiosyncratic. They reflect the personal style of administrators, unarticulated (and sometimes objectionable) local values and traditions, and historical happenstance.[24] This process of unselfconscious differentiation may end up meeting local interests quite nicely, but there is no guarantee that this will be the case. If the process is to be responsive to public interests, the decisions about whether and how to diversify educational offerings ultimately must be subjected to democratic procedures of deliberation, debate, and control. In this process, the advantages of diversification can be judged relative to other goals that are not necessarily complementary, such as providing a core of common knowledge, ensuring baseline work skills, and exposing children to the practice of pursuing common goals with others whose backgrounds and presuppositions differ from their own.

School districts seeking to diversify offerings selectively and self-consciously should take advantage of these rules of thumb. First, diversification provides the greatest advantages and least risks of danger when it presents options to older students, whose identities are more fully developed, whose skills and weaknesses are more apparent, and who are more likely to be mature decision-makers able to take responsibility for the consequences of their choices. School districts, in most instances, would be wise to begin school-choice programs at the high school level, resisting the temptation to expand them willy-nilly throughout the elementary levels. A second rule of thumb involves diversification where it takes advantage of inherently limited educational resources. A lesson can be learned here from the area of health research involving promising new therapies. Scientists have found it easier to justify engaging in human experimentation, which requires assigning some subjects to a control group in which they are denied therapies, when the treatment in question is limited in supply. In such cases, the option of providing the therapy to everyone simply is not available. The analogy may be transferable to educational options that require very expensive equipment (advanced computers, special laboratory equipment, television production facilities) or highly refined teacher expertise. It would not be possible to provide every school with an instructor who has research experience in particle physics or with a drama teacher who has directed Broadway plays. When districts are fortunate enough to have such resources, they should feel free to build special programs around them, even if access to those programs must be limited. And districts considering strategies for development should not hesitate to pursue such resources out of concern that programs that cannot be made universally available are necessarily illegitimate or politically unworkable.

Institutionalized and Improved Monitoring

Where diversity and choice already exist among classrooms, schools, and districts, they should be carefully monitored and systematically evaluated as a kind of natural experiment that can provide valuable information about what works. Improved monitoring should not mean simply taking more measurements of the kind we typically rely on now. The problem is not limited to the well-publicized tendency to promote rote lessons and "teaching to the test." Because results are so highly determined by family characteristics, *all* the standardized examinations that are in wide use are misleading when interpreted as measures of school performance. So used, they are pernicious. The surest way for schools and school districts to improve their performance (besides outright cheating) is to change their students— replacing those from low socioeconomic groups with those from higher socioeconomic groups. Replacing students is both easier and more certain of success than changing what the teachers actually do.

When researchers attribute to educational initiatives rising scores that are in fact due to population shifts, they reinforce two seductive but misleading views of education reform. First, they create the impression that the solution to problems in education is simply the adoption of known and proven techniques, when what is required is broad and sustained attention to a range of social and economic problems that we do not fully understand, that are resistant to quick fixes, and that cannot effectively be addressed without politically risky and controversial action by public leaders. Second, they reinforce a tendency to "blame the victim,"[25] in this case allowing those in more fortunate settings to evade responsibility for helping inner-city school districts, whose continuing poor performance can be shrugged off as a result of their obstinacy in clinging to outmoded techniques.

By the same token, when parents are left with standardized scores as the only readily available indicator of school performance, they are led almost inevitably to the conclusion that the "best" schools are those that have the fewest low-income and minority students. Expanding parental choice in an environment of such one-dimensional information will tend to reinforce tendencies toward racial and economic separation.[26]

Efforts already are underway to make standardized-test procedures more uniform and more sophisticated. This will involve linking tests more directly to curriculum content and including open-ended formats that allow students to demonstrate, and be evaluated on, the reasoning behind their answers. The model provided by the National Assessment for Educational Progress should be built on and expanded. The NAEP exams are anchored in clearly defined skills and normed according to objective levels of achievement. In the spring of 1988, Congress authorized expanding the NAEP to provide state-level results, but did so only on a trial and voluntary basis. By testing enough students to generate representative samples at the state level, expansion of the NAEP makes it possible to make meaningful comparisons between states, and potentially to ascribe variations in performance to differences in states' policies. Extended over time, such indicators will provide an even richer data base for determining what works and what does not. As a first step, this assessment effort should be made permanent and mandatory for every state that accepts categorical federal education aid. But the true payoff would depend on expanding the NAEP model to the district level. A reasonable next step might be to extend coverage to the large inner-city school districts, whose problematic performance is at the root of much of the nation's concerns. In order to reduce the expense, it would be possible to include districts on a rotating basis—a strategy employed by the Census Bureau and the Department of Housing and Urban Development in order to get detailed information about housing and neighborhood conditions in the largest metropolitan areas through the American Housing Survey.

Researchers interested in assessing hospital performance have recently made significant headway in developing indexes that take into account the different characteristics of the populations the hospitals serve, and education-policy experts can learn from this model. The fact that one hospital has higher mortality rates for heart-bypass operations may not mean that its doctors are doing a bad job; it may reflect that they are serving a clientele that comes to them when problems are especially advanced or with a higher incidence of other complicating health problems.[27] By using information contained in individual patient profiles, researchers can devise a mortality index that ranks hospitals as if they were serving identical groups of patients. In order to deal with the effect of parental background, the federal government should make it a priority to develop measuring instruments and procedures that can do the same for assessing schools.

Both goals—improving the tests themselves and building in controls for student background—would require collecting types of information that school systems tend to avoid as a rule, including surveys of student and parent satisfaction, assessments of the scope and reasons for withdrawals to private schools, and follow-up studies to determine alumni's long-term employment and experiences with higher education. Currently most of the smaller and more fiscally limited districts may lack the capacity to undertake such assessments. But the hardware and software required are becoming more readily available. There is a role for state and federal governments in funding the training of district personnel to collect and analyze such information. To increase feasibility, evaluations could be periodic and could focus on samples rather than entire school populations. To increase the expertise available, and to reduce concerns about possible fraud by local officials seeking to hide their inadequacies, states could fund research teams that would visit districts on a rotating basis.

Pragmatic, Selective, and Contingent Inclusion of Private Schools

Some advocates of public-school choice invest the line separating public and private schools with almost mystical significance. Crossing that line is taboo, because once it is crossed, it will be impossible to stem the flow of vital life forces from the public sector. I have suggested that this view reflects an attenuated view of the public sector as simply an alternative delivery system. It is possible to keep authority and responsibility for debate, deliberation, and decision making in the public sector without treating the line between public and private schools as inviolable.

Although claims about the general superiority of private schools have been grossly overstated, it is possible—even likely—that some private schools can provide otherwise unavailable support to at least some children at least at some times and in some places. Children with unusual needs, based on physical or psychological impairment for example, in some in-

215

stances might have their interests met more fully by a private institution with special facilities and specially trained staff. When this is the case, and when an appropriate private facility is available, and when it would not be feasible for the public system to mimic that which is readily available, there is no need to rule out an arrangement in which the public system contracts with the private provider. Similarly, as we seek better information about what works and what does not work in education, it may be reasonable and appropriate to undertake experiments—like that in Milwaukee—that involve private schools. Such initiatives can be considered appropriate and "public" so long as they: (a) are deliberately structured to further publicly defined goals, such as targeting benefits to those with the greatest need; (b) are designed and implemented to ensure that evaluation is systematic and that results of evaluations are openly disseminated and discussed; and (c) acknowledge and reaffirm the ongoing oversight, regulatory, and legislative roles of public officials.

"Seeding" Metropolitanization

One of the dubious elements of the vision of school choice promoted by market enthusiasts concerns the relationship between central cities and their suburbs. They portray choice as an explosively liberating force, blasting holes in the jurisdictional boundaries that traditionally separate low-income residents from nearby areas with richer tax bases and a richer mix of public services. In doing so, they gloss over powerful institutional and political obstacles that have proved to be dominating factors in shaping the educational landscape of the United States. The existing structure of federalism in the United States gives local jurisdictions clear incentives to create formal and informal barriers to in-migration by citizens with lower incomes and higher needs, and to protect arrangements that make it difficult for nonresidents to share in the services that are locally financed. Jurisdictions influence the class characteristics of in-migrants through formal tools such as zoning and building codes, as well as through less formal methods that communicate hostility toward racially and economically different groups. They can, and often do, make it difficult for nonresidents to take advantage of local services by, for example, charging special fees to nonresidents who use parks or attend locally sponsored events and by enforcing resident-only parking regulations.[28] Wealthier local jurisdictions have adamantly and effectively resisted efforts by state courts to mandate more progressive school-financing arrangements, have effectively preempted state and federal initiatives that would substantially encroach on local jurisdictions' discretion to "take care of their own," and have muted efforts to differentiate curriculums between schools. In this context, it is disingenuous or naive to pretend that a school-choice plan that challenged these barriers in anything other than a token manner would be politically acceptable.

A more realistic program for educational reform can—and I believe must—include a strategy for expanding the scope of responsibility beyond local boundaries. Until this is done, the incentives for local jurisdictions to pursue "beggar-thy-neighbor" policies—to protect local claims on local revenues, and to screen out families with children who will be expensive to educate or whose presence detracts from the image local boosters want to promote—guarantee inequality and social fragmentation. But a realistic program recognizes that such a strategy will depend on public leadership and authoritative governance, not market forces. In addition, it recognizes that public officials—even courageous ones—cannot implement such dramatic changes without a constituency to support them. Imposing a metropolitan solution from the top down and without democratic deliberation and debate would no doubt spark confrontation. The resulting political backlash might cause greater harm to the public-school system than programs that selectively allowed public funds to follow students to private schools.

One possibility for "seeding" the processes of metropolitanwide responses is the establishment of new interjurisdictional bodies for revenue-sharing and cooperative decision making. Building on the models of metropolitan councils of government and special districts that oversee such functions as regional transportation, the state or federal governments could encourage local school districts to join in cooperative enterprises. Categorical grants could provide the initial incentive to districts to establish these cooperative and voluntary "superdistricts." The revenues would be distributed to the local districts, with approximately half to be disbursed on the basis of need and half to support innovation and research. The superdistricts would have the primary responsibility for defining the criteria of need and evaluating the worthiness of innovation and research proposals. Some additional competitive federal education grants could require review by the superdistricts.[29] The process of negotiating and exercising these criteria might help build new habits of cooperation and alliance on which more affirmative regional policies could be built.

Ideally, the original sources of external support would be supplemented (and eventually replaced) by revenues raised on a metropolitan or regional basis. Rather than attempting to divert existing revenues—a politically intimidating prospect—superdistricts could be empowered to impose a small tax restricted to increments in the regional property-tax base. This would provide a slowly growing source of revenue, but even more importantly it could alter the structure of objectively defined fiscal interests that currently exists. Local jurisdictions today perceive themselves as competing with one another in a zero-sum pursuit of economic development, and for the most part that perception reflects reality. Sharing some portion of tax revenues can moderate both the reality and the perceptions, creating a sense in which one jurisdiction's gains are shared by the others.

Enlivening School Politics and Enriching Public Debate

School reformers overuse the crisis label and hold out the prospect of panaceas in part because they accurately gauge the public's limited attention span. Most Americans care little about education research or school politics. Those who believe education should be higher on the social agenda figure that extreme language is the only way to defeat public indifference. Once people are paying attention, the promise of quick and certain relief is the only way to entice them to support disruptive and initially costly reforms. But in adjusting to this environment, reformers make it worse. Incantations of unmitigated failure can reinforce a sense of futility, and panaceas that prove complicated to implement and slow to demonstrate impact reinforce a sense of betrayal.

The public is unlikely to play a mature and informed role in deliberation until the quality of school politics and debate is enriched and enlivened. School-board elections in most jurisdictions are fairly dismal affairs, poorly attended and attracting minimal voter response. Part of the problem can be traced to deliberate efforts to depoliticize school politics, an outgrowth of the Progressive Era's insistence on equating partisan politics with the grosser elements of machine politics. Thus school-board elections are often formally nonpartisan and deliberately timed not to coincide with other elections, when the public's attention is at its peak. Part of the problem is the overarching resonance of the spending-versus-taxes issue, which makes the cleavage between families with public-school children and other residents the dominant political reality and which drives out attention to more nuanced issues. Part of the problem lies with the highly fragmented and decentralized nature of education politics, which leaves the major media unwilling or unable to provide in-depth coverage of issues and candidates. And part of the problem is the difficulty of conducting civil discussions about differences rooted in values. Rather than being a primary focus of open and ongoing consideration, differences associated with race, religion, and class erupt spasmodically and forcefully and in the form of winner-take-all battles.

Collective deliberation about meaningful issues can be like physical exercise: it promotes health and well-being when engaged in on a regular basis, but the once-a-month jogger ends up nursing a pulled muscle or sore back. How can discussion of substantive issues be injected into the public debate about education at the local level and on a regular basis? Here, the public, the media, and officials each bear responsibility to insist that candidates for school boards take stands on difficult and controversial issues—issues that have to do with what goes on in the classroom. But improvements will be only incremental until the public gets more engaged. Local television can broadcast school-board meetings and sponsor candidate debates, but unless someone watches, this serves a symbolic purpose only. School-board candidates can issue detailed position papers, but if those who expose themselves the most prove the most vulnerable at the polls, the next generation of candidates will revert to form.

Institutional reforms might help. The most important steps could be those that relate to the collection and dissemination of more useful information about how the schools are performing. Although further research is required, it seems quite possible that public debate also would be enlivened by the breakdown of some of the barriers that have been erected between schools and the general electoral arena. Mayoral and council elections, while often dispirited affairs themselves, tend to get more attention and stir more involvement than those for school boards. Candidates for those offices have little incentive to address education issues on anything but a superficial level. There is considerable variation from jurisdiction to jurisdiction in the degree to which such offices currently have the power to shape school policy. Even where city or county councils play a key role in determining education policy through the budget process, however, this role often is obfuscated by school-board members, who have a stake in emphasizing their independence and greater expertise, and by other public officials, who may prefer not to be held responsible by the electorate for what is going on in the schools.

CIVIC CAPACITY: BUILDING A CONSTITUENCY
FOR SUSTAINED REFORM

Public-policy debates all too often start and end with the question "What should we do?" This question implies that there is a technical solution that, once identified, is readily recognized, easily put into practice, and safely left to do its good work. But there is no shortage of good policy ideas floating around in what John Kingdon refers to as the "policy primeval soup."[30] Nor is there even a shortage of policy ideas that have been proved to work, at least in some circumstances. This is no less true in the area of education than elsewhere. Indeed, just as frequently portrayed in the media as the dismal stories of systemic educational failure are anecdotes about teachers, methods, programs, and schools that have achieved stunning successes.

Making a social policy work means adjusting the original conception to local circumstance. It means investing in it the resources and effort needed to give it a chance to succeed. It means monitoring feedback, and responding to new information and changing conditions. It means resisting the temptation to lose interest once a program has been put in place and once other problems rise on the horizon. It means maintaining allegiance to collective solutions even when some individuals and groups might solve their own problems by going it alone. For many policies—especially those like education, in which the most important consequences are likely to become evident only after considerable time has passed—it means exercising the patience to wait for results without abandoning the effort prematurely.

It is true that the public often seems too fickle, flighty, uninterested, and self-interested to countenance such an approach. But the answer is not to delegate authority to a more mature or knowledgeable elite. Nor is it to give up on the prospect of collective solutions, seeking refuge in market-oriented processes that encourage us to divide up into intimate communities of like-minded individuals. Instead, we need to take seriously the task of transforming the way we conceptualize our interests and our options. This does not mean imagining ourselves suddenly changed into wiser and more social beings. It means undertaking the hard collective enterprise of identifying common interests when they may be obscure, building on alliances that are provisional and weak, and modifying institutional arrangements so that the relative rewards of cooperation and perseverance become more certain and apparent.

Clarence Stone has used the term "civic capacity" to refer to "the ability to build and maintain an effective alliance among institutional representatives in the public, private, and independent sectors to work toward a common community goal."[31] While it seems apparent that some local jurisdictions have built a greater civic capacity than others, we do not yet know much about where such capacity comes from or the factors that encourage it. Nevertheless, in the specific case of education, it seems likely that civic capacity to undertake and sustain reform depends on challenging the tendency to interpret costs and benefits *exclusively* in terms of the way they fall on discrete groups—suburbs versus central cities, businesses versus homeowners, families versus childless people, the old versus the young, teachers versus taxpayers, public versus private schools.[32] It also depends on providing the sense of stability and security that makes it more possible for citizens to leaven their deliberations with considerations of longer-term consequences rather than with those of immediate gratification.

Citizens and public officials equally share responsibility for moving us in the right direction. Because the consequences of most public policies depend ultimately on how people respond to them, the ultimate success of educational reform may require changes in the reigning culture—the norms, values, preferences, and expectations that influence the population's perceptions and responses. Deliberate government efforts to manipulate culture and values have a high failure rate, and sometimes such efforts can be downright destructive.[33] But government action and inaction send moral messages whether those messages are deliberate or not. Part of what distinguishes good government from bad government, moreover, is its ability to earn the trust and respect of the public. To maintain this source of legitimacy and authority, government must articulate and act on principles the public shares, even when those principles may be inchoate and their application uncertain. Legitimacy and authority depend on responding to the public will, but they occasionally require getting out in front of the public— exercising leadership by example. Time and time again, citizens in democratic societies have made it clear by their actions that they expect public leaders to challenge their preconceptions and biases; politicians who trim their sails to fit the prevailing winds of public opinion trade stature and respect for job security. For these reasons, as Robert Reich observes, the public official's job "is not only, or simply, to make policy choices and implement them. It is also to participate in a system in which public values are continuously rearticulated and recreated."[34]

It is because making educational choice work is an open-ended process, requiring ongoing assessment, adaptation, reconceptualization, and change, that the agenda outlined in this chapter emphasizes broad principles of decision making rather than specific pedagogical or organizational techniques. Specific techniques will come and go, working well in some places and some times, but failing to provide the universal and automatic "solution" we would prefer.

In this sense, the position staked out here is not specific to education policy. It applies generally to the application of market solutions to social problems. While market-based approaches also are open-ended in key respects, they view the process as primarily private and personal, both in practice and ideally. Government is necessary only to ensure the protection of the market framework in which these private decisions can most efficiently be played out. Both government and democracy are potential threats whose scope and potency, accordingly, must be restrained. In contrast, I have argued that market solutions are not viable or desirable without an ongoing and substantial role for the public sector. An unleashed government, admittedly, can be inefficient or malign. And raw majoritarianism can be oppressive. But the ultimate answer lies in cultivating public values, institutions, and civic arrangements that are more likely to lead to intelligent and fair decisions.

It is in this sense that education policy takes on a special significance. While today's citizens and leaders bear responsibility for setting us off in the right direction, the final measure of our success will depend on the performance by those future generations to whom we pass the baton. Public education is the institution that gives us the greatest opportunity to provide those generations with the capacity to surpass us in depth of knowledge and breadth of vision. And it is by deemphasizing such concerns that the market metaphor can be most destructive. Language is more than a neutral medium for communication. It filters and categorizes perceptions. It focuses a hot beam of light on some issues, and leaves others in the shadows.

If we face a crisis today, it is not caused only by lack of basic job skills or by unresponsive public bureaucracies. It is a crisis of social disintegration and loss of public legitimacy, authority, capacity, and will. The sad irony of the current education-reform movement is that, through overidentification with school-choice proposals rooted in market-based ideas, the healthy impulse to consider radical reforms to address social problems may be channeled into initiatives that further erode the potential for collective deliberation and collective response.

☆ *Notes* ☆

CHAPTER ONE
THE CALL FOR CHOICE AND RADICAL REFORM

1. Notebook (1935); cited in *The International Thesaurus of Quotations*, compiled by Rhoda Thomas Tripp (New York: Harper & Row, 1970), 527.

2. Louis V. Gerstner, Jr., chief executive officer of the RJR Nabisco Company, quoted in Chester Finn, *We Must Take Charge* (New York: Free Press, 1991), 53.

3. Chief executive officer of a Los Angeles company, quoted in Gary Putka, "Lacking Good Results, Corporations Rethink Aid to Public Schools," *Wall Street Journal*, June 27, 1989.

4. President of the City Club of Chicago, quoted in Thomas F. Roeser, "In Search of Educational Excellence," *Policy Review* 54 (Fall 1990): 59.

5. Thomas Kean, former governor of New Jersey and subsequently president of Drew University. The quote comes from Finn, *We Must Take Charge*, 67.

6. U.S. Department of Education, *America 2000: An Education Strategy* (Washington, D.C.: U.S. Department of Education, 1991), 59, 65.

7. The literature on privatization is extensive. Among the books providing relatively balanced and insightful assessments are John Donahue, *The Privatization Decision* (New York: Basic Books, 1989); Sheila B. Kamerman and Alfred J. Kahn, eds., *Privatization and the Welfare State* (Princeton, N.J.: Princeton University Press, 1989); and William T. Gormley, Jr., ed., *Privatization and Its Alternatives* (Madison, Wis.: University of Wisconsin Press, 1991). For more extended elaborations of my own views on privatization, see Jeffrey R. Henig, *Public Policy and Federalism* (New York: St. Martin's Press, 1985), "Privatization in the United States: Theory and Practice," *Political Science Quarterly* 104, no. 4 (Winter 1989–90): 649–70, and Jeffrey R. Henig, Chris Hamnett, and Harvey Feigenbaum, "The Politics of Privatization: A Comparative Perspective," *Governance* 1, no. 4 (October 1988): 442–68.

8. The National Commission on Excellence in Education, *A Nation at Risk: The Imperative for Educational Reform* (Washington, D.C.: U.S. Government Printing Office, 1983); this is discussed further in chap. 2.

9. John E. Chubb and Terry M. Moe, *Politics, Markets, and America's Schools* (Washington, D.C.: Brookings Institution, 1989), 225.

10. Their distinction, while tactically astute, depends on definitional idiosyncrasies that are not particularly convincing, as I will discuss later.

11. See, for example, Robert W. Poole, Jr., *Cutting Back City Hall* (New York: Universe Books, 1980); E. S. Savas, *Privatizing the Public Sector: How to Shrink Government* (Chatham, N.J.: Chatham House, 1982), 136–45; David F. Linowes, *Privatization: Toward More Effective Government: Report of the President's Commission on Privatization* (Urbana, Ill.: University of Illinois Press, 1988), chap. 6.

12. See, for example, Myron Lieberman, *Privatization and Educational Choice* (New York: St. Martin's Press, 1989).

13. Mary Ann Glendon, *Rights Talk: The Impoverishment of Political Discourse* (New York: Free Press, 1991).

14. *Washington Post*, November 25, 1991.

15. Chubb and Moe, *Politics, Markets and America's Schools*, 2.

16. Ibid., 32.

17. Mary Anne Raywid, "The Mounting Case for Schools of Choice," in *Public Schools by Choice*, ed. Joe Nathan (St. Paul, Minn.: Institute for Learning and Teaching, 1989), 32.

18. The publication, *An Exercise in Decision Making: Choosing a High School*, was prepared by the Boston school system to promote its school-choice arrangement, which is limited to public schools. It is quoted in Laura H. Salganik and Rebecca L. Carter, "Strategies for Informing Families about School Choice," prepared for the Center on Families, Communities, Schools, and Children's Learning (Washington, D.C.: Pelavin Associates, 1991), 4.

19. Deborah A. Stone, *Policy Paradox and Political Reason* (Glenview, Ill.: Scott, Foresman, 1988), 108.

20. Ibid., 118.

21. Paul Peterson, "Monopoly and Competition in American Education," in *Choice and Control in American Education*, ed. William H. Clune and John F. Witte (London, Falmer Press, 1990), 1:72.

22. Ruth Dropkin and Arthur Tobier, eds., *The Roots of Open Education in America*. (New York: City College Workshop Center for Open Education, 1976).

23. Vernon Smith, Robert Barr, and Daniel Burke, *Alternatives in Education: Freedom to Choose* (Bloomington, Ind.: Phi Delta Kappan, 1976); Mary Anne Raywid, "Family Choice Arrangements in Public Schools: A Review of the Literature," *Review of Educational Research* 55, no. 4 (Winter 1985): 435–67.

24. John E. Coons and Stephen D. Sugarman, *Education by Choice: The Case for Family Control* (Berkeley and Los Angeles: University of California Press, 1978).

25. Ibid., 21.

26. Finn, *We Must Take Charge*, 126.

27. Diane Ravitch, *The Troubled Crusade* (New York: Basic Books, 1983).

28. Allan Bloom, *The Closing of the American Mind* (New York: Simon & Schuster, 1987).

29. Discussed in Diane Ravitch, "Pluralism vs. Particularism in American Education," *Responsive Community* 1, no. 2 (Spring 1991): 40.

30. Richard John Neuhaus, ed., *Democracy and the Renewal of Public Education* (Grand Rapids, Mich.: Eerdmans, 1987).

31. Charles Leslie Glenn, Jr., *The Myth of the Common School* (Amherst: University of Massachusetts Press, 1988), 4.

32. See ibid., for a fuller development of this argument; see also the selections in Neuhaus, *Democracy and the Renewal of Public Education*.

33. Mario Fantini, Marilyn Gittell, and Richard Magat, *Community Control and the Urban School* (New York: Praeger, 1970); Ira Katznelson, *City Trenches* (New York: Pantheon, 1981); Diane Ravitch, *The Great School Wars: New York City, 1805–1973* (New York: Basic Books, 1974); David Rogers and Norman H. Chung, *110 Livingston Street Revisited: Decentralization in Action* (New York: New York University Press, 1983).

34. D. Garth Taylor, James H. Lewis, and Michael Hyatt, "The 1988 School Reform Bill: A Legislative Summary Updated to Reflect June 1989 Amendments," report prepared for the Chicago Urban League, August 1989.

35. Karen M. Thomas, "Chicago Schools Are Set for Year 2 of Reform," *Chicago Tribune*, September 2, 1990.

36. *Congressional Record*, October 13, 1989, quoted in Mary O'Connell, *School Reform Chicago Style: How Citizens Organized to Change Public Policy* (Chicago: Center for Neighborhood Technology, 1991), 1.

37. O'Connell, *School Reform Chicago Style*, 23.

38. When O'Connell asked interviewees to name three groups they felt were "most responsible" for the Chicago school reform, Designs for Change received twenty-one votes. Chicago United, an organization representing the business community, received the second highest number of mentions, sixteen. Ibid., 32. Designs for Change had conducted research on school choice as it was implemented in four cities, including Chicago; its conclusion was that magnet schools and other school-choice options tended to result in greater isolation of at-risk students and negatively to affect nonselective neighborhood schools. See Donald R. Moore, "Voice and Choice in Chicago," in Clune and Witte, *Choice and Control in American Education*, 2:180–95.

39. James H. Lewis and D. Garth Taylor, *Options without Knowledge: Implementing Open Enrollment under the 1988 Chicago School Reform Act* (Chicago: Chicago Urban League, 1990),16.

40. Stewart C. Purkey and Marshall S. Smith, "Effective Schools: A Review," *Elementary School Journal* 83 (March 1983): 427–52.

CHAPTER TWO
THE POLITICAL MEANING OF "CRISIS"

1. Besides the National Commission on Excellence in Education's *Nation at Risk*, some of the other reports by commissions, foundations, and public-interest groups include: Ernest Boyer, *High School: A Report on Secondary Education in America* (New York: Harper & Row, 1983); Education Commission of the States Task Force on Education for Growth, *Action for Excellence: A Comprehensive Plan to Improve Our Nation's Schools* (Washington, D.C.: Education Commission of the States, 1983); National Governors' Association, *Time for Results: The Governors' 1991 Report on Education* (Washington, D.C.: National Governors' Association, 1986); Research and Policy Committee of the Committee for Economic Development, *Investing in Our*

Children: Business and the Public Schools (New York: Committee for Economic Development, 1985); and Twentieth-Century Fund, *Making the Grade* (New York: Twentieth-Century Fund, 1983). Some of the important analyses by education scholars are: Mortimer J. Adler, *The Paideia Proposal* (New York: Collier, 1982); John I. Goodlad, *A Place Called School* (New York: McGraw-Hill, 1984); and Theodore R. Sizer, *Horace's Compromise: The Dilemma of the American High School* (Boston: Houghton Mifflin, 1984). For a good overview of many of the reform proposals, see Philip G. Altbach, Gail P. Kelly, and Lois Weis, eds., *Excellence in Education: Perspectives on Policy and Practice* (Buffalo, N.Y.: Prometheus, 1985).

2. Twentieth-Century Fund, *Making the Grade*, 1.

3. Ruth B. Love (superintendent of the Chicago public schools), in *Proceedings of the Second Conference of the University/Urban Schools National Task Force*, quoted in Marilyn Clayton Felt, Improving Our Schools (Newton, Mass.: Education Development Center, 1985), 1.

4. Goodlad, *Place Called School*, 1.

5. Education Commission of the States, *Action for Excellence*.

6. Paul E. Peterson, "Background Paper," in Twentieth-Century Fund, *Making the Grade*, 30.

7. Gerald W. Bracey, "Why Can't They Be Like We Were?" *Phi Delta Kappan* (October 1991): 106 (emphasis in original).

8. National Commission on Excellence in Education, *Nation at Risk*, 8–9.

9. "Changing Pool of S.A.T. Test Takers," *Washington Post*, September 11, 1991.

10. Diane Ravitch, "U.S. Schools: The Bad News Is Right," *Washington Post*, November 17, 1991.

11. Ibid. Ravitch updates this observation. In 1972, she indicates, 116,630 students scored over 600 on the verbal section of the SAT exam. This number fell by 35 percent (to 74,836) by 1991. "The high-scoring students were 11.4 percent of the test-takers in 1972, but only 7.2 percent in 1991."

12. National Commision on Excellence in Education, *Nation at Risk*, 8.

13. Ibid., 9.

14. Edward B. Fiske, "U.S. Pupils Lag in Math Ability, 3 Studies Find," *New York Times* January 11, 1987.

15. Finn, *We Must Take Charge*, 17. In fact, U.S. students outscored students from Ireland, French-speaking Ontario, and French-speaking New Brunswick in the science assessment. National Center for Education Statistics, *Digest of Education Statistics, 1990* (Washington, D.C.: U.S. Department of Education, 1991), 377.

16. Americans were tied with adults from the United Kingdom, and edged out those from Italy and Mexico.

17. "Tiny Town Refuses an Increase in Taxes to Rehire Teachers," *New York Times*, January 5, 1992.

18. Gary Orfield and Franklin Monfort, *Racial Change and Desegregation in Large School Districts: Trends through the 1986–1987 School Year* (Alexandria, Va.: National School Boards Association Council of Urban Boards of Education, 1988), table 1.

19. Between 1980 and 1988, enrollment in private elementary and secondary schools decreased by approximately 1.69 percent, while public enrollment fell about 1.77 percent (National Center for Education Statistics, *Digest of Education Statistics*, table 2).

20. The President's Commission on Privatization, for example, emphasized polls showing that, in 1986, 49 percent of parents with children in public schools said they would choose private or church-related schools if they had the financial means—up from 45 percent in 1982. Linowes, *Privatization*, 93.

21. Finn, *We Must Take Charge*, 67.

22. Linowes, *Privatization*, 85 (emphasis in original).

23. National Commission on Excellence in Education, *Nation at Risk*, 9.

24. Finn relates the Motorola and New York telephone examples (*We Must Take Charge*, 18–19). These and additional anecdotes can be found in Julie Amprano Lopez, "System Failure: Businesses Say Schools Are Producing Graduates Unqualified to Hold Jobs," *Wall Street Journal*, March 31, 1989; Mollie Rorner, "'Education Gap' Scares U.S. Chamber's Chief," *Richmond Times-Dispatch*, October 20, 1989; and Edward B. Fiske, "Impending U.S. Jobs 'Disaster': Work Force Unqualified to Work," *New York Times*, September 25, 1989.

25. "Businesses Teaching 3 Rs to Employees in Effort to Compete," *Wall Street Journal*, May 1, 1988.

26. Quoted in Kathleen Sylvester, "The Strange Romance of Business and the Schools," *Governing* (April 1991): 66.

27. Harris Education Research Center, *An Assessment of American Education: The View of Employers, Higher Educators, the Public, Recent Students, and Their Parents*, report sponsored by the Committee for Economic Development (New York: Louis Harris & Associates, 1991), tables 1, 4, 5.

28. Chubb and Moe, *Politics, Markets, and America's Schools*, 2.

29. Boyer, *High School*, 241–42.

30. Lawrence A. Cremin, *Popular Education and Its Discontents* (New York: Harper & Row, 1990), 12.

31. Michael B. Katz, *The Irony of Early School Reform* (Cambridge, Mass.: Harvard University Press, 1968); Joel Spring, *The American School, 1642–1985* (New York: Longman, 1986).

32. Cremin, *Popular Education and Its Discontents*, 15.

33. National Center for Education Statistics, *Digest of Education Statistics*, table 97. Rates dropped fairly consistently through the mid-1970s, rose incrementally in the late 1970s, and then declined to a low point of 12.2 percent in 1986.

34. The decision to use public institutions to monitor particular societal trends is itself an indirect indicator of collective priorities. It is partly because the nation set a clear goal of expanding educational attainment before it self-consciously addressed the achievement issue that a longer time-series of historical data exists.

35. Charles Murray and R. J. Herrnstein, "What's Really Behind the SAT-Score Decline?" *Public Interest* 106 (Winter 1992): 40 (emphasis in original). Murray and Herrnstein, it should be noted, are far from sanguine. They believe that this improve-

ment in results for the average student has been purchased with a decline in the quality of education provided to the elite cadre with the greatest academic potential. Even here, however, their data support a narrower claim than some have advanced. They find that the proportion of students scoring over 700 on the math SAT has rebounded "phenomenally" since the low point in 1981; this rebound, moreover, is not attributable to the increase in Asian-Americans taking the test, since it holds even when the scores of white students only are reviewed. Their concern focuses on the verbal portion of the SAT, for which they find a sharp drop in 700+ scores from 1967 to the mid-1970s that is not followed by a rebound. Their particular interpretation and policy recommendations are controversial and, I would suggest, problematic. They rest on the beliefs that the future health of the society depends most heavily on the intellectual elite, and that the proper training of this elite must emphasize the kinds of reasoning skills and knowledge base more directly related to the verbal than the mathematics exams. Whether or not they are correct in these two beliefs is less important for my argument here than is the idea (to which I believe they would also subscribe) that the priorities of public and political leaders have been just the reverse of this—emphasizing improvement for the average student over the elite student, and emphasizing mathematical skills (for their presumed relevance to scientific and technical applications) over the seemingly "softer" verbal skills. Their work, in that sense, provides further support for my general thesis that conventional mechanisms of democratic control and government implementation have led to improvement in precisely those areas that were collectively recognized as priorities.

36. In addition to being offered to a representative sample and including more substantive questions, the NAEP is a more tightly guarded test, reducing the opportunities for cheating and "teaching to the test." See Bracey, "Why Can't They Be Like We Were?" 108.

37. For seventeen-year-olds, a statistically significant decline occurred from 1970 through 1982, and a statistically significant increase followed through 1990. For thirteen-year-olds, the decline ran from 1970 to 1977, and a statistically significant increase occurred from 1977 to 1990. For nine-year-olds, the decline ended in 1973; after a level period, increases followed from 1977 through 1990. Figures are drawn from National Center for Education Statistics, *Trends in Academic Progress* (Washington, D.C.: U.S. Department of Education, 1991).

38. Seventeen-year-olds' scores declined between 1973 and 1982, while the scores of other age groups essentially were stable. For the oldest and youngest students, the recent increase began in 1982; for thirteen-year-olds it began in 1978.

39. Reading achievement increased significantly for nine-year-olds between 1971 and 1980 before falling back to earlier levels. Results for writing are only available for three test dates, beginning in 1984. Eighth-grade students showed a statistically significant decline from 1984 through 1990; scores for older and younger students showed a slight but statistically insignificant increase between 1984 and 1988, followed by a slight but statistically insignificant decline in 1990.

40. National Center for Educational Statistics, *Digest of Education Statistics*, table 8.

41. Calculated from ibid., table 119.

42. Calculated from National Center for Education Statistics, *Trends in Academic Progress*, summary report, figs. 2–4. For seventeen-year-olds, the reading, science, and math gaps decreased 42.3 percent, 17.2 percent, and 44.7 percent respectively. For nine-year-olds the comparable figures were 20.5 percent, 23.6 percent, and 15.6 percent. See also Robert L. Linn and Stephen B. Dunbar, "The Nation's Report Card Goes Home: Good News and Bad about Trends in Achievement," *Phi Delta Kappan* (October 1990).

43. Iris C. Rotberg, "What Test Scores Don't Measure," *Washington Post*, November 21, 1991. Rotberg's views are laid out more fully in "I Never Promised You First Place," Phi Delta Kappan (December 1990): 296–303, and "How Did All Those Dumb Kids Make All Those Smart Bombs?" *Phi Delta Kappan* (June 1991): 778–81. Norman Bradburn, Edward Haertel, John Schwille, and Judith Torney-Purta also respond to Rotberg's arguments in the June 1991 *Phi Delta Kappan*.

44. Rotberg, "What Test Scores Don't Measure,"

45. As evidence of the extent to which selective inclusion of regions and language groups potentially can alter rankings, consider this: in the 1988 assessment, English-speaking students from Canada's Quebec province came in fourth in math and science, while French-speaking students from Ontario province came in next to last in both exams (National Center for Education Statistics, *Digest of Education Statistics*, figs. 31 and 32). Because of the noncomparability problem, the Educational Testing Service, which conducted the study, chose not to rank the countries; the news media covering the release of the study were less inhibited.

46. In 1985, the United States spent 39.4 percent of its education dollars on higher education, versus 20.8 percent by West Germany and 21.4 percent by Japan (Michael W. Kirst, "The Need to Broaden Our Perspective Concerning America's Educational Attainment," *Phi Delta Kappan* [October 1991]: 199).

47. Ibid., 119.

48. Calculated from National Center for Education Statistics, *Digest of Education Statistics*, table 369.

49. Education Commission of the States, *Action for Excellence*.

50. National Center for Education Statistics, *Digest of Education Statistics*, table 128.

51. An exception is computer-science coursework. In 1982 public-school students took an average of 0.11 units, and private-school students took 0.08 units. In 1987, public-school students took an average of 0.43 units. Private-school students increased the units taken to 0.44 units. In foreign languages, science, mathematics, history/social studies, and English, public schools gained on private schools, although they still consistently lagged behind.

52. Stanley M. Elam, Lowell C. Rose, and Alec M. Gallup, "The Twenty-third Annual Gallup Poll of the Public's Attitudes toward the Public Schools," *Phi Delta Kappan* (September 1991): 54.

53. National Center for Education Statistics, *Digest of Education Statistics* 25 (table 17); 27 (table 19).

54. John W. Kingdon, *Agendas, Alternatives, and Public Policies* (Boston: Little, Brown, 1984), 181–93.

55. Robert B. Reich, *The Work of Nations* (New York: Alfred A. Knopf, 1991), 61.

56. Spring, *American School*, 281–96.

57. James Q. Wilson, "The Urban Unease: Community versus the City," *Public Interest* 12 (1968): 25–39.

58. Elam, Rose, and Gallup, "Twenty-third Annual Gallup Poll," 54–55.

59. Harris Education Research Center, "Assessment," tables 19, 20, 24, 27, 28.

60. The Internal Revenue Service is, perhaps, a competitor for this distinction.

61. Thomas Toch, *In the Name of Excellence* (New York: Oxford University Press, 1991), 17.

62. Education Commission of the States, *Action for Excellence*, 13.

63. Ibid., 19.

64. National Science Board Commission on Precollege Education in Mathematics, Science, and Technology, *Educating Americans for the Twenty-first Century* (Washington, D.C.: National Science Foundation, 1983), 20.

65. Ibid., v.

66. Finn, *We Must Take Charge*, 113. Finn cites John H. Bishop, "Is the Test Score Decline Responsible for the Productivity Growth Decline?" *American Economic Review* 79 (March 1989): 178–97, as the source for this estimate.

67. Bracey, "Why Can't They Be Like We Were?" 116.

68. Lester Thurow, "The Centennial Essay," *American School Board Journal* (September 1991): 41–43.

69. "Look at any natural resource you like, and you'll see a steep downward trend in use," Thurow declares (ibid., 42). Between 1960 and 1990, for example, the United States decreased its use of steel from 125 million to 85 million tons, even while the economy grew by 150 percent.

70. Ibid., 42.

71. Reich, *Work of Nations*, chap. 19.

72. Nor is it necessarily bad that we are living in a world in which economic opportunity is more widely dispersed.

73. Both Thurow and Reich argue as much.

74. Henig, *Public Policy and Federalism*, 140.

75. Edward Banfield, *The Unheavenly City Revisited*, 2d ed. (Boston: Little, Brown, 1974), 24. My acknowledgment of Banfield's perspicacity in recognizing the potential danger of misapplying the crisis label should not be mistaken for support for the specifics of his claim about improving conditions in the cities. For a discussion of the role that ideological premises played in the definition of the urban crisis, see Henig, *Public Policy and Federalism*, chap. 5.

76. Mancur Olson, *The Logic of Collective Action* (Cambridge, Mass.: Harvard University Press, 1965); Michael Lipsky, *Protest in City Politics* (Chicago: Rand McNally, 1970); David O'Brien, *Neighborhood Organizations and Interest-Group Processes* (Princeton, N.J.: Princeton University Press, 1975); Jeffrey R. Henig,

Neighborhood Mobilization: Redevelopment and Response (New Brunswick, N.J.: Rutgers University Press, 1982).

77. For an eloquent call for such a response, see Jonathan Kozol, *Savage Inequalities* (New York: Crown, 1991).

PART TWO
EVOLUTION OF AN IDEA

1. President George Bush often argued for choice; Bill Clinton, as governor of Arkansas and as a presidential candidate, made it clear that, while he also supported school choice, he opposed voucher plans that would include private schools.

2. According to the National Governors' Association, a bipartisan organization representing the governors of the fifty states, the Commonwealth of Puerto Rico, the Virgin Islands, Guam, and American Samoa, "choice, and the ensuing competition it will produce, is the force we need to ensure meaningful reform in education into the 1990s." National Governors' Association, *Time for Results*, 84.

3. Both the Reagan and Bush administrations featured choice as a facet of their national education policies. Representative Steve Bartlett, a Republican from Texas and a member of the Education and Labor subcommittee on elementary, secondary, and vocational education, labeled choice "the most potent education restructuring reform being discussed today," and concluded that "the idea works." Steve Bartlett, "Choice: The Most Effective Tool," *Roll Call*, May 21, 1990.

4. Among Democrats who have spoken favorably of educational choice are the former governor of Massachusetts and Democratic presidential nominee, Michael Dukakis, and President Bill Clinton. The Democratic governor of Minnesota, Rudy Perpich, writes that "choice is the key" to improving our schools (foreword to Nathan, *Public Schools by Choice*, 3.

5. Among the most prominent and vocal supporters are James Coleman of the University of Chicago; John Chubb of the Brookings Institution; Terry Moe of Stanford University; and Mary Anne Raywid of Hofstra University.

6. According to a 1990 Gallup poll on education, 62 percent of the American public is in favor of parental choice in public schools. Stanley M. Elam, "The Twenty-second Annual Gallup Poll of the Public's Attitudes toward the Public Schools," *Phi Delta Kappan* (September 1990): 44.

7. Among those in the education profession who have spoken out strongly for educational choice are Seymour Fliegel, a former teacher, principal, and deputy superintendent in the New York City public schools, and David Bennett, superintendent of schools in St. Paul, Minnesota. Even Albert Shanker, president of the American Federation of Teachers, has been a qualified supporter of public-school choice.

8. David T. Kearns, former chairman and chief executive officer of the Xerox Corporation, was a prominent private-sector spokesperson before being selected to become an assistant secretary of education in the Bush administration. Jerry Hume, chairman of the board of Basic American Foods, says "the most promising ap-

proaches to school reform are those that promote competition between schools and that come from providing parents a choice among schools" (U.S. Department of Education, *Choosing Better Schools: The Five Regional Meetings on Choice in Education* [Washington, D.C.: U.S. Department of Education, 1990], 2). Choice also is endorsed by the Committee for Economic Development, an organization whose membership includes many major business corporations; see *Our Children: Business and the Public Schools* (New York: Committee for Economic Development, 1985).

9. Wisconsin state legislator Polly Williams is a forceful speaker in favor of choice. (Milwaukee's school-choice policies, with which she is involved, are discussed further in chapter 5.) Robert Peterkin, who has served as superintendent in both Cambridge, Massachusetts, and Milwaukee, is a more cautious advocate. A 1990 Gallup poll indicated that support for choice among minorities was 72 percent (Elam, "Twenty-second Annual Gallup Poll").

10. Ann Lewis, "Public Schools Offer Vast Choices," *School Administrator* (September 1987): 8.

11. Chester E. Finn, then assistant secretary of education, quoted in Edward B. Fiske, "Parental Choice in Public Schools Gains," *New York Times*, July 11, 1988.

12. Savas, *Privatizing the Public Sector*, 81.

13. Kingdon, *Agendas, Alternatives, and Public Policies*.

CHAPTER THREE
APPLICATION OF THE MARKET MODEL

1. Not all school-choice proposals rest on the market analogy, however. In chap. 1, I discussed nonmarket perspectives and explained why they are significant.

2. See Milton Friedman, "The Role of Government in Education," in *Economics and the Public Interest*, ed. R. A. Solo (New Brunswick, N.J.: Rutgers University Press, 1955) and Milton Friedman, *Capitalism and Freedom* (Chicago: University of Chicago Press, 1962), chapter 6.

3. The role of "exit" in affecting the quality of goods and services provided by business and government is developed most fully by Albert O. Hirschman, *Exit, Voice, and Loyalty: Responses to Decline in Firms, Organizations, and States* (Cambridge, Mass.: Harvard University Press, 1970). For a direct application to education, see, for example, Savas, *Privatizing the Public Sector*, 137.

4. For an elaboration of this argument as it applies specifically to schools, see Lieberman, *Privatization and Educational Choice*, chap. 3.

5. On the emergence of Keynesian theories, see Peter A. Hall, ed. *The Political Power of Economic Ideas*. (Princeton, N.J.: Princeton University Press, 1989).

6. This follows from economists' conventional assumption that individuals are motivated by self-interest.

7. Olson, *Logic of Collective Action*.

8. Friedman, *Capitalism and Freedom*, 86.

9. Ibid., 87.

10. Ibid., 89.

11. Thus, farmers became an important constituency seeking to protect and expand the food-stamp program; the medical community, likewise, came around to supporting Medicare and Medicaid.

12. The formal name for the program was the Servicemen's Readjustment Act.

13. Friedman acknowledged that Virginia's plan, which was "adopted for the purpose of avoiding compulsory integration," had "many features in common" with his own. And he explicitly ruled out requiring racial integration as a criterion for a school to be eligible to take part in a voucher plan. But he argued that choice and vouchers would facilitate integration in the long run (*Capitalism and Freedom*, 118). The Southern states' reliance on vouchers and freedom of choice as a means of resisting racial integration is discussed more fully in chap. 5.

14. Writing about the British experience, Arthur Seldon speculates that the entire history of the bureaucratization of that nation's schools might have been different if the minister of education in 1955 "had been advised by his officials, scouring the world for new thinking in education, that an idea to transfer influence from the top to the bottom of the political pyramid had been launched that very year by a relatively little-known economist at the University of Chicago" (*The Riddle of the Voucher* [London: Institute of Economic Affairs, 1986], 12).

15. Indeed, none of the five 1963 reviews of *Capitalism and Freedom* that I tracked down mentioned the voucher proposal, and none devoted more than a single sentence to Friedman's views on education. An eight-paragraph review in the *Annals of the American Academy* gives education its most sustained attention: it mentions Friedman's orientation toward public schools in a single sentence ("According to his own listing, the author would gradually do away with the public operation of secondary schools, and substitute institutions run by private enterprise for profit") and does not specifically mention the voucher idea at all. A 1963 review in the *American Sociological Review* notes Friedman's views on education briefly, in this case simply listing his belief that there is insufficient justification for "the present extent and character of public school systems" as one of several examples of his challenge to the state's role. In a long review in the 1963 *Journal of Political Economy*, Paul A. Baran, similarly, alludes to education in a single clause. A seven-paragraph review in *Business History Review* groups his school proposals along with those for roads, mail service, and parks in a single sentence. And the *Economist* makes no mention of education or schools at all.

16. In the United States, early support for vouchers came from such sources as University of Chicago sociologist James Coleman, Harvard University sociologist Christopher Jencks, and University of California law professors John Coons and Stephen Sugarman. In Great Britain, early proponents included economics professors Alan Peacock and Jack Wiseman.

17. See, for example, Virgil C. Blum, S.J., *Freedom of Choice in Education* (New York: Macmillan, 1958). Not all supporters of parochial schools have favored vouchers, however; some have opposed them out of concern that government financing would open the door to government intervention.

18. In Great Britain, an early intellectual home for the education-voucher idea was found in the market-oriented Institute for Economic Affairs, founded in 1957.

19. George La Noue, "The Politics of Education," *Teachers College Record* 73, no. 2 (1971): 304–19. The article is reprinted in *Educational Vouchers: Concepts and Controversies*, ed. George R. La Noue (New York: Teachers College Press,1972), where the quoted line appears on page 138.

20. Christopher Jencks, "Is the Public School Obsolete?" *Public Interest* (Winter 1966).

21. The voucher proposal promoted by Jencks and the OEO differed from that of Friedman in important respects. Jencks proposed a highly regulated voucher system, which called upon government to take a number of steps intended to protect minorities from discrimination and to narrow the advantages enjoyed by children of wealthier families. Government was expected to provide poor children with vouchers for as much as twice the amount offered to middle-income families, require that participating schools accept the vouchers as full payment, require schools to accept any applicant as long as space was available and to allocate at least half the available slots randomly when space was not available, establish procedures for overseeing how participating schools spent their voucher money, and the like. See Christopher Jencks, *Education Vouchers: A Report on Financing Education by Payments to Parents* (Cambridge, Mass.: Center for the Study of Public Policy, 1970). The theoretical and practical distinctions between a voucher plan that explicitly acknowledges the need for strong, authoritative, and ongoing government oversight and responsibility and one—like Friedman's—anchored in a theory that disparages the capacity of government to act wisely or in the public interest are much sharper and much more consequential than contemporary debate reflects.

22. Friedman's position on the issue of redistribution comes through much more forcefully in his later book, *Free to Choose* (New York: Avon Books, 1980) (written with Rose Friedman) than in *Capitalism and Freedom*. He is explicit, in the earlier book, that parents should be allowed to add on to vouchers (89), and alludes more indirectly to different districts funding different voucher amounts (98). In the later book, he rails against the "egalitarian religion," at the same time insisting that his proposal will be more egalitarian than current educational arrangements *in effect*, if not necessarily in form (158).

23. Judith Arren and Christopher Jencks, "Education Vouchers: A Proposal for Diversity and Choice," in La Noue, *Educational Vouchers*, 53.

24. Ibid., 54.

25. Theodore R. Sizer, "The Case for a Free Market," originally published in *Saturday Review*, January 11, 1969; reprinted in *Education Vouchers: From Theory*

to Alum Rock, ed. James A. Mecklenburger and Richard W. Hostrop (Homewood, Ill.: ETC Publications, 1972), 30.

26. Testimony before the Committee on Education and Labor, April 2, 1971.

27. *Nation's Schools* (January 1971).

28. *American School Board Journal* (July 1971); results reprinted in Mecklenburger and Hostrop, *Education Vouchers*, 57.

29. John L. Puckett, "Educational Vouchers: Rhetoric and Reality," *Educational Forum* 47, no. 4 (Summer 1983): 467–92.

30. The OEO proposed to pick up the cost for any private-school students who would participate in the voucher experiment, and any additional transportation costs incurred by the participating school districts.

31. For the story of Alum Rock, see, for example, Mecklenburger and Hostrop, *Education Vouchers*, part 3; Puckett, "Educational Vouchers"; and David K. Cohen and Eleanor Farrar, "Power to the Parents? The Story of Education Vouchers," *Public Interest* 48 (Summer 1977): 72–97. The evidence about the results of the Alum Rock experiment, and the use of those findings to support the choice argument, will be discussed in chap. 6.

32. Puckett, "Educational Vouchers," 485. The full story of the state's flirtation with vouchers is found in Gordon A. Donaldson, Jr., *Educational Vouchers in New Hampshire: An Attempt at Free Market Reform* (Newton, Mass.: C.M. Leinwand Associates, 1977).

33. Laura Hersh Salganik, "The Fall and Rise of Education Vouchers," *Teachers College Record* 83, no. 2 (1981): 263–83.

34. In Great Britain, similarly, discussion of vouchers among intellectuals gradually expanded into political pressure for government action, which in turn seemed to fizzle out, at least until recently. The Friends of the Education Voucher Experiment in Representative Regions (FEVER) was formed in December 1974 to campaign for vouchers. Its efforts culminated five years later in the presentation to the secretary of state for education of a national petition for a voucher system. In the face of intense opposition from the teachers' union, however, the relevant cabinet minister announced to the Conservative party conference in October 1983 that the voucher idea was "dead" (Seldon, *Riddle of the Voucher*, 15). As in the United States, declarations of the death of vouchers in Great Britain may prove to have been premature. By 1988, efforts to increase student choice were clearly growing again in Great Britain. John E. Chubb and Terry M. Moe portray this as a seamless continuation of the efforts begun in the early 1970s. See *Lessons in School Reform from Great Britain* (Washington, D.C.: Brookings Institution, 1992), 34.

35. See E. G. West, "Tom Paine's Voucher Scheme for Public Education," *Southern Economic Journal* 33 (1966–67): 378.

36. For a recent compilation, see *Problems Concerning Education Voucher Proposals and Issues Related to Choice*, prepared for the Subcommittee on Elementary, Secondary, and Vocational Education of the Committee on Education and Labor, U.S. House of Representatives, 101st Cong., September 1990.

37. National Center for Education Statistics, *Private Schools in the United States: A Statistical Profile, with Comparisons to Public Schools* (Washington, D.C.: U.S. Department of Education, Office of Educational Research and Improvement, 1991).

38. The discussion in the next several paragraphs follows closely that presented in Henig, *Public Policy and Federalism*, 330.

39. David Selden, "Vouchers—Solution or Sop?" *Teachers College Record* 72, (1971: 365–72).

40. Peter Woll, *Constitutional Law: Cases and Comments* (Englewood, N.J.: Prentice-Hall, 1981).

41. Major cases establishing the Supreme Court's position on this issue include *Everson v. Board of Education*, 330 U.S. 1 (1947), *Board of Education v. Allen*, 392 U.S. 236 (1968), *Lemon v. Kurtzman*, 403 U.S. 602 (1971), *Committee for Public Education v. Nyquist*, 37 L.Ed.2d 948 (1973), and *Mueller v. Allen*, 463 U.S. 388 (1983).

42. Joseph E. Bryson and Samuel H. Houston, *The Supreme Court and Public Funds for Religious Schools: The Burger Years, 1969–1986* (Jefferson, N.C.: McFarland, 1990), 137.

43. Cohen and Farrar, "Power to the Parents?" 81.

44. Quoted in the *American School Board Journal* (October 1970), and reprinted in Mecklenburger and Hostrop, *Education Vouchers*, 76.

45. Mario D. Fantini, *Public Schools of Choice* (New York: Simon & Schuster, 1973), 20. He made this general argument even earlier; see *The Reform of the Public Schools* (Washington, D.C.: National Education Association, 1970).

46. Edward B. Fiske, "Reagan Agenda: Taking a New Tack," *New York Times* January 27, 1988.

47. For a review of the early Reagan years, see John L. Palmer and Isabel V. Sawhill, eds, *The Reagan Experiment* (Washington, D.C.: Urban Institute Press, 1982).

48. Leslie Maitland Werner, "Administration Drafts Third Plan for School Vouchers," *New York Times*, December 1, 1986.

49. Ibid.

50. Lee A. Daniels, "Efforts to Allow Choice of Schools Stir Debate," *New York Times*, January 11, 1989.

51. Jerry Hume, chairman of the board, Basic American Foods, quoted in U.S. Department of Education, *Choosing Better Schools*, 2.

52. Bartlett, "Choice," 23.

53. Quoted in William Snider, "The Call for Choice: Competition in the Educational Marketplace," *Education Week* June 24, 1987.

54. It was not until 1970 that the *Readers' Guide to Periodical Literature* included a separate heading for education vouchers and not until 1986 that it included a heading for school choice. Aside from those two subheads, all article titles listed under "education," "federal aid to education," and "Milton Friedman" were examined. Only titles explicitly referring to choice, vouchers, or market forces in educa-

tion were counted. This means that some articles relating to tax credits and aid to parochial schools were not included, although a substantive reading of such articles undoubtedly would have revealed much within them that relates to the school-choice issue.

55. The literature on contracting out is extensive. Early and influential studies include Savas, *Privatizing the Public Sector*, and Roger S. Ahlbrandt, Jr., *Municipal Fire Protection Services: Comparison of Alternative Organizational Forms* (Beverly Hills, Calif.: Sage, 1973). For a more recent review of the relevant evidence, see Donahue, *Privatization Decision*.

56. David W. Kirkpatrick, *Choice in Schooling: A Case for Tuition Vouchers* (Chicago: Loyola University Press, 1990), chap. 12.

57. Linda L. M. Bennett and Stephen Earl Bennett, *Living with Leviathan: Americans Coming to Terms with Big Government* (Lawrence, Kans.: University of Kansas Press, 1990): 134–35.

58. Ibid., 31–32.

59. Elam, Rose, and Gallup, "Twenty-third Annual Gallup Poll," 41–56. Eighty percent thought "the amount of money allocated to public education in this state from all sources should be the same for all students regardless of whether they live in wealthy or poor school districts"; 62 percent favored court action to equalize expenditures. Fifty-five percent (versus 40 percent) favored publicly supported preschool programs. Sixty-eight percent (versus 24 percent) favored requiring schools in their community to use a national curriculum.

CHAPTER FOUR
REPACKAGING CHOICE

1. Albert Shanker, "Choice Plans Can Bolster Public Schools, But It's No Educational Cure-all," paid advertisement in the *New York Times* (emphasis in original).

2. This experience is discussed at length in chap. 5.

3. Reagan vetoed the Civil Rights Act of 1987, which sought to negate a 1984 Supreme Court ruling (*Grove City College v. Bill*) that had the effect of undermining the government's ability to deny funds to private institutions that discriminate against minorities, the elderly, or women. This veto helped mobilize the civil-rights community, and the House overrode the veto.

4. Linowes, *Privatization*, 96.

5. Charles Murray's *Losing Ground: American Social Policy, 1950–1980* (New York: Basic Books, 1984) was perhaps the most widely read and discussed articulation of the neoconservative viewpoint. Other writers, such as Daniel Bell, Nathan Glazer, and Irving Kristol, earlier laid the intellectual foundations for neoconservatism. Peter Steinfels provides a good overview in *The Neoconservatives: The Men Who Are Changing America's Politics* (New York: Simon & Schuster, 1979). See also Henig, *Public Policy & Federalism*.

6. Murray, *Losing Ground*, 16.

7. Bryan T. Downes, "A Critical Reexamination of the Social and Political Characteristics of Riot Cities," *Social Science Quarterly* (September 1970), estimates there were 329 important riots in 257 cities between 1964 and 1968.

8. Murray, *Losing Ground*, 33 (emphasis in original).

9. Murray borrowed from economists the assumption that individuals are essentially self-interested, rational, calculating beings who seek to obtain the greatest satisfaction at the lowest possible cost. The kinds of behavior that are necessary to pursue economic success responsibly—studying hard, doing homework, saving money—are unpleasant in themselves; rational individuals engage in these behaviors only if they are convinced they will be better off if they do.

10. Murray, *Losing Ground*, 173.

11. Murray writes, "Pushing hard for academic achievement in schools with a mix of blacks and whites led to embarrassment and protests when the white children always seemed to end up winning the academic awards and getting the best grades and scoring highest on the tests. Pushing hard for academic achievement in predominantly black urban schools led to intense resentment by the students and occasionally by parents and the community" (ibid., 174–75).

12. Murray's claim that black progress did begin to decline at this time is highly questionable. There was no reliable time-series data, disaggregated by race, that could allow Murray to assess trends of this sort when he wrote the book. Admitting this, Murray compares the results of different types of tests taken by different categories of test-takers at different times. He presents the relatively poor performance of black students on the 1980 SATs as indicating a decline. While black scores were 68 percent as high as white scores on one set of tests given in 1960 and roughly 79 percent as high as white scores on a different test in 1965, Murray implies that blacks did nearly *seven times worse* than whites on the 1980 SATs. This implication derives from his unexplained decision to emphasize the percentage of test-takers scoring below a fixed point, rather than average scores, as he had for the earlier years. "Whereas only 3.5 percent of white test-takers scored less than 300, fully a quarter— 25.0 percent—of black test-takers scored in that category" (106). What Murray does not explicitly note, but what can be gleaned from the data he provides, is that the average performance of blacks on that 1980 SAT was similar to the 1965 ratio: 74.7 percent as high as white scores on both the verbal and math exams. And the much better data we have now suggests that blacks continued to make incremental progress in subsequent years.

13. Recounted in "President Reagan's Report Card," *New Republic*, November 7, 1983, 10.

14. Ibid.

15. Mary Anne Raywid, "Excellence and Choice: Friends or Foes?" *Urban Review* 19, no. 1 (1987): 35–47.

16. Raywid, "Family Choice Arrangements," 449.

17. Amy Stuart Wells, "Once a Desegregation Tool, Magnet School Becoming School of Choice," *New York Times*, January 9, 1991.

18. For a good overview of New Federalism, see Timothy Conlan, *New Federalism: Intergovernmental Reform and Political Change from Nixon to Reagan* (Washington, D.C.: Brookings Institution, 1988).

19. David Osborne, *Laboratories of Democracy* (Boston, Mass.: Harvard Business School Press, 1988).

20. For enthusiastic overviews of this literature, see Poole, *Cutting Back City Hall*, Savas, *Privatizing the Public Sector*, and Linowes, *Privatization*. For a more balanced assessment of much the same body of literature, see Donahue, *Privatization Decision*.

21. Marc Bendick, Jr., "Privatizing the Delivery of Social Welfare Services: An Idea to Be Taken Seriously," in Kamerman and Kahn, *Privatization and the Welfare State*, 107.

22. This included the replacement of categorical grants with a smaller number of block grants, giving states added discretion about how to use federal funds.

23. Conlan, *New Federalism*, 166.

24. Early in the Reagan administration, Secretary of the Interior James Watt stirred controversy with his proposals to sell off large segments of the nation's publicly held land. The President's Commission on Privatization proposed selling public housing, the U.S. Postal Service, AMTRAK, and the Navy's petroleum reserves.

25. Henig, "Privatization in the United States."

26. Chubb and Moe, *Politics, Markets, and America's Schools*. Brookings did not quietly release the book with an implicit imprimatur; it organized a major event to which it invited members of the press, education professionals, scholars, and activists.

27. Ibid., 219.

28. Ibid., 217–18.

29. Ibid., 219.

30. Ibid., 220.

31. Chubb and Moe do not consider whether such redistributory provisions are politically attainable or sustainable. This is a critical shortcoming, especially if—as I believe—adoption of the Chubb and Moe proposals would have the likely effect of weakening the political constituency that currently might support such provisions.

32. Steven V. Roberts, "Education Pledge Renewed by Bush," *New York Times*, January 19, 1989.

33. Quoted in Albert Shanker, "A Very Hard Sell: Bush Makes the Pitch for Vouchers," *New York Times*, January 19, 1992.

34. Neil R. Pierce, "School Choice Takes Careful Crafting," *National Journal*, November 3, 1990.

35. Lauro F. Cavazos, "Remarks Prepared for the Choice in Education Press Conference," Tuesday, December 4, 1990. The Milwaukee experiment is discussed in some detail below.

36. Harold Howe II, "America 2000: A Bumpy Ride on Four Trains," *Phi Delta Kappan* (November 1991): 194.

37. U.S. Department of Education, *America 2000*, 41.

38. Kenneth Cooper, "School-Choice Idea Backed Anew by Bush," *Washington Post*, January 26, 1992.

39. Andrew Rosenthal, "In a Speech, President Returns to Religious Themes," *New York Times*, January 28, 1992.

40. "Fact Sheet" distributed by the White House Office of the Press Secretary, June 25, 1992.

41. Joint Economic Committee, "A Cost-Benefit Analysis of Government Investment in Post-Secondary Education under the World War II GI Bill," staff analysis prepared for the use of the Subcommittee on Education and Health of the Joint Economic Committee, December 14, 1988.

42. Department of Veterans Affairs, "Veterans Benefits under Current Educational Programs, Fiscal Year 1989," report prepared by the Office of Planning and Management Analysis.

43. The precise mix of schools mentioned sometimes was varied to take into account the speaker's audience. Thus, when in Michigan, Alexander replaced the reference to the University of Pennsylvania with the University of Michigan. See "Secretary Lamar Alexander on Choice in Education," U.S. Department of Education Center for Choice in Education, June 19, 1992, 1–5. Also see "President Bush on Education," U.S. Department of Education Center for Choice in Education, September 23, 1992, 2–4.

44. The Minnesota tax deduction could be claimed for tuition or for textbooks and transportation costs. That it allowed those deductions to all parents, not just those with children attending private or religious schools, proved important to Justice Rehnquist's reasoning in the majority report (*Mueller v. Allen*, 463 U.S. 388 [1983]. See the discussion in Bryson and Houston, *Supreme Court*, 107–13. Bryson and Houston characterize the *Mueller* decision as "the most important Supreme Court public-education decision since Brown I."

45. In large cities, applying this cutoff would leave over 60 percent of families eligible. For example, the administration estimated that about 65 percent of students in Indianapolis, about 67 percent in Milwaukee, and about 61 percent in San Jose would qualify. U.S. Department of Education, Office of Intergovernmental and Interagency Affairs, "Q. and A.: State and Local GI Bills for Children," June 23, 1992, 5.

46. Ironically, in light of its general stance that "throwing money" at the schools was not required in order to stimulate reform, in attempting to sell the program to local school districts the Bush administration emphasized the tremendous increase in federal support that grantees might receive. Local officials and residents in Milwaukee were told that almost twice as much funding as was currently provided by the U.S. Department of Education would be injected into the district if it was selected as a grantee. The estimate for Indianapolis was more than three times the current funding, and for San Jose almost six times. Ibid., 5.

47. Chubb and Moe, *Politics, Markets, and America's Schools*, 219.

48. Chubb and Moe presume that religious schools would have to keep their sec-

tarian functions separate from their educational functions in order to meet legal objections. Ibid., 219.

49. Ibid., 225.

50. Jencks told the Senate Select Committee on Equal Educational Opportunity that "a lot of our thinking about the voucher system is based on an attempt to rethink the question of where the line between public and private should be drawn." He favored calling a school "'public' if it were open to everyone on a nondiscriminatory basis, if it charged no tuition, and if it provided full information about itself to anyone interested." See Mecklenburger and Hostrop, *Education Vouchers*, 112–13.

51. Cooper, "School-Choice Idea."

52. This was not so clearly the case with Jencks's notions. As he envisioned the application of his criteria, many existing private and public schools were too discriminatory, too secretive, too economically restrictive to earn the label "public."

53. Chubb and Moe, *Politics, Markets, and America's Schools*, 218.

54. Henig, "Privatization in the United States."

55. For an extended discussion of the manner in which a view of an apolitical public interest influenced the thinking of the "common school" reformers of the 1830s and 1840s and the turn-of-the-century Progressive reformers, see Jeffrey R. Henig, "Ideas and Interests in Educational Reform," presented at the annual meeting of the American Political Science Association, Atlanta, September 2, 1989.

56. Classic statements of the pluralist position include Arthur F. Bentley, *The Process of Government* (Chicago: University of Chicago Press, 1908); David Truman, The Governmental Process (New York: Alfred A. Knopf, 1971); Robert Dahl, *Who Governs?* (New Haven: Yale University Press, 1961); and Nelson Polsby, *Community Power and Political Theory* (New Haven: Yale University Press, 1963).

57. For example, James Buchanan and Gordon Tullock, *The Calculus of Consent: Logical Foundations of Constitutional Democracy* (Ann Arbor: University of Michigan Press, 1962); *Logic of Collective Action*; and Gordon Tullock, *Politics of Bureaucracy* (Washington, D.C.: Public Affairs Press, 1965). Some more contemporary applications of this perspective include James T. Bennet and Manuel H. Johnson, *Better Government at Half the Price* (Ottawa, Ill.: Caroline House, 1981); Thomas E. Borcherding, ed., *Budgets and Bureaucrats: The Sources of Government Growth* (Durham, N.C.: Duke University Press, 1977); and Savas, *Privatizing the Public Sector*.

58. Chubb and Moe, *Politics, Markets, and America's Schools*, 30.

CHAPTER FIVE
EVOLVING PRACTICE: PROBLEMATIC LESSONS
FROM HISTORY

1. The two decisions—commonly referred to as *Brown I* and *Brown II*—are *Brown v. Board of Education*, 347 U.S. 483 (1954), and *Brown v. Board of Education*, 349 U.S. 2994 (1955).

2. Benjamin Muse, *Ten Years of Prelude* (New York: Viking, 1964), 20. The discus-

sion of the Southern response to *Brown* also draws on such valuable sources as Benjamin Muse, *Virginia's Massive Resistance* (Bloomington: University of Indiana Press, 1961); Robbins L. Gates, *The Making of Massive Resistance* (Chapel Hill: University of North Carolina Press, 1964); Bob Smith, *They Closed Their Schools* (Chapel Hill: University of North Carolina Press, 1965); Gary Orfield, *The Reconstruction of Southern Education* (New York: John Wiley & Sons, 1969); and David L. Kirp and Mark G. Yudof, eds., *Educational Policy and the Law* (Berkeley: McCutchan, 1974).

3. Muse, *Ten Years*, 24.

4. Ibid., 65.

5. Orfield, *Reconstruction*, 17–18.

6. Robert Crain et al., *The Politics of School Desegregation* (New York: Anchor Books, 1969), 259.

7. In September 1958, Virginia's governor, J. Lindsay Almond, acted on the provision, ordering the compulsory closure of the Warren County High School just hours after a Friday afternoon federal court ruling that would have integrated the school the following Monday. Muse, *Ten Years*, 151–52.

8. Kirp and Yudof, *Educational Policy and the Law*, 307.

9. Ibid., 310.

10. Orfield, *Reconstruction*, 121; Raymond Wolters, *The Burden of Brown* (Knoxville: University of Tennessee Press, 1984), 151. See also note 5 of *Green v. County School Board*, 391 U.S. 430 (1968), in which the U.S. commissioner on civil rights indicates that "during the past school year [1966–67], as in the previous year, in some areas of the South, Negro families with children attending previously all-white schools under free choice plans were targets of violence, threats of violence and economic reprisal by white persons and Negro children were subjected to harassment by white classmates notwithstanding conscientious efforts by many teachers and principals to prevent such misconduct."

11. *Goss v. Board of Education*, 373 U.S. 683 (1963), at 687.

12. Orfield, *Reconstruction*, 120.

13. Muse, *Ten Years*, 24.

14. Ibid., 186.

15. During the first year that the schools were closed, as many as sixty-eight black students went to school at an African Methodist Episcopal college located in North Carolina. But most received little or no education. Special training centers were established, but these had limited academic offerings, and suffered sharp declines in attendance from year to year. Special crash courses were offered to volunteers during the summers, and the American Friends Service Committee organized a program to send sixty-seven children to live with northern families and attend school there. Others attended school in neighboring counties. Of about seventeen hundred black children, however, an estimated eleven hundred had virtually no formal education during the period in which the schools were closed. Smith, *They Closed Their Schools*, 170, 251–55.

16. *Griffin v. County School Board of Prince Edward County*, 377 U.S. 218 (1964).

17. Smith, *They Closed Their Schools*, 186.

18. Orfield, *Reconstruction*, 235.

19. In *Lee v. Macon County*, 267 F. Supp. 458 (1967), the Court found that Alabama was trying "to support a separate and private school system for white students," and noted, moreover, that the governor had "officially encouraged private contributions to support the many private schools throughout the state as alternatives to the public desegregated school system." In *Poindexter v. Louisiana Financial Assistance Commission*, 275 F. Supp. 833 (1967), the federal district court noted that forty-four of the sixty private schools for white children in Louisiana had been formed after desegregation of the public schools began in 1960, and concluded that "the State is so significantly involved in the discrimination practiced by the private schools in Louisiana that any financial aid from the State to these schools or newly organized schools in the form of tuition grants or similar benefits violates the equal protection clause of the Fourteenth Amendment."

20. *Green v. County School Board*, 391 U.S. 430 (1968).

21. *Poindexter v. Louisiana Financial Assistance Commission*, 275 F. Supp. 833 (1967).

22. Michele L. Norris, "In Line for P.G. Magnet Schools, No Margin for Mercy," *Washington Post*, March 17, 1989.

23. Leah Y. Latimer, "Suitland Bursts with Pride over Reagan's Visit," *Washington Post*, January 21, 1988.

24. Donald R. Waldrip, "Alternative Programs in Cincinnati; or 'What Did You Learn on the River Today?'" in *The Future of Big-City Schools*, ed. Daniel U. Levine and Robert J. Havighurst (Berkeley: McCutchan, 1977), 97.

25. Daniel J. Monti, *A Semblance of Justice: St. Louis School Desegregation and Order in Urban America* (Columbia: University of Missouri Press, 1985), 140–41.

26. Rolf K. Blank, Robert A. Dentler, D. Catherine Baltzell, and Kent Chabotar, *Survey of Magnet Schools: Analyzing a Model for Quality Integrated Education*, final report prepared by James H. Lowry and Associates for the Office of Planning Budget, and Evaluation, U.S. Department of Education, September 30, 1983, appendix 3.

27. Daniel U. Levine and Connie Campbell, "Developing and Implementing Big-City Magnet School Programs," in Levine and Havighurst, *Future of Big-City Schools*, 247.

28. Blank et al., *Survey of Magnet Schools*.

29. Smith, Barr, and Burke, *Alternatives in Education*, 36–37.

30. Nicholas Lemann, "Magnetic Attraction: Magnet Schools' Unfulfilled Potential," *New Republic*, April 13, 1987.

31. See Gary Orfield, *Must We Bus?* (Washington, D.C.: Brookings Institution, 1978), 140.

32. Robert A. Dentler, "The Boston School Desegregation Plan," in *School Desegregation Plans that Work*, ed. Charles Vert Willie (Westport, Conn.: Greenwood Press, 1984), 64.

33. The parents brought suit in March 1972 (the same month that the Boston suit was filed), and in December of that year U.S. District Court Judge Frank A. Kaufman ordered implementation of a mandatory busing plan. At that time, black students made up just about one-quarter of the county's public-school enrollment. Nine years later the parents asked that the case be reopened; schools remained segregated, they said. In September 1983, Judge Kaufman issued new desegregation guidelines that would have required that the county ensure that no school had black enrollment less than 10 percent or greater than 80 percent. Efforts to overturn that decision eventually failed, and in the spring of 1985 the board finally offered a new plan of its own; it proposed instituting thirty magnet schools as a way to eliminate the need for massive mandatory busing. By then black enrollment had reached about 60 percent. That same year, the board hired John A. Murphy as superintendent; Murphy built a national reputation in part through his aggressive efforts to make the magnet plan work. Michele L. Norris, "P.G. Not Alone with Racial Trends Hurting Magnet Strategy," *Washington Post*, January 25, 1990. See also Sarah Glazer, "Magnet Schools," *Editorial Research Reports* (Washington, D.C.: Congressional Quarterly, 1987).

34. Charles V. Willie, "Desegregation in Big-City School Systems," *Educational Forum* 47, no. 1 (Fall 1982): 83–96.

35. Olson, *Logic of Collective Action*.

36. For example, the Ford Foundation provided some of the initial support for Berkeley's "alternative schools," which Mario Fantini calls the first effort to launch a full-scale version of public schools of choice. Fantini, *Public Schools of Choice*, chap. 4.

37. Blank et al., *Survey of Magnet Schools*.

38. Cambridge is a predominantly white (80 percent) city of just under one hundred thousand people. Although the minority population in the city is relatively small, it has been growing rapidly as a proportion of public-school students. Between 1982 and 1990, the Asian population attending the district's public schools increased by 76.5 percent, the Hispanic population increased 30.6 percent, and the black population grew 15 percent. Of the approximately seventy-five hundred students attending the thirteen public elementary schools and one public high school in the 1989–90 school year, 50 percent were white. See Norma Tan, *The Cambridge Controlled Choice Program: Improving Educational Equity and Integration* (New York: Center for Educational Innovation, Manhattan Institute, 1990).

The demographic characteristics of Montclair, New Jersey, located about twelve miles from New York City, are quite similar to those of Cambridge. Its median income is about 133 percent of that for all of New Jersey, and approximately 40 percent of its adult residents have college degrees. The black population for the city as a whole increased 29 percent in 1980, but the black population in the public schools was 45 percent. By 1988, 49 percent of the public-school enrollment was black. Beatriz C. Clewell and Myra F. Joy, *Choice in Montclair, New Jersey* (Princeton, N.J.: Educational Testing Service, 1990), 5.

39. The community districts were established in 1970, as part of an effort to decentralize the administration of the city's schools. The central administration delegates to each of the thirty-two districts certain responsibilities for hiring staff and managing budgets in elementary and junior high schools.

40. This discussion draws on Sy Fliegel, "Parental Choice in East Harlem Schools," in Nathan, *Public Schools by Choice*, 95–112.

41. Susan Chira, "The Rules of the Marketplace Are Applied to the Classroom," *New York Times*, June 12, 1991.

42. The two organizations are the Twin Cities Citizens League, a policy-research organization funded by business and the Minnesota Business Partnership, which represents the eighty largest corporations in the state.

43. This discussion draws primarily on Ross Corson, "Choice Ironies: Open Enrollment in Minnesota," *American Prospect* (Fall 1990); Tim L. Mazzoni, "Analyzing State School Policymaking: An Arena Model," *Educational Evaluation and Policy Analysis* 13, no. 2 (Summer 1991): 115–38; Jessie Montano, "Choice Comes to Minnesota," in Nathan, *Public Schools by Choice*, 165–80; and Michael C. Rubenstein, Rosalind Hamar, and Nancy E. Adelman, *Minnesota's Open Enrollment Option* (Washington, D.C.: Policy Studies Associates, 1992).

44. This exception applies only to districts with state-approved desegregation plans (Minneapolis, St. Paul, and Duluth). Rubenstein, Hamar, and Adelman, *Minnesota's Open Enrollment Option*, 3.

45. Ibid., 3.

46. The state legislature provided that funds would be available to reimburse transportation expenses incurred by families falling below the federal poverty level. Only nineteen families applied for this reimbursement in 1990–1991. (ibid., 31 n. 2). It is not clear whether this reflects the unwillingness or incapacity of the poor to take part in the program, or a failure on the part of public officials to inform parents adequately about this option.

47. William Snider, "'Choice' Proposals Make Headway in Statehouses in 1990," *Education Week*, September, 5, 1990.

48. The amount is the equivalent of the per-student state aid normally provided to the public-school district. Most of the information in this paragraph is drawn from John Witte, "First Year Report, Milwaukee Parental Choice Program," report submitted to the Department of Public Instruction, November 1991.

49. Students' families' incomes must not exceed one and three-quarters times the national poverty level. Using the 1 percent of enrollment standard, about 980 students could have been funded in the 1990–91 school year.

50. *Newsweek*, May 27, 1991, 60.

51. Ben Wildavsky, "Hero of Choice," *New Republic*, October 22, 1990, 14.

52. Witte, "First Year Report," 3.

53. Jennifer L. Hochschild, *The New American Dilemma: Liberal Democracy and School Desegregation* (New Haven: Yale University Press, 1984). Hochschild credits

Gunnar Myrdal with providing the most important statement of this thesis. "The Negro problem in America represents a moral lag in the development of the nation," he wrote in *An American Dilemma* in 1944. But he also saw hopeful signs to "antici-pate fundamental changes in American race relations, changes which will involve a development toward the American ideals" (1).

54. Ibid., 203.

55. The results of nearly twenty surveys addressing choice in education are re-viewed in Center for Choice in Education "Public Opinion on Choice and Educa-tion," prepared by the Office of Intergovernmental and Interagency Affairs, U.S. Department of Education, March 18, 1992. Many of these surveys disaggregate by race, but none is designed to distinguish class, educational, or generational differ-ences within the minority community. My inference from the overall patterns is that support appears to be greater among blacks in large cities, lower-income blacks, and younger blacks who did not directly experience the civil-rights movement and its emphasis on integration.

56. Quoted in Wildavsky, "Hero of Choice," 22. Wildavsky considers the implica-tions of Williams's association with Milwaukee alderman Michael McGee, who has been charged with advocating the violent overthrow of the U.S. government. See also Mark Lawrence Ragan, "An Enigma Fights for School Choice," *Insight*, August 26, 1991.

57. National Center for Education Statistics, *Digest of Education Statistics*, table 43. Figures were from fall 1986 enrollments. The states with smaller minority popu-lations were Vermont, Maine, New Hampshire, West Virginia, and Iowa. Minne-sota's 93.9 percent white enrollment compared to 70.4 percent for the nation as a whole.

CHAPTER SIX
USES OF EVIDENCE: THE EMPIRICAL CASE THAT "CHOICE WORKS"

1. Carol F. Steinbach, "Public Schools 'Choice' Gathering Momentum," *National Journal*, January 26, 1991, 205.

2. Blum, *Freedom of Choice in Education*.

3. Friedman, *Capitalism and Freedom*, 99. An even more emphatic analogy be-tween vouchers and the GI Bill is drawn in Friedman and Friedman, *Free to Choose*, 151.

4. E.g., Arren and Jencks, "Education Vouchers," 49.

5. Coons and Sugarman, *Education by Choice*, 217.

6. Christopher Jencks and Associates, *Education Vouchers*, excerpted in Meck-lenburger and Hostrop, *Education Vouchers*, 216.

7. Coons and Sugarman, *Education by Choice*, 217.

8. Kirkpatrick, *Choice in Schooling*, 138.

9. Gary Bridge and Julie Blackman, *Family Choice in Schooling, A Study of Alter-*

natives in American Education, prepared for the National Institute of Education (R–2170/4–NIE) (Santa Monica, Calif.: Rand Corporation, 1978), 16.

10. Robert L. Bish and Vincent Ostrom, *Understanding Urban Government* (Washington, D.C.: American Enterprise Institute, 1973), 40 (emphasis in original).

11. Gary Bridge, "Information Imperfections: The Achilles' Heel of Entitlement Plans," *School Review* (May 1978): 504–29.

12. Denis P. Doyle, "Public Funding and Private Schooling: The State of Descriptive and Analytical Research," in *Private Schools and the Public Good,* ed. Edward McGlynn Gaffney, Jr. (Notre Dame, Ind.: University of Notre Dame Press, 1981), 74.

13. Chubb and Moe, *Politics, Markets, and America's Schools,* 309 n. 50.

14. Friedman and Friedman, *Free to Choose,* 161–63.

15. Background on the Milwaukee case can be found in Michael Barndt, Rick Janka, and Harold Rose, "The West and the Midwest: Milwaukee, Wisconsin: Mobilization for School and Community Cooperation," in *Community Politics and Educational Change,* ed. Charles V. Willie and Susan L. Greenblatt (New York: Longman, 1981), 237–59; David A. Bennett, "A Plan for Increasing Educational Opportunities and Improving Racial Balance in Milwaukee," in Willie, *School Desegregation Plans that Work,* 81–118; and David A. Bennett, "Choice and Desegregation," in Clune and Witte, *Choice and Control in American Education,* 2:125–52.

16. Bennett, "Choice and Desegregation," 2:135–36.

17. For example, Michael Winerip, "School Integration in Buffalo Is Hailed as a Model for U.S.," *New York Times,* May 13, 1985.

18. Christine H. Rossell, "The Buffalo Controlled Choice Plan," *Urban Education* 22, no. 3 (October 1987), table 7.

19. Ibid., 347.

20. Willis D. Hawley et al., *Strategies for Effective Desegregation* (Lexington, Mass.: Lexington Books, 1983), cites Racine, Wisconsin, and Tacoma, Washington, as examples of districts that have successfully desegregated using primarily magnet schools (33). Bennett, "Choice and Desegregation," cites as recent examples Yonkers, New York, and San Jose, California 2:136.

21. The primary contractor for this research was James H. Lowry and Associates. Abt Associates was a major subcontractor. The results have been released in a number of reports and publications. The most comprehensive version is Blank et al., *Survey of Magnet Schools.*

22. Ibid., Executive Summary, 33–34.

23. Christine H. Rossell and Ruth C. Clarke, *The Carrot or the Stick in School Desegregation Policy?* report to the National Institute of Education, March 1987.

24. Mandatory plans couple magnets with techniques (such as pairing, clustering, and rezoning) that authoritatively reassign students to promote racial balance. Voluntary plans combine magnets with open enrollment or majority-to-minority transfer plans, both of which attempt to maximize students' freedom to choose their own schools as long as such choices do not exacerbate racial segregation.

25. Measures of interracial exposure differ from measures of racial balance. The former assess the proportion of whites in the average minority child's school (or vice versa); the latter assess how well individual schools' racial compositions mirror that of a district as a whole. Rossell and Clarke argue that, "if the instrumental goal of school desegregation is to bring whites and minorities into contact with each other," exposure is the more meaningful indicator of the success of desegregation. A school in which 90 percent of the students are black will get a perfect score on a measure of racial balance if the district as a whole is 90 percent black. Racial-exposure measures take into account the possible harm caused by white flight. See Rossell and Clarke, *Carrot or the Stick*, 13–18.

26. Ibid., 70.

27. On a scale on which a score of 22 means that the school equaled its district average, the thirty-two magnet schools for which appropriate data was available averaged 34.78 for reading and 33.25 for math achievement. About one-fifth of the schools exceeded the district average by 30 points or more. Ibid., tables 3.2 and 3.3.

28. Rolf K. Blank, "Educational Effects of Magnet High Schools," in Clune and Witte, *Choice and Control in American Education*, 2:77–109. The twelve studies were the only ones with educational-impact data that Blank could obtain from evaluation directors in thirty-three large urban districts known to have magnet schools.

29. Ibid., 2:99.

30. The issues of research design and measurement are further discussed later in this chapter.

31. Michael J. Alves and Charles V. Willie, "Controlled Choice Assignments: A New and More Effective Approach to School Desegregation," *Urban Review*, 19, no. 2 (1987): 67–88.

32. Christine H. Rossell and Charles L. Glenn, "The Cambridge Controlled Choice Plan," *Urban Review* 20, no. 2 (1988): 75–94.

33. Tan, *Cambridge Controlled Choice Program*.

34. Clewell and Joy, *Choice in Montclair, New Jersey*.

35. Ibid., 12.

36. Former governor of Minnesota Albert Quie (*Education Week*, May 20, 1987), quoted in Fliegel, "Parental Choice in East Harlem Schools," 107.

37. Fliegel, "Parental Choice in East Harlem Schools," 104; William Raspberry, "Real Choice for Better Schools," *Washington Post* June 12, 1989.

38. Amy Stuart Wells, "Quest for Improving Schools Finds Role for Free Market," *New York Times*, March 14, 1990.

39. Chira, "Rules of the Marketplace," reports the district placed 23 percent of its high school class in the eight top selective schools, compared to a citywide average of 9 percent.

40. Raspberry, "Real Choice for Better Schools." But see below for a discussion of this as a distortion.

41. Quoted in Snider, "Call for Choice."

42. Gary Putka, "Parents in Minnesota Are Getting to Send Kids Where They Like," *Wall Street Journal*, May 13, 1988.

43. "Teachers vs. Kids," *Wall Street Journal*, June 6, 1990.

44. Isabel Wilkerson, "For 345, Poverty Is Key to Door of Private School," *New York Times*, December 19, 1990.

45. Jeanne Allen, "Nine Phoney Assertions about School Choice: Answering the Critics," *Heritage Foundation Backgrounder* (Washington, D.C.: Heritage Foundation, 1991), 6.

46. James S. Coleman, Thomas Hoffer, and Sally Kilgore, *High School Achievement* (New York: Basic Books, 1982).

47. Torsten Husen, "Coleman II—Another Case of Politics and the Professors," *Change: The Magazine of Higher Learning* 13, no. 3 (September 1981): 11–12.

48. "Gain scores measure only the learning that takes place during high school whereas scores for the sophomore and senior years alone are contaminated by many years of prior learning . . . it is especially important to factor out of the analysis those influences—school, family, peer groups—that precede the high school years." Chubb and Moe, *Politics, Markets, and America's Schools*, 71.

49. The improvement for Catholic schools was from 76.69 to 85.67; for other private schools, it was from 78.48 to 87.31. James S. Coleman and Thomas Hoffer, *Public and Private High Schools* (New York: Basic Books, 1987), table 3.2. There are two apparent inconsistencies in Coleman and Hoffer's table 3.2. They involve the gain in science for Catholic schools and the gain in civics for other private schools. I present corrected figures, based on the premise that the "gain" scores are wrong and the item counts correct.

50. In mathematics and writing, Catholic schools performed better, but other private schools did not.

51. Besides much richer detail, the ATS drew its measures of school environment from a presumably more reliable source than had studies based solely on HS&B; previously, such information came principally from students' impressions.

52. Chubb and Moe, *Politics, Markets, and America's Schools*, chap. 5.

53. Coleman and Hoffer, *Public and Private High Schools*, 242.

54. Coleman and Hoffer write, "The possibility must be entertained that the very individualism that is embodied in the choice of a private school (unless that school is surrounded by a functional community) may destroy some of the remaining social capital that can still be found in residential neighborhoods, and impose costs upon the student whose family makes such a choice" (ibid., 242).

55. Chubb and Moe, *Politics, Markets, and America's Schools*, 38.

56. A series of reports prepared by the Veterans Administration provides basic information about use of the GI Bill benefits. The reports include: "Vietnam Era Veterans: Usage of GI Bill Education Entitlement" (March 1983), "Historical Data on the Usage of Education Benefits, 1944–1983" (April 1984); and Department of Veterans Affairs, "Veterans Benefits" (undated).

57. Department of Veterans Affairs, "Veterans Benefits," table 1.

58. Ibid., table 2.

59. Richard Hammond, *1979 National Survey of Veterans: Summary Report*, Reports and Statistics Service (Washington, D.C.: Office of the Controller, undated), appendix G, table 8.

60. Ibid., 60–61.

61. "A Cost-Benefit Analysis of Government Investment in Post-Secondary Education under the World War II GI Bill," published in *The Future of Head Start*, Hearing before the Subcommittee on Education and Health of the Joint Economic Committee, February 26, 1990. Dave O'Neill, "Voucher Funding of Training Programs: Evidence from the GI Bill," *Journal of Human Resources* 12, no. 4 (Fall 1977): 428–45, focuses on vocational-technical training.

62. The study estimates how much more college-educated men old enough to fight in World War II earned per year than those without college educations (the estimate growing from four hundred dollars in 1952 to nineteen thousand dollars by 1987). Treating these gains in income as program benefits, the study concludes that the net gain attributable to the bill was about $125 billion ($59 billion in constant 1952 dollars) against a program cost of about $7 billion. To this net gain is added an assessed $12.8 billion (in 1952 dollars) in added taxes presumably paid to the federal government by program beneficiaries on the higher incomes they earned. This gain was then discounted using an estimated long-term discount rate of 2.5 percent. The study's estimated 12.5-to-1 benefit-to-cost ratio is based on the assumption that *all* the net income gains associated with the supported education should be attributed to the program. The lower 5-to-1 ratio reflects an adjustment made because some percentage of these veterans would have gone on to college even without the bill's support. Fifteen percent of eligible veterans attended college or graduate school under the GI Bill. In 1940, only 9 percent of college-age men attended college. Based on these figures, the study concludes that 40 percent of the beneficiaries of the GI Bill would not have gone to college without the bill's financial support.

63. Phone interview with Bill Buechner, Joint Economic Committee staff, March 23, 1992.

64. The first concerns the critical estimate that 40 percent of GIs who used the bill to attend college would not have done so without the support. College attendance was becoming increasingly expected and likely during the decades after the war; therefore using the prewar figure of 9 percent as a baseline expectation is questionable. Even more significantly, the 15 percent who subsequently pursued higher education includes all eligible veterans who went on to receive higher education *at any time*, whereas the 9 percent figure was based on rates of attendance within the relevant age group in a single year. Second, the attempt to use gains in personal income as a measure of the program's benefit needs to be regarded with caution; it is by no means obvious that higher salaries earned by beneficiaries should be treated as equivalent to national increases in output that benefit the public at large. Using this type of reasoning, the "benefits" of a government failure to monitor the performance

of defense contractors would include the higher salaries and bonuses earned by the contractors' management teams.

65. David Kershaw and Jerilyn Fair, *The New Jersey Income-Maintenance Experiment* (New York: Academic Press, 1976).

66. George L. Kelling, Tony Pate, Duane Dieckman, and Charles E. Brown, *The Kansas City Preventive Patrol Experiment* (Washington, D.C.: Police Foundation, 1974).

67. Katharine L. Bradbury and Anthony Downs, eds., *Do Housing Allowances Work?* (Washington, D.C.: Brookings Institution, 1982).

68. Advocates of systematic policy analysis sometimes treat this impatience with scorn. But their claim on the public's patience would be a stronger one if they could demonstrate that systematic policy analysis, allowed to percolate gently until done, generates conclusions that are firm, sharp, and conducive to action. That has not been the case. Even the biggest and best studies have been controversial and ambiguous, requiring careful judgment and interpretation before application.

69. Putka, "Parents in Minnesota." The postsecondary plan gives eleventh and twelfth graders the choice of taking courses at public or private colleges and universities.

70. Nancy Livingstone, "Use of Open Enrollment Program Doubles in Minnesota This Year," *St. Paul Pioneer Press*, October 26, 1990.

71. Witte, "First Year Report," 10.

72. Alan Lupo, "Flexibility for Schools," *Boston Globe*, August 10, 1988. Fiske used the same figures in "Parental Choice in Public Schools Gains," Both attribute them to Cambridge officials.

73. Tan, *Cambridge Controlled Choice Program*, 12. For new kindergartners the figures were more impressive, showing an increase from 78 percent to 89 percent. Some might argue that this is the true test of the appeal of choice, since it excludes from consideration older students who might be staying in private schools out of inertia, habit, or loyalties already formed. This is a reasonable premise, although one would wish to observe evidence of retention before drawing a conclusion to that effect. Again, the point is not that one set of estimates is conclusively better than another, but that early declarations of success often trumpet exaggerated gains.

74. Snider, "Call for Choice."

75. Fiske, "Parental Choice in Public Schools Gains."

76. This lower estimate came in response to the charge by critics that gains in test scores are inflated by outsiders. Chira, "Rules of the Marketplace."

77. For example, Wells, "Quest for Improving Schools." William Raspberry uses approximately the same figures: 15 percent in 1974 to "over 65 percent" (presumably in 1989) (William Raspberry, "Real Choice for Better Schools").

78. Chira, "Rules of the Marketplace."

79. Raspberry, "Real Choice for Better Schools."

80. Raspberry's column is generally built on Nathan, *Public Schools by Choice*, in which the article by Fliegel appears.

81. Fliegel explains that "the rest went to specialized, option, or choice schools" (111). Even the 7 percent figure is likely exaggerated, since it appears to be based on only 7 percent of the entering class being graduated from the school, which may mean that others who simply transferred elsewhere were classified as dropouts.

82. Bridge and Blackman, *Family Choice in Schooling*, xiv.

83. Witte, "First Year Report," 22. Witte speculates that any of several factors might account for this: dissatisfaction with poor test scores, uncertainty about the program's long-term viability, residential mobility, or a response bias that overstated parental satisfaction.

84. Kansas City, Missouri, School District, *Desegregation Plan for the 1988–89, 1989–90, 1990–91 School Years*, March 15, 1988. For example, the Volker Elementary School was given an emphasis in enriched learning in laboratories and through the use of community resources; the number of nonminority students initially increased, but it declined to only sixty-six students by 1985.

85. Gary A. Orfield, "Do We Know Anything Worth Knowing about Educational Effects of Magnet Schools?" in Clune and Witte, *Choice and Control in American Education*, 2:120.

86. Blank, "Educational Effects," 101.

87. Livingstone, "Use of Open Enrollment Program."

88. William Myers and Michael Schwartz, "State of Choice: Minnesota Leads the Nation in Public School Options," *Policy Review* 54 (Fall 1990): 67–69.

89. Donald Moore and S. Davenport, "The New Improved Sorting Machine," paper prepared for the National Center on Effective Secondary Schools, University of Wisconsin, Madison (1988); Jeffrey R. Henig, "Choice in Public Schools: An Analysis of Transfer Requests among Magnet Schools," *Social Science Quarterly* 71, no. 1 (March 1990): 69–82. Although they do not comment on it, Clewell and Joy's data on Montclair indicate a slight erosion of racial balance in the year following the implementation of the citywide controlled-choice program.

90. Isabel Wilkerson, "Des Moines Acts to Halt White Flight after State Allows Choice of Schools," *New York Times*, December 16, 1992.

91. Montgomery County, Maryland, provides racial breakdowns for its subschool magnets at the intermediate and high school levels. In 1990, Blair High School, with an overall minority population of 66 percent, had 43 percent minority in the magnet; Eastern Intermediate, with 62 percent overall, had 24 percent minority in the magnet; Takoma Park Intermediate, with 59 percent minority in the school, had 40 percent in the magnet. Memo from Superintendent of Schools Harry Pitt to members of the Board of Education, "Plans for Assessing Current and Future Needs of Magnet Programs," January 22, 1990.

92. Blank et al., *Survey of Magnet Schools*, 91–95; Clewell and Joy, *Choice in Montclair, New Jersey*, 11.

93. Toch, *In the Name of Excellence*, 219.

94. The Council of Great City Schools, *Results 2000* (Washington, D.C.: Council

of Great City Schools, 1990). The table reports the results for forty-four cities; the relevant information was not available for Phoenix.

95. See Fliegel, "Parental Choice in East Harlem Schools," 104–5.

96. Fliegel mentions the change, but makes no effort to take it into account. Other do not mention it. In 1984, the last year for which he reports California Achievement Test results, the number of students at or above grade level in reading was 48.5 percent. In 1986, the first year in which the city used the Degrees of Reading Power exam, the figure jumped to 62.2 percent.

97. One of the earliest and strongest explications of this point is found in John F. Witte, "Understanding High School Achievement: After a Decade of Research, Do We Have Any Confident Policy Recommendations?" prepared for delivery at the 1990 annual meeting of the American Political Science Association, August 30–September 2, 1990.

98. Chubb and Moe, *Politics, Markets, and America's Schools*, 73, table 3–1.

99. Witte, "Understanding High School Achievement," 11. Chubb and Moe's decision to present most of their findings as a comparison between the highest quartile and the lowest quartile of schools further exaggerates the differences, since, as Witte observes, "by using means and medians of quartiles, this technique compares schools at approximately the 12.5 and 87.5 percentiles" (32). This is somewhat akin to assessing the relationship between a person's height and his or her success in basketball by comparing people seven feet tall to people five feel tall.

100. William R. Morgan compared the HS&B sample to a broader private-school sample (the National Longitudinal Survey of Youth Labor Market Behavior). Among other differences, he found the twenty-seven HS&B non-Catholic schools to be more selective and to have students who performed better than would appear to be typical of that genre. Morgan, "Learning and Student Life Quality of Public and Private School Youth," *Sociology of Education* 56 (October 1983): 187–202. Glen G. Cain and Arthur S. Goldberger argue strongly that the non-Catholic-school sample is simply "too small, heterogeneous and erratically collected to permit reliable inferences" (208), in "Public and Private Schools Revisited," Sociology of Education 56 (October 1983): 208–18. Their criticisms are more telling for Coleman's analyses, which attempt to treat Catholic and non-Catholic private schools separately, than for Chubb and Moe's, which do not. But Witte observes that the oversampling of elite schools, combined with the weighting estimate applied, and the decision to focus on comparisons between high and low quartiles, cumulatively may skew Chubb and Moe's estimation of the effects of school organization.

101. H. W. Riecken and R. F. Boruch, eds., *Social Experimentation: A Method of Planning and Evaluating Social Intervention* (New York: Academic Press, 1974).

102. The classic source is Donald T. Campbell and Julian Stanley, *Experimental and Quasi-Experimental Designs for Research* (Skokie, Ill.: Rand McNally, 1963).

103. Blank et al., *Survey of Magnet Schools*, p 23.

104. Blank, "Educational Effects," 77–109.

105. The study achieving the highest level of sophistication in research design was John C. Larson and Brenda A. Allen, *Pupil and Parent Outcomes*, vol. 2 of *A Microscope on Magnet Schools, 1983 to 1986* (Montgomery County, Md.: Department of Educational Accountability, Montgomery County Public Schools, 1988). Blank, "Educational Effects," seemingly mischaracterizes this study, implying that its control group comprised students who "chose to enroll in a magnet program but are currently on a waiting list" (89), which would be an even stronger form of control for self-selection.

106. Larson and Allen, *Microscope*, 3–5.

107. Tan, *Cambridge Controlled Choice Program*, 15. Tan notes in the text that "the performance of Cambridge elementary students in grades 6 and 9 ranked higher than the performance of students in similar urban schools in the state," but she does not present any such comparison data to substantiate this point. She adds 1988 Cambridge test data to demonstrate that scores continued to improve, but she does not provide the statewide data for that year, making it impossible to determine if Cambridge was gaining ground due to its choice program, or simply sharing in a broader statewide improvement.

108. Glenfield Elementary, with 70 percent minority students, was closed in 1977, as was Southwest Elementary, with 59 percent nonminority students. Grove Elementary, with 82 percent minority students, was closed in 1983.

109. Alves and Willie, "Controlled Choice Assignments," 85.

110. Interracial exposure (Smw) indicates the proportion of whites at the school attended by the average minority student. Racial imbalance (Dm) measures the degree to which the racial makeup of individual schools differs from that of the district as a whole. The data used to compile the figure are drawn from Rossell and Glenn, "Cambridge Controlled Choice Plan," table 5.

111. Fliegel asserts that outsiders "have not unduly influenced our measures of improvement," noting that highest-ranking school in District No. 4 drew fewer than 2 percent of its students from outside. But, in another context, Fliegel notes: "I could take you to a school on 100th Street where 49 per cent of the youngsters are white, middle-class kids." Quoted in Carol Steinbach and Neal R. Peirce, "Multiple Choice," *National Journal*, July 1, 1989, 1697. At the Talented and Gifted School, where at least 75 percent of the students read at or above grade level, 40 percent of the students were white. Over a third of Manhattan East's students came from outside the district. David L. Kirp, "What School Choice Really Means," *Atlantic Monthly*, November 1992, 127.

112. Kirp, "What School Choice Really Means," 127.

113. Richard F. Elmore, "Public School Choice as a Policy Issue," in Gormley, *Privatization and Its Alternatives*, 71.

114. Jacques Steinberg, "Reading Test Results Show Progress at Many Schools," *New York Times*, March 25, 1992.

115. On average, the twenty schools dropped 23.8 points in rank.

116. Joseph Berger, "Test Scores in Reading and Math Drop across New York Districts," *New York Times*, June 26, 1992. This figure left District No. 4 ranked twenty-second among the thirty-two districts.

117. Coleman and Hoffer, *Public and Private High Schools*, 30–31.

118. Karl L. Alexander and Aaron M. Pallas, "Private Schools and Public Policy: New Evidence on Cognitive Achievement in Public and Private Schools," *Sociology of Education* 56, no. 4 (October 1983): 170.

119. Witte, "Understanding High School Achievement," table 11.

120. Ibid., 29.

121. For example, only 6 percent of parents who chose their children's schools reported that they did not read with or to their children in the year before the children entered the program, compared to 13 percent of Milwaukee public-school parents. Seventy-one percent reported working with their children on arithmetic or math three or more times per week, compared to 50 percent of other public-school parents. Ibid., table 12.

122. Because of its self-policing elements, it is less likely to hold onto misinformation. But there is no guarantee that misinformation will be identified as such. Misinformation that escapes refutation may gain an air of added legitimacy that over time makes it more difficult to dislodge.

123. Charles E. Lindblom, *Inquiry and Change* (New Haven, Conn.: Yale University Press, 1990).

CHAPTER SEVEN
REINTERPRETING THE LESSONS OF EXPERIENCE

1. Clint Bolick, "A Primer on Choice in Education: Part I. How Choice Works," *Heritage Foundation Backgrounder* 760, March 21, 1990, 6.

2. Stone, *Policy Paradox and Political Reason*, 118.

3. For the reasons why these claims must be tentative, see the discussion in the previous chapter.

4. On the point that popular pressure from the citizenry often worked against moderate, choice-oriented desegregation efforts, see Hochschild, *New American Dilemma*.

5. Rossell and Clarke, *Carrot and the Stick*, table 3.1.

6. Monti, *Semblance of Justice*, 100.

7. Ibid., 136–37.

8. Ann LaGrelius Siqueland, *Without a Court Order: The Desegregation of Seattle's Schools* (Seattle: Madrona, 1981), 100–102.

9. Ibid., 23–24.

10. Ibid., 71.

11. For example, Friedman and Friedman, *Free to Choose*, 154; Gary S. Becker, "What Our Schools Need Is a Dose of Healthy Competition," *Business Week*, De-

cember 18, 1989, 28; Dwight R. Lee, "An Alternative to Public Schools: Educational Vouchers," *Current* (October 1986): 26–32; and Allen, "Nine Phoney Assertions," 12–13. Among the few exceptions, Lieberman, *Privatization and Educational Choice*, acknowledges that implementing voucher systems in states that have high proportions of students currently in private schools would impose substantial financial obligations, leading to the ironic result that vouchers would be fiscally most feasible in those states in which there is the least political support for them (242).

12. School District of Kansas City, "Motion for Approval of Desegregation Plan for 1988–89 through 1990–1991," in *Kalima Jenkens et al. v. State of Missouri*, case no. 77–0420–CV–W–4, before the United States District Court for the Western District of Missouri.

13. Ibid.

14. Blank et al., *Survey of Magnet Schools*, 52–53.

15. Denis P. Doyle and Marsha Levine, "Magnet Schools: Choice and Quality in Public Education," *Phi Delta Kappan* 66 (December 1984): 265–70. They use the example of D.C.'s Dunbar High school to show that efforts to sustain magnetlike programs sometimes failed. Dunbar, which "was a magnet school of its day, drawing able black students from across the city" and even some from beyond the city's borders, was converted to a conventional neighborhood school in the mid-1950s, in the aftermath of the Brown decision.

16. Mary Haywood Metz, *Different by Design: The Context and Character of Three Magnet Schools* (New York: Routledge & Kegan Paul, 1986). Her reference here was to the district she labels "Heartland," a large midwestern district integrating under court order.

17. William Maynard, "The Seattle Plan for Eliminating Racial Imbalance," in Willie, *School Desegregation Plans that Work*, 125.

18. Blank et al., *Survey of Magnet Schools*, 206. The authors present evidence that such "skimming" is less prominent in practice than in perception.

19. "Busing without Tears?" *New Republic*, November 7, 1983, 19.

20. The collective decision was the one to launch an aggressive and innovative choice-based scheme; the individual decisions were those made by families of students regarding the schools they would apply to and attend.

21. Bennett, "Plan for Increasing Educational Opportunities," 88–89.

22. Blank et al., *Survey of Magnet Schools*, 92–93.

23. See, for example, Robert L. Crain and Rita Mahard, "Some Policy Implications of the Desegregation–Minority Achievement Literature," in *Assessment of Current Knowledge about the Effectiveness of School Desegregation Strategies*, ed. Willis D. Hawley (Nashville, Tenn.: Vanderbilt University Center for Education and Human Development Policy, 1981); and Willie and Greenblatt, *Community Politics and Educational Change*.

24. Charles E. Lindblom, "The Science of 'Muddling Through,'" *Public Administration Review* 19 (Spring 1959): 79–88.

25. A fuller description of the county and its experience with magnet schools can be found in Henig, "Choice, Race, and Public Schools: The Adoption and Implementation of a Magnet Program," *Journal of Urban Affairs* 11, no. 3 (Fall 1989): 243–59.

26. Leila Sussmann, *Tales out of School: Implementing Organizational Change in the Elementary Grades* (Philadelphia: Temple University Press, 1977), chap. 13.

27. David L. Kirp, *Just Schools: The Idea of Racial Equality in America* (Berkeley and Los Angeles: University of California Press, 1982).

28. Ibid., 149.

29. Robert Peterkin and Dorothy Jones, "Schools of Choice in Cambridge, Massachusetts," in Nathan, *Public Schools by Choice*, 142.

30. Nine Massachusetts cities—Boston, Chelsea, Fall River, Holyoke, Lawrence, Lowell, Northampton, Salem, and Springfield—adopted districtwide controlled-choice plans between 1987 and 1991. Charles L. Glenn, "Why Are They So Afraid of School Choice? (And What They Could Learn from Massachusetts)," *Public Interest* (January 1991).

31. Jack L. Walker, "The Diffusion of Innovations among the American States," *American Political Science Review* 63 (September 1969).

32. Virginia Gray, "Innovation in the States: A Diffusion Study," *American Political Science Review* 67 (December 1973).

33. Robert Albritton, "Social Services: Welfare and Health," in *Politics in the American States*, ed. Virginia Gray, Herbert Jacob, and Robert B. Albritton, 5th ed. (Glenview, Ill.: Scott, Foresman, 1990): 426–27.

34. In 1987–88, Massachusetts spent $5,471 per pupil (based on average daily attendance) for elementary and secondary education. This placed it fifth among the fifty states, behind Alaska, New York, New Jersey, and Connecticut. National Center for Education Statistics, *Digest of Education Statistics*, table 155.

35. The moralistic political culture, according to Daniel Elazar, views government as a commonwealth, considers social as well as economic regulation to be legitimate, and regards both politics and bureaucracy positively. In contrast, an individualistic political culture views government as a marketplace, sees economic but not social intervention as legitimate, regards politics as "dirty," and is ambivalent toward bureaucracy; a traditionalistic culture sees government as an instrument for maintaining order, regards as legitimate only those governmental activities that maintain traditional patterns, sees politics as a privilege reserved for an elite, and regards bureaucracy negatively. Elazar names Minnesota and Wisconsin as two of nine states with relatively pure moralistic cultures. Daniel J. Elazar, *American Federalism: A View from the States*, 3d ed. (New York: Harper & Row, 1984), chap. 5.

36. Albritton, "Social Services," 426–27.

37. Minnesota and Wisconsin spent $4,386 and $4,747 per pupil in average daily attendance in 1987–88. The average among the midwestern states was $4,057. National Center for Education Statistics, *Digest of Education Statistics*, table 155.

38. See, for example, Charles R. Morris's critical, but generally sympathetic, assessment of New York's proclivity for bureaucratic and programmatic responses to perceived social problems. Morris, *The Cost of Good Intentions: New York City and the Liberal Experiment* (New York: W. W. Norton, 1980).

39. As Ken Auletta notes: "No other city enjoys its own vast City University and provided its students [for many years] with free tuition. No other city offered the same poor and middle-income housing subsidies. No other city has such an extensive municipal hospital system. No other city so richly supplements its welfare and Medicaid benefits" (Avletta, *The Streets Were Paved with Gold* [New York: Random House, 1979], 203).

40. U.S. Bureau of the Census, *County and City Data Book, 1988* (Washington, D.C.: U.S. Bureau of the Census, 1989). Three of the four cities that outstrip Montclair on this measure are far larger municipalities, with much more pressing social needs: Atlantic City, Elizabeth, and Jersey City.

41. Seymour Fliegel, "Creative Non-Compliance," in Clune and Witte, *Choice and Control in American Education*, 2:199–216. Fliegel emphasizes the broad support, but quotes also from an early appraisal that characterizes the first school as having "no base of support in the poor, largely Hispanic community where it would be located" (2:202–3).

42. Mazzoni, "Analyzing State School Policymaking," 121.

43. Joe Nathan, a leader in the Minnesota and national movements for public-school choice, cites his personal experience with the St. Paul Open School as central in shaping his ideas.

44. Coons and Sugarman, *Education by Choice*, 118.

45. Bennett, "Plan for Increasing Educational Opportunities."

46. Blank et al., *Survey of Magnet Schools*, 11.

47. Ibid., 30.

48. Rolf K. Blank, Robert A. Dentler, D. Catherine Baltzell, and Kent Chabotar, "Guide to Magnet School Development," final report prepared by James H. Lowry and Associates for the U.S. Department of Education, Office of Planning, Budget, and Evaluation, September 1983, 10.

49. Phale D. Hale and Daniel U. Levine, "Kansas City, Missouri School District Long-Range Magnet School Plan," presented to Dr. Claude G. Perkins and the Board of Education, July 28, 1986, 26–32.

50. Blank et al., *Survey of Magnet Schools*, chap. 5. They found some indication that the cost difference narrows over time, but this was accounted for at least in part by cutbacks occasioned by the declining availability of federal support.

51. Peterkin and Jones, "Schools of Choice in Cambridge, Massachusetts," 142.

52. Chira, "Rules of the Marketplace."

53. "Not by Choice Alone," *Washington Post*, October 21, 1989.

54. Advocates of choice point to the high percentage of families in Cambridge and

Montclair that succeed in getting into their first choice. But achieving this has depended on large and ongoing public-sector investments in the initially less-attractive schools. Moreover, there have been some claims that school officials may discourage parents from making selections that are likely to be denied.

55. For a fuller discussion of the measures and methods employed in this study, see Henig, "Choice in Public Schools."

56. Metz, *Different by Design*, 207–8.

57. The Twin Cities area's unusual support for values of regional cooperation is reflected in its innovative regional tax-sharing arrangements. Tim L. Mazzoni recounts the story of political coalition-building that was necessary. "Analyzing State School Policymaking," 115–38.

58. The experimental Milwaukee voucher program is the only one to come close; as mentioned above, one of the private schools participating in that program did discontinue operation in the middle of the first year. But the reaction to that closing was pressure on officials to put into place stronger reporting, governance, and accountability procedures to make it less likely this would happen again. See Witte, "First Year Report," 24.

59. Blank et al., *Survey of Magnet Schools*, 31.

60. Quoted in Snider, "Call for Choice."

61. In addition, in 1989–90 New Hampshire Estates was assigned four special magnet-staff faculty members, five magnet aides, and three faculty members funded from the county's program for Quality Integrated Education, essentially doubling its regular staff allotment of eleven ("Plans for Assessing Current and Future Needs," appendix 5).

62. Laurel Shaper Walters, "'Choice' Pioneer Fine-tunes Plan," *Christian Science Monitor*, March 11, 1991. Margaret Gallagher, the director of the Parents' Information Center in Cambridge, holds special meetings at Head Start facilities and even goes so far as to stand outside schools when parents come to pick up their children in the evening in order to hand out information. According to Gallagher, "All the TLC [tender loving care] you can give parents helps."

63. Rebecca L. Carver and Laura H. Salganik, "You Can't Have Choice without Information: Strategies for Reaching Families," *Equity and Choice* 7, nos. 2–3. (Spring 1991): 71–75; Salganik and Carter, "Strategies," 18.

64. Carver and Salganik, "You Can't Have Choice"; see also Salganik and Carver, "Strategies."

65. Carver and Salganik, "You Can't Have Choice," 75.

66. Salganik and Carver, "Strategies," 24.

67. Carver and Salganik, "You Can't Have Choice," 75.

68. In Montgomery County, Maryland, for example, school officials rejected parents' request for a math/science high school in the northern section of the county, for fear that it would negatively affect the thriving math/science magnet at Blair High School.

CHAPTER EIGHT
HOW MARKET-BASED PLANS WILL FAIL

1. Mary H. Metz, "Potentialities and Problems of Choice in Desegregation Plans," in Clune and Witte, *Choice and Control in American Education* 2:111.

2. Richard Elmore, "Choice as an Instrument of Public Policy," in Clune and Witte, *Choice and Control in American Education*, 1:297. Speaking of variations in voucher plans, Henry Levin observes, in the same volume, that "different specifics can lead to radically different results" ("The Theory of Choice Applied to Education," 1:260).

3. If they are not required to provide lunch, will this mean that some schools will become informally closed to those currently benefiting from the federal free and reduced-cost lunch program?

4. There is little information available to allow one to do more than guess about how schools would evaluate the relative attractiveness of different types of students. Based on economic modeling, John Witte concludes that "differential voucher levels based on income are essential to avoid increased inequity" ("Market versus State-Centered Approaches to American Education: Does Either Make Much Sense?" prepared for delivery at the 1991 annual meeting of the American Political Science Association, August 29–September 1, 1991, 9). Experience in job training and place-ment programs may also be relevant. There, government officials have consistently underestimated the willingness of private employers to hire the long-term unem-ployed—even when various subsidies make the nominal cost close to zero. Joleen Kirschenman and Kathryn M. Neckerman, "'We'd Love to Hire Them, But . . .': The Meaning of Race for Employers," in *The Urban Underclass*, ed. Christopher Jencks and Paul E. Peterson (Washington, D.C.: Brookings Institution, 1991): 203–32.

5. Coons and Sugarman, as well as Chubb and Moe, oppose parental add-ons because of their potential to undermine efforts to protect lower-income families from isolation. See Coons and Sugarman, *Education by Choice*, 191; Chubb and Moe, *Politics, Markets, and America's Schools*, 220.

6. Eugene Bardach, *The Implementation Game: What Happens after a Bill Be-comes Law* (Cambridge, Mass.: MIT Press, 1977); D. Mazmanian and P. Sabatier, eds., Implementation and Public Policy (Chicago: Scott, Foresman, 1983); Robert K. Nakamura and Frank Smallwood, *The Politics of Policy Implementation* (New York: St. Martin's Press, 1980); Jeffrey Pressman and Aaron Wildavsky, Implementation, 3d ed. (Berkeley and Los Angeles: University of California Press, 1984); W. Williams, ed., Studying Implementation (Chatham, N.J.: Chatham House, 1982).

7. Martha Derthick, *New Towns In-Town* (Washington, D.C.: Urban Institute, 1972), xiv.

8. Pressman and Wildavsky, *Implementation*, 93.

9. Ibid., 69.

10. Ibid., 109.

11. Sussmann *Tales Out of School*; see also Henig "Choice, Race, and Public Schools."

12. Giandomenico Majone and Aaron Wildavsky, "Implementation as Evolution," in Pressman and Wildavsky, *Implementation*, 174.

13. Chubb and Moe, for example, are adamant in denying that the changes they propose "have anything to do with 'privatizing' the nation's schools" (*Politics, Markets, and America's Schools*, 225).

14. Considering implementation politics in this way challenges David Truman's thesis that "potential groups" play nearly as important a role as do formally organized groups in shaping public policy. While acknowledging that formal organization is important in the short run, Truman suggests that the difference between an unmobilized and a mobilized interest is one of "merely a stage or degree of interaction." Truman, *Governmental Process*, 36.

15. Chubb and Moe, *Politics, Markets, and America's Schools*, 309 n. 51.

16. Ibid.

17. Pressman and Wildavsky, *Implementation*, 132.

18. Richard Scher and James Button, "Voting Rights Act: Implementation and Impact," in *The Implementation of Civil Rights Policy*, ed. Charles S. Bullock III and Charles M. Lamb (Monterey, Calif.: Brooks/Cole, 1984), 41.

19. Charles S. Bullock III, "Equal Education Opportunity," in Bullock and Lamb, *Implementation of Civil Rights Policy*, 65, table 3.2.

20. Second-generation discrimination involves the separation of white and black students *within* schools, through the designation of ability groups, tracking, disproportionate assignment of minorities to classes for the educable mentally retarded, and the like.

21. Charles S. Bullock III, "Conditions Associated with Policy Implementation," in Bullock and Lamb, *Implementation of Civil Rights Policy*, 184–207.

22. Robert P. Stoker, *Reluctant Partners: Implementing Federal Policy* (Pittsburgh, Pa.: University of Pittsburgh Press, 1991).

23. Ibid., 58–59.

24. Ibid., 55.

25. Ibid., 128.

26. See Gordon P. Whitaker, "Co-production: Citizen Participation in Service Delivery," *Public Administration Review* 40, no. 3 (May–June 1980): 240–46, and Richard C. Rich, "The Interaction of the Voluntary and Governmental Sectors: Toward an Understanding of Coproduction of Municipal Services," *Administration and Society* 13 (May 1981): 59–76.

27. See Hirschman, *Exit, Voice, and Loyalty*.

28. Clarence Stone, *Regime Politics: Governing Atlanta, 1946–1988* (Lawrence, Kans.: University of Kansas Press, 1989); quoted in Stoker, *Reluctant Partners*, 92.

29. Lindblom, "Science of 'Muddling Through,'" 81.

30. Robert B. Reich, ed., *The Power of Public Ideas* (Cambridge, Mass.: Harvard University Press, 1988).

31. The question was worded as follows: "Do you favor or oppose allowing students and their parents to choose which public schools in this community the students attend, regardless of where they live?" Sixty-two percent indicated they favored such freedom of choice; 33 percent were opposed. Support was relatively consistent across income, education, and region. Nonwhites were more supportive than whites (69 percent to 60 percent). Respondents between the ages of eighteen and twenty-nine were much more responsive than respondents over fifty (71 percent to 50 percent). Elam, Rose, and Gallup, "Twenty-third Annual Gallup Poll," 47–48.

32. The wording was as follows: "In some nations, the government allots a certain amount of money for each child's education. The parents can then send the child to any public, parochial, or private school they choose. This is called the 'voucher system.' Would you like to see such an idea adopted in this country?" The wording of the question can be important.

33. The theoretical link to decentralization is forged most directly through the analogy between competition among firms for customers and that between localities for taxpayers. Presumably, mobile households and businesses can exert pressure on local governments to provide efficient, responsive, and high-quality services through the exercise of their right to "shop" elsewhere. See Charles Tiebout, "A Pure Theory of Local Expenditures," *Journal of Political Economy* 64 (1956): 416–24, for the classic statement; for a contemporary restatement and empirical assessment, see Mark Schneider, *The Competitive City: The Political Economy of Suburbia* (Pittsburgh, Pa.: University of Pittsburgh Press, 1989). Market solutions tended to be associated with greater centralization in Margaret Thatcher's Great Britain; this raises the possibility that this link is based on political expedience as well as theoretical inevitability.

34. The question was phrased thus: "It has been proposed that the public schools make preschool programs available to 3- and 4-year-olds whose parents wish such programs. These programs would be supported by taxes. Would you favor or oppose such programs?" Support was greatest among minorities, younger respondents, professionals, and parents of school-age children. Elam, Rose, and Gallup, "Twenty-third Annual Gallup Poll," 45.

35. Support for the sales tax was greatest even though the question linked it to a 1 percent increase, while the state income-tax question was pegged to a .5 percent figure.

36. Elam, Rose, and Gallup, "Twenty-third Annual Gallup Poll," 45–46.

37. This formulation acknowledges the potential for a less conventional, more sophisticated market theory, one that acknowledges fully the extent to which markets and their achievements are entirely dependent on socially defined and maintained institutions and practices.

CHAPTER NINE
PUTTING EDUCATIONAL CHOICE IN ITS PLACE

1. Chubb and Moe, *Politics, Markets, and America's Schools* (emphasis in original).

2. Despite all the reasons to be concerned about the overselling of market solutions and educational restructuring in general, advocates of school choice at least have been offering something to get enthused about. This may in itself account for some non-negligible portion of the movement's political appeal.

3. Charles Glenn, "Putting Choice in Place," in Nathan, *Public Schools by Choice*, 149–64.

4. A. Stephen Stephan, "Prospects and Possibilities: The New Deal and the New Social Research," *Social Forces* 13 (May 1935), reprinted in *Readings in Evaluation Research*, ed. Francis G. Caro (New York: Russell Sage Foundation, 1977), 40.

5. An early and influential work is Daniel Lerner and Harold D. Lasswell, eds., *The Policy Sciences* (Stanford, Calif.: Stanford University Press, 1951). For historical overviews, see Carol H. Weiss, *Using Social Research in Public Policy Making* (Lexington, Mass.: Lexington Books, 1977), and Richard P. Nathan, *Social Science in Government: Uses and Abuses* (New York: Basic Books, 1988), especially chap. 2.

6. "Social science inquiry embraces the same variety of explanations that ordinary people construct for themselves and exchange with each other. Not at all distinctive to social science, the explanatory methods constitute the ways in which we all try to make sense of the world and go about the pursuit of our own purposes, the solutions to our own problems. In their efforts at explanation, social scientists and researchers only try to do much better what everyone else does." Lindblom, *Inquiry and Change*, 142. Lindblom argues that the proper role for professional analysts is supplementary to lay inquiry: "This does not mean an unimportant role but an adjunct role," 161.

7. For an elaboration of the intellectual history of the interest-group perspective, see Henig, "Ideas and Interests in Educational Reform."

8. Aaron Wildavsky, "Choosing Preferences by Constructing Institutions: A Cultural Theory of Preference Formation," *American Political Science* Review 81 (1987): 4.

9. Although economists rely on presumed changes in "tastes" to account for consumer behavior that does not otherwise fit the pattern predicted by income and prices, "they admittedly have no useful theory of the formation of tastes" (Gary S. Becker and Robert T. Michael, "On the New Theory of Consumer Behavior," in Gary S. Becker, ed., *The Economic Approach to Human Behavior* [Chicago: University of Chicago Press, 1976], 133). That most conventional economists do not find troubling the lack of a theory of where interests come from is explainable in part by their satisfaction that the specific nature and realism of their theoretical premises are not of concern so long as their models "work." What is more, conventional economists see the parsimony of their deductive framework to be one of its most valued

advantages; to delve into the muddy and mysterious process by which people come to define their interests and desires might draw them far from the solid scientific ground on which they feel they have built their successes.

10. Jane Mansbridge, *Beyond Adversary Democracy* (New York: Basic Books, 1980); Benjamin Barber, *Strong Democracy: Participatory Politics for a New Age* (Berkeley and Los Angeles: University of California Press, 1984).

11. Writing about the history of the common-school movement, for example, some—such as Katz, *Irony of Early School Reform*, Joel Spring, *Education and the Rise of the Corporate State* (Boston: Beacon Press, 1972); and Samuel Bowles and Herbert Gintis, *Schooling in Capitalist America* (New York: Basic Books, 1976)—emphasize the economic and political values the emergent bourgeoisie sought to inculcate in a potentially resistant working class. Others, like Glenn, *Myth of the Common School*, emphasize the religious doctrine they sought to impose on immigrant Catholics.

12. My characterization of the relation between education and democracy is informed by Amy Gutmann, *Democratic Education* (Princeton, N.J.: Princeton University Press, 1987).

13. The rapid unraveling of the Communist regimes in the Soviet Union and Eastern Europe are testimony to the limited power of government institutions to proscribe certain ideas.

14. Chubb and Moe, *Politics, Markets, and America's Schools*, 217 (emphasis in original).

15. Even in older cities undergoing population loss, the supply of available seats may be insufficient to accommodate demand. Lewis and Taylor, *Options without Knowledge*, for example, concluded that, of the roughly 14,700 empty seats, nearly two-thirds were in the worst schools; only 5,228 empty seats were in schools where quality was high enough that "student 'consumers' might improve by 'purchasing' them—i.e., changing enrollment" (16). Since over 164,000 students attended the lowest-quality elementary schools, the Urban League reasoned that at most one child in fifty who might benefit from choice would really have the opportunity to do so.

The notion that new schools can fill such vacuums is one of the most problematic assumptions of the advocates of market choice; at least we can be certain that the likelihood of this occurring will depend on other conditions: the size of vouchers or scholarships, the extent of regulation, the intensity of crime, other costs of doing business, and so forth. In Milwaukee, where low-income students are eligible for vouchers that can be applied to private schools, ten private schools expressed an interest in participating, only seven enrolled any applicants, and only five accounted for over 92 percent of the placements. Over one-third of those who applied were refused admission because of lack of space. The second year the number of participating schools was even lower, with only four private schools accounting for over 92 percent of the placements. See Witte, "First Year Report."

16. Hirschman, *Exit, Voice, and Loyalty.*

17. For a balanced discussion of what markets and governments do well and do poorly, see Charles E. Lindblom, *Politics and Markets* (New York: Basic Books, 1977).

18. For a fuller consideration of the kinds of obstacles that can prevent personal distress from culminating in pressure for a government response, see Henig, *Neighborhood Mobilization*,

19. E.g., Otis Dudley Duncan, *Toward Social Reporting* (New York: Russell Sage Foundation, 1969); Leslie D. Wilcox, Ralph M. Brooks, George M. Beal, and Gerald E. Klonglan, *Social Indicators and Social Monitoring* (San Francisco: Jossey-Bass, 1972).

20. Garry D. Brewer and Peter deLeon, *The Foundations of Policy Analysis* (Homewood, Ill.: Dorsey Press, 1983), 133.

21. Carver and Salganik, "You Can't Have Choice"; Chubb and Moe, *Politics, Markets, and America's Schools*, 221.

22. Parents are likely to hesitate more about sending their child to a different school than switching their child to a different classroom. If choices do not work out, the costs of reversing the error are much lower as well.

23. Studies of service delivery in urban areas show that bureaucracies tend to favor rules relating to equal treatment and to buffer against political demands for favoritism based on economic or political clout. See, for example, Robert L. Lineberry, *Equality and Urban Policy: The Distribution of Municipal Public Services* (Berkeley, Calif.: Sage, 1977); Bryan D. Jones, Saadia R. Greenberg, Clifford Kaufman, and Joseph Drew, "Service Delivery Rules and the Distribution of Local Government Services: Three Detroit Bureaucracies," *Journal of Politics* (May 1978): 332–68; and Kenneth R. Mladenka, "The Urban Bureaucracy and the Chicago Political Machine: Who Gets What and the Limits to Political Control," *American Political Science Review* 74 (December 1980): 991–98.

24. The last can occur, for example, when school districts go through periods of sudden growth, forcing them to hire large numbers of teachers. Such generational cohorts may carry with them the pedagogical fashions then in vogue in the schools of education in which they were trained. Similarly, systems that built or rehabilitated school buildings during the period in which open education and unwalled classrooms were popular can carry with them a physical legacy that exercises an ongoing constraint on educational strategies.

25. On this general phenomenon, see William Ryan, *Blaming the Victim* (New York: Vintage, 1971).

26. Such resegregation can be avoided when public officials make dramatic, redistributive investments in magnet schools or impose and enforce strict racial-balance criteria that effectively limit transfers.

27. Jesse Green, Neil Wintfeld, and Phoebe Sahrkey, "The Importance of Severity of Illness in Assessing Hospital Mortality," *Journal of the American Medical Association* 263 (January 1990): 241–46; Jesse Green, Leigh Passman, and Neil Wintfeld,

"Analyzing Hospital Mortality: The Consequences of Diversity in Patient Mix," *Journal of the American Medical Association* 265 (April 1991): 1849–53.

28. See, for example, Michael Danielson, *The Politics of Exclusion* (New York: Columbia University Press, 1976).

29. During the 1960s and 1970s Congress and the executive branch took steps similar to this in order to promote regional cooperation, especially on land-use and transportation issues. Section 204 of the Demonstration Cities and Metropolitan Development Act of 1966, the Intergovernmental Cooperation Act of 1968, and Circular A-95 issued by the Office of Management and Budget are credited with having spurred the formation of regional councils of government.

30. Kingdon, *Agendas, Alternatives, and Public Policies*, chap. 6.

31. This definition of civic capacity was developed as part of an ongoing, multi-researcher project, in which I am a participant. The project—a multicity study of "Civic Capacity and Urban Education"—is directed by Clarence N. Stone and has received sponsorship from the Department of Government and Politics at the University of Maryland, the Joint Center for Political and Economic Studies, and the National Science Foundation.

32. This is not to say that we should ignore the differing objective circumstances that distinguish these groups, disallow the legitimacy of their expressing those differences in public debate and deliberation, or ignore the distributional implications of specific policies.

33. Benjamin Barber warns that "when moral and political leadership overlap, the need for social cohesion becomes confused with the disposition toward political unanimity, and inspirational persuasion becomes charismatic aggression by manipulation." This leads him to conclude that "in the ideal participatory community, moral leadership must therefore be exercised outside the political arena, in a public but nonpolitical fashion that is conducive to fraternal affection and common values yet hostile to conformity" (*Strong Democracy*, 241).

34. Robert B. Reich, "Policy Making in a Democracy," in Reich, *Power of Public Ideas*, 124.

✩ *Index* ✩